# Carr and Latham's
# Technology of Clothing

# Carr and Latham's
# Technology of Clothing Manufacture

## Fourth Edition

## Revised by
## David J. Tyler

**Blackwell** Publishing

Blackwell Publishing editorial offices:
Blackwell Publishing Ltd, 9600 Garsington Road, Oxford OX4 2DQ, UK
Tel: +44 (0)1865 776868
Blackwell Publishing Inc., 350 Main Street, Malden, MA. 02148-5020, USA
Tel: +1 781 388 8250
Blackwell Publishing Asia Pty Ltd, 550 Swanston Street, Carlton, Victoria 3053,
Australia
Tel: +61 (0)3 8359 1011

First edition published by BPS Professional Books
Second edition published 1994 by Blackwell Science
Third edition published 2000 by Blackwell Publishing
Fourth edition published 2008 by Blackwell Publishing

ISBN: 978-1-4051-6198-5

Library of Congress Cataloging-in-Publication Data

Carr, Harold.
Carr and Latham's technology of clothing manufacture / Revised by
David J. Tyler. – 4th ed.
p. cm.
Includes bibliographical references and index.
ISBN-13: 978-1-4051-6198-5 (pbk. : alk. paper)
ISBN-10: 1-4051-6198-1 (pbk. : alk. paper)
1. Clothing trade.  2. Sewing.  3. Dressmaking.  I. Latham, Barbara.
II. Tyler, David J.  III. Title.

TT497.C33 2008
338.4'7687–dc22
2007036941

A catalogue record for this title is available from the British Library

Set in 10 on 12.5 pt Avenir by SNP Best-set Typesetter Ltd., Hong Kong
Printed and bound in Singapore by C.O.S. Printers Pte Ltd

The publisher's policy is to use permanent paper from mills that operate a sustain-
able forestry policy, and which has been manufactured from pulp processed using
acid-free and elementary chlorine-free practices. Furthermore, the publisher ensures
that the text paper and cover board used have met acceptable environmental
accreditation standards.

For further information on Blackwell Publishing, visit our website:
www.blackwellpublishing.com

# Contents

Colour plate section appears between pages 276 and 277

# About the Author

David J. Tyler graduated in physics from Southampton University and started working for an industrial research association serving the textiles and clothing industry. Afterwards he moved into industry as a technologist and later became a manager. He is currently Reader in Apparel Systems and Technologies in the Department of Clothing Design and Technology at Manchester Metropolitan University.

# Preface to the Fourth Edition

It is now 20 years since the first edition of this book was published. Since that time, much has changed. Early in 2007, I asked one of my ex-students to speak on the subject of garment technology to a current student group. During this talk, she reflected on the changes since 1984, when she started work in the UK industry. These thoughts are worth sharing.

Twenty five years ago, the garment technologist's job was concerned with garment fit and conformance to specification. This was the case whether the technologist was working in the supply chain or for a retailer. Then we witnessed the great expansion of globalisation!

Now, the technologist's role has expanded to include commercial and practical inputs to the new product development process, ensuring products conform to legislation, and addressing manufacturability issues. Quality assurance activities continue, but there is much more effort given to build quality into products at the development stage.

The technologist is uniquely equipped to interpret the requirements of designers and buyers, who typically do not have a technical vocabulary. This extends to checking that the product looks right over the whole size range and helping to resolve any issues that arise. Technologists can be found assessing prototype garments alongside the buyer, appraising make-up, fit and product presentation. Any decisions arising from this will be communicated to the manufacturer (who has not been involved in the fit session) by the technologist.

More and more, garment technologists are expected to deal with fabric information and be able to interpret test results on shrinkage, dye-fastness and other performance-related matters. Technologists will receive submissions for sealed samples and evaluate them. They will be involved with bulk stocks in the retailer's distribution centre, to assess any problems and to contribute to decision-making about them. With mail order business, technologists will take the lead in analysing customer returns so that appropriate action can be taken.

Some garment technologists may get involved in appraising the capabilities of potential suppliers, and this is likely to incorporate aspects of ethical auditing. Some may be involved in implementing appropriate information systems, such as product data management software. The diversity of work makes the technologist's job very demanding.

Globalisation does mean that there are two types of garment technologist: those based in retail organisations (or brand owners) and those based in manufacturing organisations (the supply chain). The work of retail based technologists is directed to achieving conformance to quality standards and ensuring the suppliers understand what the products should be like. Those working in the supply chain gain far more first-hand experience of problem solving, as they are working with the people, the fabrics and the machinery on a regular basis.

An important skill for technologists is to be able to communicate across cultures and across the design/technology divide. The language problems are only part of the story. People in different cultures may have different expectations and different judgments on what is an acceptable standard. There may be different views on what is aesthetically pleasing. Since the brand owner is setting the standard, the supply chain needs the style of communication that will help it understand the customer requirements and the consumer markets that are being served.

This book has focused on the technology of clothing manufacture, leaving issues of fit and quality systems for others. However, the technologies have changed with time, and this shift is reflected in the way different editions have been updated. In the third edition, the role of the garment technologist in new product development was introduced. The new chapter in this edition (Chapter 8) concerns the technology of colour and its management. The chapter that has seen the most change is that on alternative joining technologies (Chapter 6), because of the major expansion of interest in welded seams and the use of adhesives. Chapter 10 has been introduced on the solution of sewing problems, drawing on material previously in Chapter 3 and introducing checklists in tabular form.

The initial work on this book by Harold Carr and Barbara Latham was extensive and their contribution has always been the key to making this book useful and successful. My role in revising the book has been one of editing a proven resource and, I hope, maintaining its value within education and industry.

# Acknowledgements

I am grateful to Lorraine Hall of Apparel Matters for useful discussions on developments in the industry. Colleagues in the Department of Clothing Design & Technology and in the industry are thanked generally for creating an environment where innovation is valued, discussed and implemented. Raf Mulla of X-rite Inc. provided helpful feedback on numerous aspects of colour management.

David J. Tyler
2008

# Chapter One
# Background to
# the Clothing Industry

Clothing manufacture is an activity dominated by the need for human skills, with a great range of raw materials, product types, production technologies, production volumes, retail markets and brands. Companies range from small family businesses to multinationals. Supply chains are typically global, with materials being sourced in many different countries. This diversity is difficult to match in any other industry.

In Europe and the USA, the past 20 years have seen dramatic changes in the structure of the apparel industry. Large-scale domestic manufacturing belongs to the past: the emerging industry has the core skills of design, product development, sourcing, logistics and supply chain management. Domestic manufacturing continues to exist, normally supplying niche markets using specialist skills.

The wide variations of company size and type within the clothing industry are due to three special features of the fashion industry:

*Fashion requires a quick response*   The world of clothing incorporates a broad spectrum of products, ranging from high fashion exclusives to mass-produced commodity products.

Fashion may be couture garments, setting the trends for a season and made in small quantities at high cost. The pool of fashion houses is currently about 100, all of which are seeking to make an impact in the market. Celebrity fashion has grown in importance, particularly with young people. However, designers do not overlook the importance of street fashion, and look also for 'home-grown' fashions that spring up unpredictably and create demand for products of a particular style and look. Low-cost retailers have emerged with clothes that are fashionable but which are not designed for a long life.

At the other end of the spectrum are those clothing types normally referred to as *staple*. These include underwear, shirts and schoolwear, where the influence of fashion is minimal and there is a constant demand for large quantities. In particular, they include the garment types where a consumer makes multiple purchases, often of exactly the same thing.

Between these extremes are the garments produced in hundreds or thousands with varying levels of style change between each batch. They may be ladies' or children's dresses, men's suits, leisure and sportswear, and many other types. Consumer demand in this area is increasingly for more fashionable garments, but made to the standards of make-up and performance that are more easily achieved in high volume.

Fashion trends are rarely technology led. Most designers do not have a strong element of technology in their education, courses often having a greater emphasis on creativity than on technological content. There is a substantial interest in 'visual images', providing stimulus and excitement, but this affects only a small section of the market for clothing. The larger market is for retail- and manufacturer-label goods that draw inspiration from the fashion designers and much else besides. For this sector, technology is employed not primarily to do things that cannot be done on basic machinery, but to reduce costs, to improve quality and to reduce the requirement for human skill.

The technology that is applied to clothing must increasingly allow for versatility and responsiveness to market demand, except in the limited number of garment types such as shirts, where long runs will probably always be the case. This technology makes the management of clothing manufacture relatively uncertain in respect of output, quality and delivery. It makes economies of scale small, except sometimes in the cutting room. The technology must also cope with a continuous input of products which vary in colour, fabric, shape, feature and size, changing even more frequently to meet opportunities in a competitive marketplace. The point which will be made throughout this book is that the levels of technology used in clothing manufacture are closely related to the quantity and length of manufacturing run of a style of garment that is made.

*The clothing industry is labour intensive and has a relatively low requirement for fixed capital* Entry into the clothing industry is relatively easy. A new entrepreneur needs primarily design flair, a niche in the market, some working capital, but only a small amount of fixed capital. The reason for this relates to the simplicity of the central process in clothing manufacture, which is sewing. Although fabric must be cut before it can be sewn, and pressed after it has been sewn, it is the process of sewing that dominates the output of a clothing factory, however large or small it is.

The sewing machine is no more than a power-operated needle, with other mechanisms in synchronisation, which produces a series of stitches continually. All the rest is left to the operator. The operator controls the size of the stitch, the tension of the sewing threads and the rate of stitch formation. The operator controls the shape of the sewing line and hence the shape of the finished garment part, as well as the matching and fitting of one ply against another. In addition, the operator must interpret instructions on a work ticket about different styles, have the knowledge to thread up the machine correctly, often a highly complex process, and be able to judge acceptable quality during and after the operation. Thus, apart from a small number of operations where some form of automatic machine can be used, the operations in clothing manufacture are largely operator-controlled. This does not apply to quite the same extent in cutting and pressing.

A sewing factory produces low added value, because it is generally limited to a one operator/one machine organisation. In addition, the machine's output is constrained by the speed of stitch formation, as well as the machine speed the operator can effectively use, especially on short bursts of sewing. This is not, however, as significant as the fact that however sophisticated the engineering of stitch formation, its time requirement is only about one-fifth of the time of the average sewing operation. The other four-fifths are occupied in activities such as preparing the fabric to be sewn, trimming, folding, creasing, marking, disposal after sewing and bundling. These activities are often referred to as ancillary handling. In fact, they are the core of the typical clothing operation. Mechanisation/automation generally achieves productivity increases by reducing the ancillary handling of operators.

The reasons for the continuing dominance of the human hand stem largely from the nature of the raw materials used in clothing. First, fabrics are limp: in particular, they bend in all directions. It is therefore much more difficult and expensive to invent jigs and automatic equipment for performing sewing operations than it is for operations on the rigid materials used in other industries. Second, fabrics vary in extensibility. A certain minimum extensibility of yarn is necessary in order that the needle may penetrate the fabric satisfactorily, but extensibility that is less than that minimum and very high extensibility both give trouble in making up. This extensibility then varies, not only from fabric to fabric, but also according to the angle of the line of sewing to the lengthwise grain of the fabric. One of the difficulties inherent, for example, in the operation of sewing a sleeve into an armhole – following a complete circle around the armhole – is that the line of sewing includes all degrees of bias in the fabric and therefore all degrees of extensibility in it. Third, fabrics vary in thickness. There are problems associated with sewing very thin or very thick fabrics, and within one garment the overall thickness the operator is required to handle will vary as different numbers of plies are sewn. Fourth, because the joining must achieve compatibility with the flexibility, drape and handle of fabrics, no satisfactory general alternative to sewing has yet been generally applied. In mechanical terms, a stitch is a flexible universal joint, and it is still the only type of joint whose properties approach those of fabrics.

Machinery suppliers have sought to enhance the ability of automated machinery to be flexible. During the 1980s, large projects were funded in the USA, Japan and the EU that had the goal of increasing the competitiveness of domestic manufacture via automation. None of these projects was particularly fruitful. All have found the challenge of working with limp, deformable materials to be enormous. In principle, automation is possible, but the cost is prohibitive.

A contrast with the sewing room situation described above is provided by the activity of cutting which precedes it. The cutting room must produce as many accurately cut pieces as are required by the sewing room but, instead of working to join together single sections of garment in a three-dimensional form, the cutting process operates on flat fabric. This is significantly easier to handle and, if many plies of fabric can be piled up and some kind of vertically operating knife used, it is possible to cut out garment parts in large quantities at a time. This has led to a great deal of technical development in the various processes relating to cutting, the spreading of fabric, as well as the actual cutting itself. This in turn has led to extensive investment in computerised cutting room equipment by the larger manufacturers who are able to cut large amounts of garments using only a small staff. This is in sharp contrast to the labour-intensive nature of sewing. Visually, a cutting room is an extensive area with large tables and few operators while a sewing room always seems relatively crowded with people.

The economies of scale that are now available to companies requiring to cut large quantities of garments are such that it makes financial sense to concentrate the cutting for several sewing units into one large cutting factory which, as is explained above, will not need to employ a very large number of people. Cut garments are transported to sewing factories by road, with completed garments frequently being brought back to a central warehousing facility.

A further significant factor in the differences between the cutting and sewing activities in clothing manufacture relates to costs. The cutting room may employ a small number of people for the amount of work it produces but, because about half of the wholesale cost of a garment is in the materials, the cutting process consumes about half the company's turnover when it cuts cloth. The result of this is a strong emphasis on economy of materials in everything the cutting room does, though it will be seen that this must sometimes be compromised to fulfil the overriding need to keep the sewing room supplied with cut work. By contrast, the typical major cost in the sewing room is that of labour which, in developed countries, generally contributes 20 to 25 per cent of the total cost of a garment. Of that labour cost, 95 per cent is likely to be incurred in the sewing room and only 5 per cent in the cutting room. This leads to pressure on the productivity of sewing room labour and on labour cost. The work of the managers in many companies involves improving the efficiency of training methods so that operators may become productive as soon as possible.

*The industry has developed globalised supply chains*   Much product development is now retailer led. In such cases, at the time of establishing garment specifications, decisions may not have been made regarding *where* manufacturing is to take place. In the absence of a domestic manufacturer, the question needs to be asked: how are the technological aspects of product development going to be handled? This is a major emerging role for clothing technologists.

As far as the UK, EU and USA markets are concerned, all are experiencing large import penetration from low-cost-labour countries. However, the need to reduce lead times in the supply chain has led to a resurgence of interest in more local suppliers, and low-cost-labour countries near to the EU and the USA are seeing increasing investment in manufacturing facilities. All these global changes have implications for technology. The issues may be concerned with product specifications, quality assurance, production flexibility, short lead times, and the use of innovative technologies to create novel products, all of which need to be translated into processes and procedures that can be effectively co-ordinated from a distance. Here again, it can be expected that clothing technologists will play a crucial role in these supply chains.

# Chapter Two
# Cutting

With the exception of one-piece knitted garments, clothing is assembled from several parts. This is necessary to introduce shape, to overcome the limitations of fabric width, and because a piece of fabric wrapped around the body must be joined somewhere. The first stage in the manufacture of garments is the cutting of the materials into the necessary pattern shapes. These are then joined together by means of seams to create three-dimensional garments.

When a single garment is cut out, the garment pattern is attached to one or two plies of the fabric in a way that allows for any special requirements such as matching of the design on the fabric. The garment parts are then cut out with hand shears, electric cutters or dies. Where large quantities of a garment style must be cut, a lay is created which consists of many plies of fabric spread one above the other. From this must then be cut all the garment pieces for all the sizes planned to be cut from that lay. The pattern shapes for these garments may be drawn on a paper marker placed on top of the lay, or information as to their shape and position may be held within a computer, to be plotted similarly on a paper marker or used to drive an automatic cutter. Depending on the method of cutting that is used, there is not always a need for the pattern shapes and positions to be physically drawn on a paper marker, but whether the marker is drawn out or not, a marker plan must be made in which the pattern pieces are closely interlocked to achieve the minimum usage of fabric. In spreading the fabric to form a lay, the plies of fabric in the lay will be nominally the same length as the marker plan. A diagram of a lay, showing a paper marker, is given in Fig. 2.1.

The sizes that will be cut and the number of plies of fabric in the lay are determined by the requirements of the order for the garments, the availability of materials and the constraints of physical equipment. This is not discussed in detail here. The purpose of this chapter is to

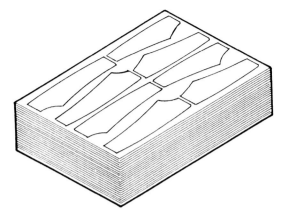

**Figure 2.1** A lay with paper marker on top.

study the technology of the cutting room which has as its objective the cutting of garment parts accurately and economically and in sufficient volume to keep the sewing room supplied with work. The four processes involved are:

- planning and, if appropriate, drawing and reproduction of the marker
- spreading of the fabric to form a lay
- cutting the fabric
- preparation of cut work for the sewing room

## Planning, drawing and reproducing the marker

It is useful to break down marker making into:

1. Marker planning, or the placement of pattern pieces to meet technical requirements and the needs of material economy.
2. Marker production, which may include drawing the marker plan directly on to fabric, drawing it on to a paper marker by pen or automatic plotter, or, where the cutting method allows it, recording pattern piece information on the paper marker or on the fabric without actually drawing pattern lines on it. Provision may have to be made for the same marker plan to be used many times.

Although the original diagram of a lay and a marker implied a large sheet of paper on which were drawn the edges of all the pattern pieces, this is appropriate only when cutting is by manually controlled knife and a line must be provided for the cutting operator to follow. Even then, it is sometimes more appropriate to mark the pattern lines directly on to the fabric rather than on to paper. Increasingly though, cutting is by computer-controlled knife and drawn pattern shapes are unnecessary.

Where a paper marker is used, it is normally stabilised on the top ply of the lay by stapling or by ironing so that an adhesive backing on the paper may lightly stick to the surface of the fabric. The paper marker is cut along with the fabric plies, and thus destroyed. Since a marker may be required for use more than once, this method needs an economical way of duplicating to provide copies. Where marking is done directly on to the fabric, it must, of course, be repeated for each spread of fabric.

## The requirements of marker planning

The industry has always paid great attention to marker planning, because when the cutting room cuts cloth it processes materials representing about half the company's turnover. Any reduction in the amount of cloth used per garment leads to increased profit.

Marker planning is a conceptualising, intuitive, open and creative process, in contrast to making up a jigsaw puzzle, which is an analytical, step-by-step and closed process. There is no final solution to a marker-planning problem, only a more tightly packed and therefore a shorter marker the more time is spent on it. In order to plan efficiently, it is necessary to visualise the marker as a whole to see it at a glance. Consequently, marker planning is a highly skilled activity and different people have different aptitudes for this kind of work. The best marker-makers can be expected to achieve utilisations one to four per cent higher than the average. Computerised marker-making systems can assist, but rarely replace, skilled people.

The planner proceeds by first positioning the larger pattern pieces in a relationship which looks promising and then fitting the smaller pieces into the gaps. Since most of the pieces are irregular and often tapered, one skill lies in discovering those edges which fit together most neatly, and placing side by side across the marker those pieces that fill the width most nearly. The planner will then try a number of pattern placements, selecting the one that gives the shortest marker. The work of the marker planner is subject to a number of constraints relating to:

♦ nature of the fabric and the desired result in the finished garment

- ♦ requirements of quality in cutting
- ♦ requirements of production planning

*Nature of the fabric and the desired result in the finished garment*

*Pattern alignment in relation to the grain of the fabric* Pattern pieces normally carry a grain line. When pattern pieces are laid down the piece of cloth, as is commonest with large pattern pieces, the grain line should lie parallel to the line of the warp in a woven fabric or the wales in a knitted fabric. Where pattern pieces are laid across the piece, the grain line should lie parallel to the weft or course direction. In bias cutting, which is often used in large pattern pieces as part of the garment style in ladies' dresses and lingerie, as well as in small pattern pieces such as pocket facings and undercollars in menswear as a requirement of satisfactory garment assembly, the grain lines will (normally) be at 45° to the warp. The designer or pattern cutter may define a tolerance that allows the marker planner to swing the grain line a small amount from parallel. If the marker planner lays down a pattern outside the stated rules for grain lines, the finished garment will not hang and drape correctly when worn. This requirement to follow grain lines restricts the freedom the marker planner has in choosing how to lay the patterns in the marker.

*Symmetry and asymmetry* Many fabrics can be turned round (through 180°) and retain the same appearance; these are designated '*two-way*' or '*symmetrical*'. They require no special action on the part of the marker planner. More restricting are fabrics with some asymmetry. In this case, if a fabric ply is turned round it does not retain the same appearance, especially when the two opposite ways are sewn together. However, in some cases, as long as the pattern pieces of an individual garment all lie in the same direction, the direction they lie in does not matter. Examples of such fabrics are those with a nap or pile which is brushed in one direction and thus presents surfaces which show different reflection of light; knitted fabrics where the loops of the wales always point in the same direction; and fabrics with a surface design which does not run the same way when turned round but where either direction is acceptable. Because of the frequently tapered shape of pattern pieces, an economical marker is usually still possible provided an even number of sets of patterns are fitted together. Even more restricting are fabrics which are '*one way*' or '*asymmetrical*'. These have a surface pile or nap or a print design which includes a recognisable object which can only be used one way up. Typical of the former would be velvet which should be cut with the pile pointing upwards. The marker planner must ensure that the top ends of the pattern pieces, as they will be worn in the garment, all face the same way.

This is likely to be less economical than other markers. It will be seen later that care must be taken to spread the fabric in the lay in such a way that effects built into the marker are retained.

*Design characteristic of the finished garment* For example, if a vertical stripe does not show a complete mirror image repeat, the right and left sides of a garment may be designed to be mirror images of each other. In this case, a marker that uses a half-set of patterns is planned, and the required effect is created in the spreading of the fabric which places pairs of plies face to face.

### Requirements of quality in cutting

For the majority of cutting situations where a knife blade is used, the placements of the pattern pieces in the marker must give *freedom of knife movement* and not restrict the path of the knife so that it leads to inaccurate cutting. A blade, which has width, cannot turn a perfect right angle in the middle of a pattern piece and space must always be allowed for a knife to turn such corners. Also, in practice a curved part of a pattern such as a sleevehead, when placed abutting a straight edge, leads to either a shallow gouge in the straight edge or the crown of the curve being straightened. The amount of space that must be left will depend on the actual cutting method employed.

*A pattern count* must always be made at the completion of the planning of a marker to check that the complete menu of patterns has been included. This is not just a formality when, for instance, a 12-garment trouser marker (where each garment may have 16 pattern pieces) signifies a complete marker of 192 pattern pieces.

*Correct labelling of cut garment parts* is essential if, in sorting and bundling a multi-size lay after cutting, operators are to identify correctly the parts which make up whole garment sizes. It is the responsibility of the marker planner to code every pattern piece with its size as the marker is planned.

### Requirements of production planning

When an order is placed for a quantity of garments, it normally specifies a quantity of each size and colour. For example, a contract for 6000 blouses may include 2400 red, 2400 blue and 1200 green, across sizes 12, 14, 16 and 18 in the ratio 2:4:4:2. The requirements of production planning and control will be to supply the sewing room with an adequate amount of cut garments at sufficiently frequent intervals, consistent with availability of fabric and the best utilisation of cutting room resources. Among the latter considerations are that, for a given quantity of garments, a high lay rather than a low lay gives a lower cutting labour cost per garment. The higher lay will, of course, also be shorter, giving a lower overall cutting time which is important if the sewing room requires the cut work urgently. The shorter lay will also require a shorter marker and in the above example the marker planner may make two markers, each containing six garments, one with two size 12s, two size 14s and two size 16s and the other with two size 14s, two size 16s and two size 18s. The planning of two shorter markers may not take more time than the planning of one long one, and since shorter markers are easier for the planner to work on, a more tightly packed and efficient marker could result. For complex garments, however, long markers generally offer more opportunities for savings than do short ones.

The mixing of sizes in a marker is to be encouraged because in general the more sizes that are included in a marker, the greater is the scope for fabric savings. If, in the above example, the marker planner could create a marker which contained the pattern pieces for a dozen garments, it would include the pieces for two size 12s, four size 14s, four size 16s and two size 18s. Unfortunately, there are a number of reasons, in addition to the production planning restrictions given above, why this may not be possible. The marker will be long and may even be too long for the cutting tables. A piece of cloth when spread to this length will not give many plies before it runs out, and it may not be possible to mix garments cut from it with garments cut from another piece because the shade may not be exactly the same. In many sewing rooms, the operators work on bundles of garments, a bundle consisting of garments that are all the same style, size and colour. Small numbers of plies of one colour spread in a lay lead to small bundles and increased costs of handling those bundles.

An alternative to the marker described above, when order quantities do not reduce to a simple ratio, is the use of single size markers on a stepped lay. If it is required to cut 95 singles of a size 14 dress and 65 singles of a size 12 dress, all in the same colour, two markers would be made with one containing the size 12 pattern pieces and one containing the size 14 pattern pieces. Sixty-five plies of the fabric would be spread to a length to include both markers, followed on top and at one end by a further 30 plies of a length to fit the size 14 marker. The marker containing the size 12 patterns would then be placed on top of the 65 plies and the marker containing the size 14 patterns on top of the 95 plies. This is illustrated in Fig. 2.2. Greater fabric savings, and often lower total cost, although with more time taken, would normally result from cutting this stepped lay as some combination of lays with mixed-size markers.

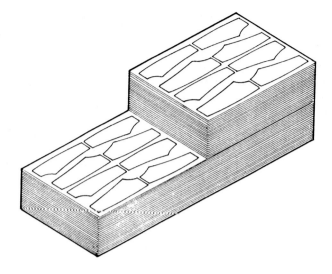

**Figure 2.2** A stepped lay with paper markers on top.

## Maximising marker utilisation

Marker planners measure their success by the utilisation (or efficiency) of the marker plan created. A formula describes this:

$$\text{Marker utilisation} = \frac{\text{Area of patterns in the marker plan}}{\text{Total area of the marker}}$$

Since the reduction in fabric cost is so important, the company expects the planner, perhaps in collaboration with a garment technologist, to discover opportunities for improvements in marker utilisation. This involves suggesting alterations to patterns and cloth, the two elements brought together in marker planning. The first sort of opportunities are commonly designated pattern engineering. Chief among these is an examination of seam location to ensure the best possible placement of patterns in the marker. In one case the shift of a seam might allow the placement of small parts in areas otherwise wasted, for instance in the armhole of a jacket or shirt lying next to the edge of a marker. In another case the seam is moved to enable the better placement of large panels across the whole width of the fabric. It goes without saying that the seam shift should not affect the appearance or balance in such a way that the designer's intentions are significantly diverted. If no change is made, however, at least the effect of not changing can be analysed, and the costs of the two alternatives presented will be known at the time the decision is made.

Again the planner may spot opportunities arising from needlessly generous seams, turnups, hems and alteration allowances. Sometimes there is an opportunity to 'piece' a pattern. This means dividing a large, awkwardly shaped pattern into two pieces, the better to accommodate it in the marker. One example is the fork on the underside of trousers, which projects from the main contour very prominently. It is common practice to cut off from the point of the fork a nearly triangular pattern piece, adding the seam widths to both new edges. This allows both the closer placement of the larger piece and the 'hiding' of the smaller piece in a waste area of the marker. The cost saving in this instance is greater than the cost of seaming the parts together.

The second sort of opportunity arises in the influence the marker planner has on the selection of fabric widths where a choice is available. The 'best' width depends among other factors on the costs of various fabric widths per square metre, the typical number of sizes in a marker, the potential pattern engineering changes at various widths and the utilisation of a series of test markers.

An important consideration is the value of the material. Low-cost linings promise much smaller savings than worsted suitings at many pounds per metre. The possibility of bigger material savings should stimulate more effort to achieve higher marker efficiency through longer lays. On the other hand, if the more expensive fabric is commonly only cut in lays a few plies high, whereas the cheaper fabric is cut several hundred plies high, the situation reverses, because what is significant is the total value of the fabric in the lay.

The range of markers used varies from perhaps shirt markers containing up to 20 garments in many sizes, through 6 to 12 garment trouser markers and 2 to 6 garment dress markers to single suit markers. However, there is considerable variation in practice even within one sector of the industry.

## Methods of marker planning and use

### Manual marker planning with full-size patterns in a full-size marker

Before the development of computerised marker planning systems, all markers were planned by working with full-size patterns. This method may still be used where companies make only short or single garment markers (e.g. customised tailoring) and the planner can see the whole of the plan relatively easily. The planner works by moving around the full-size patterns until a satisfactory plan is obtained.

Sometimes this planning is done directly on the fabric to be cut and the pattern shapes marked in immediately.

More commonly a paper marker is used for cutting; in this case the pattern lines and style and size information are usually drawn on 'spot and cross' paper to ensure adherence to grain lines. It is still essential that patterns do not become worn but a satisfactorily fine line is easier to achieve than when marking directly on to fabric as a pencil or a ballpoint pen can be used.

Multiple copies of the paper marker are normally needed. These copies can either be made when the marker plan is first drawn, or the master marker can be reproduced as needed by a variety of methods.

*Non-computerised methods*   *Carbon duplicating* is used when small numbers of copies are to be made as the original is drawn. Double-sided carbon paper or special NCR-type (no carbon required) paper can be used. In either case, six to eight copies can be made without too great a deterioration in the fineness of the line.

In *spirit duplicating* or *hectograph carbon system*, the master marker is drawn on paper with a layer of special hectograph paper underneath it. This paper transfers a blue line on to the back of the master as it is drawn. The master is then used to make one copy at a time in a duplicating machine. The machine uses alcohol to wet a plain white paper which is then passed with the master between two rollers, transferring the lines onto the copy.

The *diazo photographic method* makes as many copies of the marker as are needed, one at a time, following the drawing of a master marker. The master marker and a light-sensitive paper are passed under high intensity ultraviolet light and the light-sensitive paper is developed using ammonia vapour. The lines and other markings on the master marker prevent exposure of the light-sensitive paper which forms the copy; when developed the lines remain visible.

These copying methods were used widely in the 1970s, but have been steadily overtaken in popularity by computerised plotting. After computerised marker planning, markers are plotted out as required. This procedure has proved far more versatile and more appropriate for responsive manufacturing than any of these predecessors.

*Computerised marker planning*   This method is normally part of an integrated system which includes digitising or scanning of full-size patterns into the computer, facilities for pattern adaptation and, by inputting appropriate grade rules, the means to generate all the sizes required. The planner uses a visual display unit (VDU) with keyboard, tablet and data pen, puck or mouse.

Methods and equipment vary slightly between manufacturers but a typical example is as follows. The planner specifies the exact make-up of the marker plan: the width of the fabric, the pattern pieces to be used, the sizes to be included and all constraints to be applied, including any matching of checks. The system produces a marker plan automatically or interactively. Automatic marker planning involves calling up data defining the placement of pieces in markers previously planned, and selecting from a series the marker conformation that gives the highest marker utilisation. There is no guarantee that the best marker plan will be achieved, but this is an automatic method of achieving a plan which can then be screened by the operator.

Interactive marker planning is more common and is the process by which the operator plans markers by interacting directly with the system through a VDU screen. All the pattern pieces are displayed in miniature at the top of the screen. In the middle of the screen are two horizontal lines defining the marker width and a vertical line at the left representing the beginning of the marker. The right end is for the moment open. At the bottom of the screen is a written marker identification, with marker length and utilisation constantly updated during the planning process. A view of a computer system for marker planning, and pattern development and grading, is shown in Fig. 2.3.

A data pen (or mouse), tablet and computer keyboard are used to manipulate the pattern pieces. The tablet, which rests on the desk in front of the operator, represents the display screen and consists of a grid of fine wires immediately below the surface. When using a data pen, the pen is touched on the surface of the tablet and it registers a position on the grid which shows as a position on the screen. A combination of movements of the pen and commands via the keyboard enable pattern pieces to be moved about the screen and positioned in the marker. The system finally positions the pattern

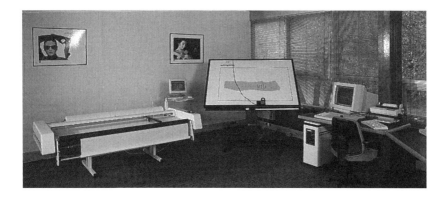

**Figure 2.3** Computer system for pattern development and grading, and marker planning and plotting. (Reproduced by permission of Lectra Systems Ltd.)

pieces precisely according to the marking rules specified. This process enables the planner to produce a trial marker very rapidly and accurately, thus enabling the planner to run through the feasible placements of pattern pieces more quickly than with non-computerised systems. After selecting the most economical marker plan devised in the time available, the computer will provide an accurate piece count, calculate a marker plan efficiency percentage and total the length of the pattern peripheries. When the marker plan is complete it will be stored in a marker plan file for future retrieval.

The quality of computerised marker planning is more consistent than that of manual methods, because instructions regarding grain lines are always followed, the butting of pattern pieces is precise with no overlapping, and the pattern count is automatic – a boon in complex markers.

It is difficult to compare the capital cost of the computer system used in marker planning with the other methods described previously because in all cases the computer system provides a pattern development and grading facility as well. In combination with a plotter, it also enables the reproduction of as many copies of a marker as are required without resorting to additional methods of reproduction such as the manual methods require. However, despite the cost of a package of computer equipment being many times that of a manual marker planning and reproducing system, computer systems have steadily become the normal way of working in the sector.

After planning the marker on the computer, the marker planner instructs the computer to plot the marker automatically on to paper. Granted a well-maintained mechanical plotter, this provides the most accurate marker. The plotter operates on a dual axis system; the x direction is determined by a beam travelling along the table, and the y direction by the pen's travel along the beam. The process requires minimum attention since the plotter uses a continuous roll of paper, and a series of markers can be plotted continuously. In practice, plotters are commonly left to run overnight. If required, markers may also be plotted to a slightly larger scale, such as a 1 per cent increase lengthwise, to allow for shrinkage on certain fabrics. Reference copies in miniature can also be plotted. It is, of course, the cleanest system of marker making. As was stated before, the planning and plotting systems involve a high capital cost, which is justified by its potential to achieve the most economical use of fabric, its ability to operate in a responsive way to customers, its savings in expensive marker planning and plotting time, and its storage of large amounts of information.

It is possible, with further investment, to feed the marker plan to a computer-controlled cutting knife. This knife does not require that the pattern shapes are drawn on paper. Indeed, it does not require a

**Figure 2.4** Top-ply labelling system. (© Lectra Systems Ltd., reproduced by permission.)

marker at all. However, for the cut work to be sectioned off correctly into garment parts and sizes, there is a need to identify the size code of each garment part the knife cuts. In such cases, the plotter will not actually draw the pattern outlines, but will write only the size codes in the correct positions on the marker and mark a corner reference point which gives an initial position to the knife. The plotting of markers by computer is shown, along with the rest of the system, in Fig. 2.3.

If cutting will be by computer-controlled knife, it is possible not to plot any of the marker but to attach adhesive labels to the top ply of fabric to give the information necessary to section garment parts into bundles. This saves both the time of plotting and the cost of plotter and paper. Instead, a system is mounted over the lay of fabric, similar in principle to the plotter described above. A beam travels along the table and a label dispenser travels along the beam, the x and y co-ordinates again giving the position. In some systems the label dispenser also prints the labels; in others they are printed separately and loaded into the dispenser. Positioning is faster when printing is done separately. The labels carry bar-coded or alphanumeric information.

An example of equipment for top-ply labelling is shown in Fig. 2.4.

## Spreading the fabric to form a lay

The objective of spreading is to place the number of plies of fabric that the production planning process has specified to the length of the marker plan, in the colours required, correctly aligned as to length and width, and without tension. Although in certain sections of the clothing industry, notably bespoke menswear, it remains necessary to cut single garments, most of the industry is able to cut garments in bulk and by doing so achieves the savings in fabric that are available through the use of multi-garment marker plans and the savings in cutting time per garment that result from cutting many plies at the same time. However, there are a number of prices to be paid for this saving in the time and cost of cutting and the cost of materials.

First, the spreading of multi-size lays of many plies demands strong tables (Fig. 2.5), usually with steel legs and braced frames, a heavy laminated, smooth wood top, and sometimes centre legs. A 10-metre lay of shirting fabric with 200 plies can weigh up to 600 kg and with 150-cm wide fabric can exert a downward pressure of up to approximately 40 kg per square metre on the table surface. The table may also bear the weight of a spreading machine, travelling on steel rails at the edge of the table. The type of table surface is critical for the spreading and cutting operations. It is usually covered with a plastic laminate or tempered hardboard, which provide a low level of friction, but in more sophisticated examples the table incorporates a source of compressed air, giving the facility of air flotation through perforations in the table surface. This enables heavy sections of lay to be moved easily along the surface of the table to the cutting operation. It is also possible to fit tables with a vacuum facility so that a high lay may be sucked down, compressed and stabilised before cutting.

Second, spreading is a time-consuming operation. With the highest lays it can consume more time in total than cutting, especially if the

**Figure 2.5** Standard 2 m spreading table. (Reproduced by permission of Macpi Group.)

cutting is by computer-controlled knife. Just as with the marking and cutting operations, the efforts of engineers have produced sophisticated equipment designed to reduce spreading time and make the operation more automatic. Before the advent of computerised marker making and computer-controlled knives, the largest capital expenditure in the cutting room was usually the purchase of spreading equipment. With a few exceptions, spreading machines can spread only one ply at a time and most developments have had the objective of simply spreading individual plies more quickly and accurately. It has to be remembered that spreading is no more than a sophisticated method of material handling, adding nothing to the manufacture of garments, yet in conventional cutting rooms it is the technological bottleneck.

A study of spreading must include the following considerations:

- requirements of the spreading process
- methods of spreading
- nature of fabric packages

## Requirements of the spreading process

Spreading must achieve a number of specific objectives:

### Shade sorting of cloth pieces

Lays commonly require more than one roll of cloth, those which include several colours normally require more than one roll of each colour to achieve enough plies in total. It is likely that cloth pieces that are nominally the same colour will have been dyed separately and are not an exact shade match. A garment made from parts cut from these different pieces would be likely to show a shaded effect between its different panels. Thus when deliveries of a number of rolls of cloth of the same colour are received, they should be sorted into batches such that shade differences between them are undetectable. This is normally done by a trained colourist but can be done more easily by a computer after measurement of the colour has been carried out using a spectrophotometer or a colorimeter (see Chapter 8).

It was stated earlier that the size of bundles of garments supplied to the sewing room is related to the number of plies of fabric of the same shade in the spread lay. Batching together rolls of the same shade gives a greater number of plies that in turn give larger bundles. Where rolls of cloth of the same colour but different shades do have to be spread adjacent to each other in the lay, they are separated by a layer of interleaving paper, a roughened tissue in a bright colour that can be seen easily at the edge of each cut stack, and which assists in easy separation of the plies for bundling. (Lays containing more than one colour are spread with the colours changing from one roll to the next to make bundling very easy.) Occasionally the relationship between roll length and marker length gives bundles that are too large for convenient handling in the sewing room. In this case the plies would be separated at suitable intervals of perhaps 10 or 12 plies with interleaving paper. The paper can also assist in holding the spread firm where fabric surfaces may slip against each other.

### Correct ply direction and adequate lay stability

These two factors must be considered together as the opportunities for achieving them are related. They depend on fabric type, pattern shape and the spreading equipment that is available.

The various types of fabric, in terms of surface direction, that are available (designated two-way and one-way) were described in the section on marker planning. For one-way fabrics, where the pattern pieces have been positioned in a particular direction in the marker plan, it is essential that the fabric is spread in a way that maintains that direction.

In addition to the visual effects of a surface design or fabric construction, problems of instability and creep can arise with fabrics with special frictional characteristics such as those with a nap or a pile surface. This can require that some fabrics are spread with all the plies face up, some with all the plies face down and some face to face.

As far as pattern shape is concerned, many garments are constructed from symmetrical pattern pieces, in which case the fabric may be spread all the same way up or face to face. If the pattern pieces are asymmetrical, however, the fabric can only be spread with all the plies face up or face down as a face to face spread will result in half the garments being asymmetrical the wrong way and produce, for instance, a double-breasted garment fastening the wrong way.

If fabric is being spread by hand or if a spreading machine with a turntable is available, there are four possible types of spread which can be achieved, combining the two directional possibilities with the face up, face down, and face to face possibilities. Some are faster than others but, aside from the question of speed, the possibilities depend on the various constraints described above. Fortunately a great many garments have symmetrical pattern pieces and fabrics which are completely plain; the fabrics are also stable spread in any configuration. The fabrics for these garments can be spread in any of the four ways provided the necessary machinery is available.

Figure 2.6 shows the spreading possibilities diagrammatically, with the unrolling of the fabric piece giving a ply laid with a

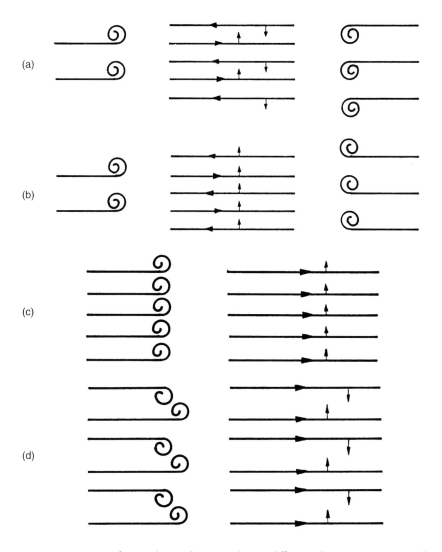

**Figure 2.6** Types of spread. (a) Alternate plies in different directions; symmetrical pattern pieces; fabric stable face to face. (b) Alternate plies in different directions; fabric stable face up; turntable spreader. (c) All plies in the same direction; fabric stable face up. (d) All plies in the same direction; symmetrical pattern pieces; fabric stable face to face; turntable spreader.

length-wise direction, and an up or down direction, as indicated by the arrows.

Methods of spreading which lay alternate plies in different directions can only be used for two-way fabrics. In this case the pattern pieces can face in either direction in the marker and the following opportunities are available:

- ◆ For symmetrical pattern pieces, and fabric that is stable spread face to face, the fabric can be spread along face up and immediately back again face down.
- ◆ For asymmetrical as well as symmetrical pattern pieces, and fabric that is stable spread all the same way up, the fabric can be spread along and immediately back again but the roll must be turned on a turntable before returning.

Methods of spreading that lay each ply in the same lengthwise direction can be used for any surface direction of fabric, but if the fabric was one-way the pattern pieces would be positioned appropriately. These represent the other two spreading opportunities:

- ◆ For asymmetrical as well as symmetrical pattern pieces, and fabric that is stable when all are placed the same way up, the spreader spreads in one direction only, returns to the starting point and spreads the next ply in the same direction.
- ◆ For symmetrical pattern pieces, and fabric that is stable face to face, the spreader spreads in one direction only but after returning to the starting point, a turntable is required to rotate the roll before the next ply is spread in the same direction.

### Alignment of plies

Every ply should comprise at least the length and width of the marker plan, but should have the minimum possible extra outside those measurements. The nature of textile materials means that pieces of fabric delivered from suppliers vary in width, both from piece to piece and to a lesser extent within single pieces. The marker plan is made to fit the narrowest width. The surplus width is usually distributed outside the edge of the marker plan farthest from the spreading operator by aligning the straight edges of the plies nearest the operator. Alternatively, plies are centred and the surplus distributed equally to both edges. Inaccuracy in this alignment could mean that plies do not cover the whole area of the marker plan and parts of some pattern pieces would be missing when cut. In addition the ends of the plies must be cut off squarely, allowing the smallest possible loss at both ends, and having regard to the weft grain.

### Correct ply tension

If the plies are spread with too slack a tension they will lie in ridges with irregular fullness. If plies are spread in a stretched state they will maintain their tension while held in the lay, but will contract after cutting or during sewing, thus shrinking the garment parts to a smaller size than the pattern pieces. In a non-stretch fabric practically all elongation of the fabric occurs in such a manner that rapid relaxation and recovery ensues. Thus the use of spreading machines with positive feed to give tension-free spreading normally obviates stretched plies being bound into the lay. On the other hand stretch fabrics containing elastic or texturised yarns or knitted fabrics designed to have 10 to 50 per cent stretch present special problems.

In addition to the tension that may be produced by a conventional spreading machine, there are likely to be tensions inherent in the fabric roll arising from the twist, texturising or elasticity of the yarn and the relationships of loops in the knitted structure. These elements of stretch do not allow rapid relaxation and recovery. Stretch fabric plies used to be positioned by hand, and, although the fabric may be dispensed from a travelling spreader, it may in some cases be unrolled and allowed to relax overnight before spreading. The width of most fabrics meant that two operators were normally required for spreading. In recent years, more attention is given to finishing and storing fabrics to keep them in a relaxed state. Full use is made of spreading machinery with good tension control.

A further difficulty lies in building an accurate edge to the spread, since knitted fabric plies, once spread on top of each other, cannot easily be shifted without localised distortion. To make use of the speed of spreading in a modern spreading machine and the accuracy of placement that comes from an alignment shifter actuated by photo-electric guides, it is necessary not only to avoid adding to the tension in the fabric but also to reduce or eliminate the inherent tensions in a stretch fabric. This can be done by agitating, flexing and vibrating the fabric in a regular manner between its dispensing from the rolled piece and its placement on the spread, just as the operators do by hand in a somewhat irregular manner.

### Elimination of fabric faults

Fabric faults (flaws, holes, stains, etc.) may be identified by the fabric supplier, and additional faults may be detected during examination of the fabric by the garment manufacturer before spreading. In either situation a 'string' or plastic tag is attached to the fabric edge level with the fault. It is possible that the spreading operator may also discover faults missed in previous examinations.

The faults which concern the cutting room are those that downgrade the garment and make it less than acceptable to the customer. First, localised defects to the fabric are considered which, unless removed, would produce substandard garments. Second, fabric faults affecting whole pieces are discussed.

There are three basic ways of responding to localised fabric faults: make-through, cut out at the lay, and sort and recut. The methods can be used in combination and there are minor options to consider that are dependent on available technology.

Make-through means leaving faults in garments and 'inspecting-out' at the end of manufacture. In other words, a policy decision is made to let faults into the sewing room and to produce substandard garments. This option is possible where there is a market for substandards and where the fault rate is not high.

Cutting out at the lay involves creating a splice. The spreader cuts across the ply at the position of the fault and pulls back the cut end to overlap as far back as the next splice mark. Splice marks are marked on the edge of the spreading table before spreading, by reference to the marker, and ensure that whenever a splice is created the overlap of fabric is sufficient to allow complete garment parts rather than sections only to be cut. The amount of fabric wasted when a splice is made thus depends not just on the size of the fault but on the size of the garment panels in that part of the marker.

Several suppliers offer computerised systems to reduce the material losses associated with cutting out at the lay. The operator is provided with a display of the marker plan on a computer screen. A reference light is mounted on the crossbar of the machine which can be moved to a position directly over the fault each time the spreading operator stops the machine at a string on the selvedge. Various options are available to the operator to deal with the fault, once it can be seen where it will come in relation to the marker plan. If the fault lies in an area of waste then no action is needed. Alternatively, a conventional splice may be seen as the best option or a fabric patch of sufficient size may be added over the flaw so that a separate recutting operation is avoided later.

The third course of action is sort and recut. Faults are normally marked with a strip of contrasting fabric but no further action is taken at spreading. After cutting is completed, the blocks are inspected (sorted) for faults and any defective pieces are recut from remnant fabric. This option can be cost-effective when the fabric costs are high, when the garment pieces are large, and when the fault rate is high. The most significant variant procedure is to place metallic stickers on the faults and to find them after cutting using a metal detector.

Three other types of fabric fault affect the fabric as a whole, and require the spreader to respond in appropriate ways. These are tight selvedges, static electricity, and fusion during cutting. Tight selvedges cause fullness in the central area of the spread. They can be corrected by cutting into the selvedge to release the tightness. Static electricity can build up within a lay, particularly with man-made fibres on dry days. In such cases, difficulty will be experienced controlling the spreading process. Fusion during cutting is not a spreading problem, but there are things that can be done during spreading to help. Cut edges of thermoplastic fibre fabrics may fuse together during cutting if the cutting knife becomes hot as a result of friction with the fabric. To help reduce the problem, anti-fusion paper can be inserted into the lay. This contains a lubricant that lubricates the knife blade as it passes through the spread, thus reducing the generation of heat energy and the temperature of the knife.

In these three cases, only partial solutions to the problems are possible. The basic problem is either poor fabric development or inadequate control of the finishing process. Clothing technologists and fabric technologists need to communicate about such problems and resolve them by ensuring the fabric is in a fit state to be processed in the cutting room.

### Avoiding distortion in the spread

Spreaders are required to lay up the fabric tension-free, so that the garment pieces do not shrink in unpredictable ways before cutting. But there are other ways that distortion can be introduced to a lay, and these need to be controlled carefully.

A layer of glazed paper is normally placed glazed side down at the bottom of the spread. This helps to avoid disturbing the lowest plies of material in the spread when the base plate of a straight knife passes underneath, and also gives stability to the lay if it is to be moved on a flotation table. In addition, it prevents snagging of the fabric on the table surface which often becomes roughened with use.

Where lays are moved by flotation, it is important that there is no differential movement of one ply against another. This will occur, for example, if the lay is moved up or down a ramp or over a ridge in the table. In the past, some transfer tables (used with computerised cutting) have been designed with several levels, with ramps to link to the spreading tables and to the cutting tables. Movement up and down these ramps has introduced distortion and has affected cutting quality adversely.

## Methods of spreading

Before describing the methods of spreading that can be used, we must look at the different forms of spread that can be created. The commonest form of spread in bulk production is one where all the plies of fabric are the same length, underlying the complete marker plan. Although this plan can contain the parts for only one garment style, it normally contains the pattern pieces for a number of garments, usually in different sizes, interlocked together in the most economical manner.

An alternative type of spread is the stepped spread in which a series of separate, usually single-size markers are positioned on top of varying numbers of plies. This was shown in Fig. 2.2. Spreading a stepped lay may take less time than the alternative of several mixed-size lays, and this shorter time may be crucial if the sewing room is to be fed with cut parts on time.

The methods of spreading that the industry uses can be classified as:

 ♦ spreading by hand
 ♦ spreading using a travelling machine

*Spreading by hand*

Despite the advent of spreading machinery which will cope with a wide variety of fabrics, there is still a frequent need to spread fabrics by hand. It is a time-consuming method, usually requiring an operator at each side of the table.

The fabric is drawn from its package which, if it is a roll, may be supported on a frame, and carried along the table where the end is secured by weights or a clamp. The operators work back from the end, aligning the edges and ensuring that there is no tension and that there are no wrinkles. The ply is normally cut with hand shears or with a powered circular knife mounted on a frame, though a few fabrics are ripped at the end of the ply to discover the exact weft grain and enable some straightening of a slightly crooked fabric to take place. Typical fabrics that are spread by hand are checks, crosswise stripes and other regularly repeating patterns, as well as those with a repeating design at intervals of a garment length. If accurate 'stacking up' of the design vertically through the spread is necessary, the fabric may be 'spiked' on to a series of sharp spikes set vertically on the spreading table. These are available with an adjusting mechanism that controls the amount of spike showing above the table, and which also enables the complete spikes to be lowered after spreading to allow for cutting or for moving of the lay along the table to a different cutting site.

The cost of hand spreading is partly offset by the ability to cut a fabric in bulk which might otherwise have to be cut in single garments.

*Spreading using a travelling machine*

Spreading machines carry the piece of fabric from end to end of the spread, dispensing one ply at a time on to the spread. Their basic elements consist of a frame or carriage, wheels travelling in guide rails at the edge of the table, a fabric support, and guide collars to aid the correct unrolling of the fabric. In the simpler versions, the operator clamps the free end of fabric in line with the end of the spread, pushes the spreader to the other end, cuts off the ply in line with that end, clamps the beginning of the next ply, pushes the spreader to the other end and so on.

More advanced spreading machines may include a motor to drive the carriage, a platform on which the operator rides, a ply-cutting device with automatic catcher to hold the ends of the ply in place, a ply counter, an alignment shifter actuated by photo-electric edge guides, a turntable, and a direct drive on the fabric support, synchronised with the speed of travel, to reduce or eliminate tension in the fabric being spread.

The maximum fabric width that can be handled is normally 2 m, although extra wide machines capable of handling up to 3 m are available. The maximum weight of cloth roll that can be carried by the larger spreading machines is 120 kg, the maximum spreading speed around 100 m/min and the maximum height of spread cloth 28 cm. When a spreading machine dispenses fabric when travelling in one direction but returns to the first end without spreading to begin the next ply, the return pass is known as 'dead heading'. Many spreaders will travel at a considerably higher speed when 'dead heading'. Heavy piece machines are usually automatic, incorporating specialised braking facilities. A modern spreading machine is shown in Fig. 2.7.

The advent of microprocessor control has enabled the development of more automatic functions on spreading machines. Thus a spreader can be preset to a selected number of plies, emitting an audible signal when it has reached the selected number or has come to the end of a piece of fabric. Automatic turntabling gives automatic spreading even for corduroys which are normally spread face to face. With automated spreading, when the piece is finished, the spreader returns to an auto-lifter at the end of the table, transfers the empty centre bar to the lifter which then advances the next piece to the spreader. It repeats the process until it achieves the required number of plies. This method can be used in conjunction with the automatic sensing of previously marked flaws and damages. As the flaw moves past the sensor, the spreader will halt, the ply cutter will cut across the ply, the spreader will reverse direction and move back to the nearest splice mark on the marker plan, and then it will continue its run to the end of the ply.

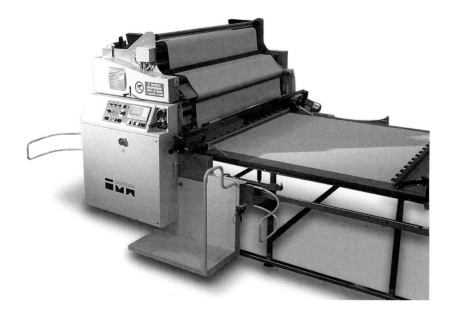

**Figure 2.7** Fully automated spreading machine with edge alignment and tension-free operation. (Reproduced by permission of Macpi Group.)

Rolls of cloth have increased in length and hence in weight over the years and even without the level of automation described above there is a need for mechanical assistance with lifting rolls of cloth from warehouse to cutting room and with loading them on to the spreading machines.

Some machines are specifically designed to lay up tubular knitted fabric (Fig. 2.8). A specially designed former is placed inside the fabric and then threaded through two nip rollers that feed the fabric on to the spreading table. The former ensures that control is maintained over the fabric tube and that no differential movement takes place.

## Nature of fabric packages

Fabric packages vary in length, width and make-up. The choice of package to be delivered to a cutting room relates to the characteristics of the fabric and the method of spreading employed. The forms of fabric piece that can be used are as follows.

### Open fabric – rolled

Most fabrics are supplied rolled as a single ply directly on to a disposable, tubular cardboard core about 7 to 8 cm in diameter. The packages are suitable for spreading by machine. When spread by hand they often require two spreading operators, one each side of the table. Open fabric may vary from less than 75 cm wide to over

**Figure 2.8** Spreading machine for tubular knitted fabric (Reproduced by permission of the Konsan Machinery Co.)

3 m, especially with knitted fabrics. Over time, the width of fabric has tended to increase, since its manufacturing costs per square metre tend to decrease with increasing width. This process is limited by the size of processing machinery and by what the garment manufacturer is prepared to handle. To reduce the manual demands of the task, a variety of cloth loading systems have been devised. A fully automated system is illustrated in Fig. 2.9.

*Tubular knitted fabric – rolled and plaited*

This is usually used for the manufacture of garments such as underwear, sports shirts and tee shirts. Often, the fabric width is that required to fit the wearer's body. The fabric fits the designed girth rather than vice versa. Plaiting (presenting the fabric in widthwise folds rather than in a roll) helps to avoid tension in the fabric.

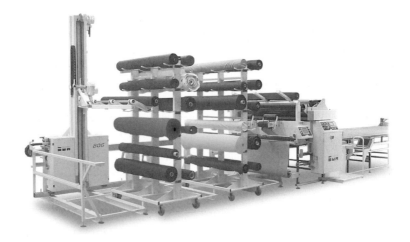

**Figure 2.9** Automated system for handling open-width rolls. (Reproduced by permission of Macpi Group.)

### Folded fabric – rolled and plaited

This form is traditional with the woollen and woollen mixture fabrics used in tailored garments. The fabric is rolled on to a disposable, flat board approximately a centimetre thick. It is not suitable for spreading by machine, but its lesser width allows it to be spread manually by one spreader on narrower tables. Its width commonly varies from about 70 to 80 cm folded. With folded fabric the marker contains only a half set of patterns, since the fabric by its attitude is spread face to face.

Plaited (or cuttled) folded fabric occurs usually with checks and some tubular knits, and aims to avoid the distortions that may result from tight rolling. The doubled fabric is folded accurately backwards and forwards in lengths of approximately 80 to 90 cm, the end of the piece being wrapped around the pile of folds or cuttle.

### Velvet – hanging

More rarely, some velvets may be delivered wound on specially constructed frames to prevent the pile becoming crushed.

There has been a trend towards heavy pieces of 500 or even 1000 metres. Generally, the longer the piece of fabric, the lower the cost of manufacture and packaging per square metre. This benefits the fabric supplier, but in a competitive market part of the benefits will be passed on to the garment manufacturer as lower priced fabric. In addition, garment manufacturers can reduce handling costs although specialised handling equipment is required. In spreading, the heavy piece reduces total loading and threading times on the travelling spreader, and increases the number of plies available from each piece. With effective control of shading over a larger area, it will also reduce the garment maker's costs in demarcating different shades from piece to piece. Finally, the longer the piece, the smaller is the percentage of wastage through remnants. This trend is being obviated by the prevalence of smaller contracts and the need for smaller batch production.

## Cutting the fabric

The use of the term cutting can present a difficulty. It is often used in the sense of 'cutting room', an area that normally includes the activities of marker planning, spreading and preparation for sewing, as well as being used to refer to the actual cutting out of garment parts from the lay.

### The objective of cutting

The objective of cutting is to separate fabric parts as replicas of the pattern pieces in the marker plan. In achieving this objective, certain requirements must be fulfilled:

*Precision of cut*

Garments cannot be assembled satisfactorily, and they may not fit the body correctly, if they have not been cut accurately to the pattern shape. The ease with which accuracy is achieved depends on the method of cutting employed and in some cases on the marker planning and marker making, as described earlier. In manual cutting using a knife, accuracy of cut, given good line definition, depends on appropriate, well-maintained cutting knives and on the skill and motivation of the cutter. In both die cutting and computer-controlled cutting, the achievement of accuracy comes primarily from the equipment.

*Clean edges*

The raw edge of the fabric should not show fraying or snagging. Such defects come from an imperfectly sharpened knife.

It is possible for the knife blade to heat up sufficiently to damage the fabric. The problem arises from the friction of the blade passing through the fabric. In extreme cases, it leads to scorching of the fabric and, more likely, to the fusing of the cut edges of fabrics with thermoplastic fibres. In such cases, the cutter is unable to separate individual plies from the pile of cut parts. Forced separation causes snagged edges and, in any case, the hard edge is uncomfortable in wear. Solutions to this problem lie in well-designed fabric finishing and in a well-sharpened blade. Some help may be obtained from using a blade with a wavy edge, the use of anti-fusion paper during spreading, spraying the blade with air coolant/lubricant, slowing down the speed of the blade, and reducing the height of the lay.

### Support of the lay

The cutting system must provide the means not only to support the fabric but also to allow the blade to penetrate the lowest ply of a spread and sever all the fibres.

### Consistent cutting

The cutting system will cut lays up to a specified height, but this may need to be reduced as a response to deteriorating cutting quality. There may be mechanical or human reasons, involving toppling or leaning, for the height of the lay to be limited.

## Methods of cutting

Numerous attempts have been made over the years to develop methods of cutting cloth other than by means of some kind of metal blade. Work continues in this direction and the main alternatives will be described later, but in the majority of cutting rooms today, the cutting process makes use of hand shears, a mechanised knife blade in one of several possible types, or a die press that stamps out the garment shapes.

In all of these methods, a sharp blade is pressed against the fibres of the fabric. The blade must present a very thin edge to the fibres, to produce a bearing pressure high enough to shear the fibres without exerting a force that will stretch or deform the fabric. All fibres must be severed to allow the blade to pass through the fabric and produce free-standing cut parts. The act of cutting dulls the blade, which must be sharpened regularly to renew the thin sharp edge. This wears the blade and leads to its eventual replacement. Where an upright, mechanised knife blade is used, the blade must point in the direction of travel through the fabric when cutting straight or at a tangent to the line of cut on a curve. These methods of cutting remove no material between the cut parts (in contrast to the act of sawing wood which creates sawdust). The blade opens the cut after the fibres are severed, and the rest of the blade passes through the cut by compressing the material on either side (especially when cutting a curve). Normally fabrics return to their original shape after cutting. The following cutting systems are currently in use, separately or in combination.

## Hand shears

Hand shears are normally used only when cutting single or double plies. The lower blade of the shears passes under the plies, but the subsequent distortion of the fabric is only temporary and accurate cutting to the line can be achieved with practice. Left-handed shears are available since the cutting line will not be seen easily if right-handed shears are used by a left-handed person. This method is flex-ible enough to accommodate any fabric construction and pattern shape. The obvious disadvantage of the method lies in the time it consumes and the consequent high labour cost per garment, but it is appropriate for made-to-measure garments.

## Straight knife

Most cutting rooms that cut garments in bulk make use of straight knives. The elements of a straight knife consist of a base plate, usually on rollers for ease of movement, an upright or standard carrying a straight, vertical blade with varying edge characteristics, and an electric motor above it, a handle for the cutter to direct the blade, and a sharpening device. The base plate on its rollers slides under the glazed paper which is spread below the bottom ply of fabric in the lay. A typical straight knife is illustrated in Fig. 2.10. Both this and the round knife mentioned later are hand-held power tools requiring an overhead cable feed and statutory safety precautions.

Two kinds of power are required to operate a straight knife. Motor power drives the reciprocating blade, and operator power drives the knife through the lay. The motor power needed is determined by the height of the lay, the construction of the fabric, the curvature of the line being cut (which causes the rear of the blade to press against the cut fabric plies) and the stroke of the blade. The greater the power of the motor, the heavier the machine. The taller the standard, the thicker its cross-section and the greater its width, adding resistance to the forward movement on a curve. Normally available blade heights

**Figure 2.10** Straight knife. (Reproduced by permission of Eastman Machine Co. Ltd.)

vary from 10 cm to 33 cm. Normally available strokes vary from 2.5 cm to 4.5 cm. The greater the blade movement, the faster the blade cuts the fabric and the more rapidly and easily the operator can push the machine, although proportionately greater motor power is required.

The most important consideration in selecting a straight knife is the power required from the operator to move the knife through the lay. Operator effort is affected by the weight of the motor, the shape of the standard, handle height (awkward if too far above the lay), stroke, sharpness of blade, and the effect of the baseplate rollers on the table surface. The first four are involved in the choice of machine and the remainder in effective maintenance at the workplace. In particular, the sharpness of the blade and its constant bevel is most consistently achieved by the use of a continuous abrasive belt, available in a series of grits from coarse to fine. The normal blade has a straight edge, varying from coarsely ground for use with densely woven and coated fabrics, through various grades of roughness to a fine edge for cutting synthetic fabrics, knits and loose wovens. As stated previously, knife blades are also available with wavy edges to reduce heat generation and the possibility of fusing synthetic materials. Variable speed machines are available, allowing the same machine to be used to cut natural and thermoplastic fibres as well as allowing for a change of speed between long straight cuts and tight curves. The option of selecting a machine with a different blade stroke provides another way of solving the problem of the fusing of synthetics, as an alternative to varying the machine speed.

The straight knife is a common means of cutting lays in conventional cutting rooms because it is versatile, portable, cheaper than a band knife, more accurate on curves than a round knife, and relatively reliable and easy to maintain. Even if a band knife is used for the main cutting operation, a straight knife will be used to separate the lay into sections for easier handling.

A more recent development has been a travelling suspension system equipped with a modified straight knife. This system supports the knife from above, which allows the heavy base plate and rollers to be replaced with a small, flat base, reducing the possibility of distortion during cutting which can arise from the thickness of the conventional base plate. Suspension from above also reduces the need for a heavy gauge standard behind the knife, and the width of the blade is also reduced, allowing easier cutting of sharper curves. The drive trolley of the support arm moves automatically along rails on the side of the table supports as the straight knife is moved during the cutting process, allowing the best support to the knife at any part of the lay. These servo knife systems enable a much higher degree of cutting accuracy than unsupported straight knives, with less operator skill required. In many cases they allow a standard of cutting to be achieved with a straight knife that is normally only achievable by transporting roughly cut work to a band knife. The system is shown diagrammatically in Fig. 2.11.

### Round knife

The elements of a round knife, pictured in Fig. 2.12, are a baseplate, above which is mounted an electric motor, a handle for the cutter to direct the blade, and a circular blade rotating so that the leading edge

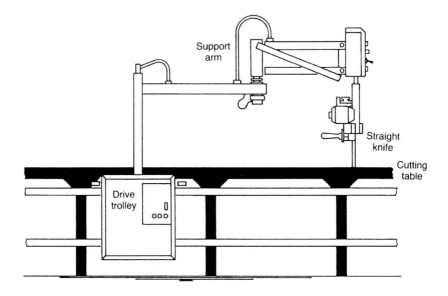

**Figure 2.11** Straight knife with servo-assisted arm support.

cuts downwards into the fabric. Blade diameters vary from 6 cm to 20 cm. Knives with smaller diameter blades are termed 'electric shears' and are used for cutting simple pieces of fabric (Fig. 2.13). Round knives are not suitable for cutting curved lines in high lays because the blade does not strike all the plies simultaneously at the same point as a vertical blade does. Therefore a round knife is used only for straight lines or lower lays of relatively few plies. It is naturally much more difficult for a circular blade to negotiate a tight curve, such as an armhole.

*Band knife*

A band knife comprises a series of three or more pulleys, powered by an electric motor, with a continuously rotating steel blade mounted on them. One edge of the blade is sharpened. The principle of operation is different from a straight or a round knife in that the band knife passes through a slot in the cutting table in a fixed position and the section of lay to be cut is moved past it. The blade is usually narrower than on a straight knife and there is no standard behind it, both factors which assist the cutting of tight curves. A band knife workplace may be arranged so that the operator either pushes or pulls the section of

Figure 2.12 Round knife. (Reproduced by permission of Eastman Machine Co. Ltd.)

lay towards the knife. The latter is most common in Britain. A band knife is shown in Fig. 2.14.

Band knives are used when a higher standard of cutting accuracy is required than can be obtained with a straight knife. Space must be left around garment parts when planning the marker so that they can be sectioned out using a straight knife and then cut exactly using the band knife. When small parts such as collars, cuffs and pockets are cut, a template of metal or fibre board in the shape of the pattern piece may be clamped to the section of lay on top of the marker,

**Figure 2.13** Electric shears. (Reproduced by permission of Eastman Machine Co. Ltd.)

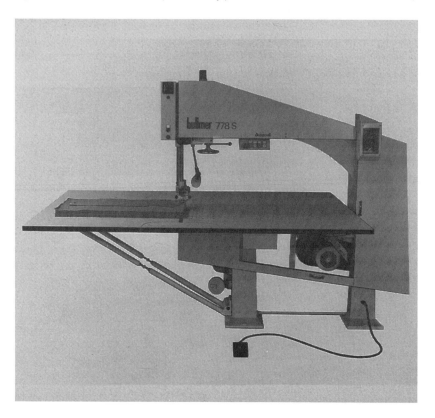

**Figure 2.14** Band knife. (Reproduced by permission of Pfaff Bellow Ltd.)

which is then drawn past the band knife blade, cutting exactly along the hard edge. Band knives are used more in menswear than in womenswear and are often used to cut large garment parts such as the large panels of jackets and overcoats.

### Computer-controlled cutting knives

In describing the use of computer systems for marker planning and marker making, the possibility of using the information stored in the computer to drive a cutting knife was mentioned. This method provides the most accurate possible cutting, at high speed, and to keep the larger systems fully occupied they are used frequently in a central cutting facility that supplies a number of separate sewing factories. Increasingly, though, smaller, cheaper systems are being developed which are suitable for companies wanting to cut lower lays of smaller quantities of garments and these are appropriate for a single-factory operation. The main elements of a computer-controlled cutting system are shown in Fig. 2.15.

A typical computer cutting system has a table with a cutting surface consisting of nylon bristles, which support the fabric lays but are flexible enough to permit penetration and movement of the knife blade

**Figure 2.15** Computer-controlled knife cutting and table. (© Lectra Systems Ltd., reproduced by permission.)

which is supported only at the top. The bristles also allow the passage of air through the table to create a vacuum, reducing the height of the lay and holding it in place. The carriage supporting the cutting head has two synchronised servo-motors which drive it on tracks on the edges of the table. A third servo-motor positions the cutting head on a beam across the width of this carriage. These two movements are co-ordinated to give a knife position at any point on the table. The cutting head (Fig. 2.16) contains a knife, automatic sharpener and a further servo-motor which rotates the knife to position it at a tangent to the line of cut on curves. A further facility controls the deflection of the knife which inevitably occurs on curves by adjusting the angle to equalise the pressure on each side of the blade. This ensures accurate cutting through all layers. A sheet of airtight polyethylene covers the top of the lay which assists the creation of a vacuum and allows significant compression of the lay. A control cabinet houses the computer and the electrical components required to drive the cutter, its carriage and the vacuum motor.

The spreader spreads the lay on a conventional cutting table equipped with air flotation. Paper is spread below the bottom ply so that the lay can be moved on to the cutting table without distortion

**Figure 2.16** Computer-controlled cutting head in action. (© Lectra Systems Ltd., reproduced by permission.)

and so that the bottom plies are supported during the cutting operation. This paper is perforated to enable the vacuum on the cutting table to operate to compress the lay.

After loading the disc into the computer, the operator positions the cutting head's origin light over the corner of the spread. This provides the computer with a reference point. A lift and plunge feature enables the knife to negotiate sharp corners; straight or V-shaped notches can also be cut. A motorised drill behind the cutting head can provide drill holes as required. Different systems are available, designed to cut different heights of compressed plies. The maximum height is usually 7.5 cm when compressed, with the height before compression, and hence the number of plies, being dependent on the nature of the fabric. The type of powerful cutting head designed to cut this high is more costly than one designed for lower ply heights and it cannot cut as fast. A manufacturer who cuts only low lays, e.g. 2 cm compressed, would invest in the less expensive, faster system. Quoted figures for actual knife speeds can be as high as 80 m/min but the overall speed of cutting garment parts is generally between 5 and 12 m/min, with the higher overall speeds being obtained when cutting large rather than small garment parts.

Different arrangements of cutting room tables are possible, but they must allow for the fact that in this situation the cutting process takes much less time than spreading and somewhat less time than bundling. A typical arrangement would consist of four spreading tables supplying each cutting table. The cutting table and its carriage and cutting head is able to move between the spreading tables by means of tracks on the floor and has, beyond it, four bundling tables on to which the cut garments are moved. When the cutting table is lined up with a table on which a lay has been prepared, the lay is floated on to it in sections which are then cut and moved on to the bundling table. The cutting table does not need to be as long as the lay and its bristle surface can consist of a conveyor that assists in the transfer of the lay, in sections, from the spreading table and of the cut work on to the bundling table. The rotation of the conveyor with its bristle surface also assists in cleaning waste material from the surface. An alternative arrangement is for a flotation cutting table to be used as a transfer table to a fixed cutting table carrying the cutting head. The transfer table has to be as long as the lay and a table for bundling would be required beyond the cutting table.

Since it is possible to cut a lay in sections, machinery suppliers have developed bite cutting systems. The cutting table is mobile and can be connected directly to spreading tables. The lay is moved to the cutting zone using air flotation, and thereafter the conveyor system takes over. The lay is cut in bites, and operators have to remove each bite of cut work during the time the cutter is working on the next bite. Meanwhile, the spreading table is prepared for the next lay. This mode of operation has reduced cost and space requirements and is fully compatible with the need for small batch production.

Since the computer-controlled knife cuts according to instructions from the computer rather than by following a pattern line drawn on a marker, it is possible, as indicated previously, to dispense with the use of fully plotted paper markers and either just plot the information necessary for bundling on the marker, or elimininate the marker completely and just label the garment parts that are being cut. Care must be taken that the correct disc is loaded into the computer so that the correct garments are cut. An error here would be costly in wasted fabric and, without a plotted marker on top of the lay, it may not be immediately obvious that the computer-controlled knife is cutting a different style from that intended.

### Die cutting

In contrast to the fast-moving blades used in the methods of cutting previously described, die cutting involves pressing a rigid blade through the lay of fabric. The die (called a clicker in the shoe industry) is a knife in the shape of a pattern periphery, including notches. One or more tie bars secure its stability. Free standing dies generally fall into two categories. They can be made of strip steel, manufactured by bending the strip to the shape required and welding the joint. These cannot be sharpened and must be replaced when worn. Alternatively, they can be heavier gauge, forged dies that can be resharpened but which are about five times the price of strip steel. The position of the tie bars determines the depth of cut, which is generally greater with forged dies.

Free standing dies cut the small parts of larger garments such as collars and trouser pocketing or the parts of smaller garments such as bras. They can also be used for part of a larger garment part, such as the neck area of a coat front. They provide a high standard of accuracy of cutting but, because of the cost of the dies, they are only appropriate to situations where large quantities of the same pattern shape will be cut. Die cutting also offers much faster cutting than knife cutting for the same depth of cut. It is proportionally more economic for small parts, which have a greater periphery in relation to their area than do large parts. In addition, the level of accuracy demanded of small parts is not only greater but correspondingly more difficult to achieve with conventional knives.

The die press generally has a cutting arm supported by a single pillar at the back of the machine. It swings to the side to allow the placing of dies on top of the fabric. The downward cutting stroke of the press should be controlled so that the edge of the die just penetrates the cutting pad or surface in order that the fibres of the lowest ply are separated completely. Die presses are of two types: impact, which make a single press on the die, and, more commonly, hytronic (hydraulic and electronic), which exert continuous pressure on the die until it has cut the fabric and made contact with the soft metal or nylon pad. Once the pad, after repeated cutting, reaches an unsatisfactory state of wear, its surface is recut and relevelled (or replaced).

For die cutting, the spreader spreads a lay to the required number of plies and may place a marker on top to guide the placement of dies. The spread is cut into sections to allow transport to the cutting pad. In some cases, no marker is used, the operator placing the dies by eye to the correct grain line and as close together as this method allows.

One important disadvantage of die cutting is its greater use of fabric. When the die press forces the dies through the fabric it also forces a narrow wedge of fabric between the dies. The narrow wedge exists because the sharpened cutting edge of the die is necessarily of narrower gauge than the top of the die. Thus if dies are butted together, they touch at the top but show a small gap at the level of the cutting edges. The action of the press will compress this narrow wedge of fabric to the point where it will rupture the dies. Hence it is necessary to leave a significant gap between two dies, say 2–3 mm. Similarly a single die will not cut satisfactorily if placed closer than 3–4 mm to a previously cut edge.

Large area die cutting presents a number of technical problems. A complete lay of free dies several metres long on top of the fabric could be cut by a twin pillar or four pillar press extending across the lay. For economic and engineering reasons, the depth of the press is limited. Hence the lay is cut in sections, the downward stroke of the press alternating with the forward movement of a conveyorised bed. This gives partial coverage of larger dies at certain strokes of the press, causing the dies to break. One solution is the die forme, for instance a plywood backing with strip steel dies set in it blade upwards. The fabric plies are spread on top of the die forme and the strokes of the die press successively press the fabric down on to the blades. Foam inserts within the dies assist the operation of stripping out after cutting. Some fabric stretch may result when the press head does not completely cover a die, because while part of the fabric is pressed on to the die, the area just outside the head remains on the surface. The capital cost of large area die presses is high but more importantly, the cost of tooling up with die formes, to cover all markers in all styles and fabric widths, is prohibitive in a frequently changing market. Hence the circumstances where large area die cutting is profitable are rare. An exception is the cut-and-sew knitwear industry.

All the cutting methods described so far have made use of a metal blade in some form, powered by hand or machine. This is not the only way to separate materials, but it is reliable in that a cut is assured whichever of the methods is used. Several high energy sources that can be concentrated into a moving point have been tried for the cutting of fabric. It will be seen that some of them can be used effectively but all carry the possibility of insufficient energy and hence poor quality cutting or even complete lack of cutting. All are controlled in a similar way to the computer-controlled knife already described.

Single or low ply die cutters are available, which have proved particularly successful with knitted products from both V-bed and circular machines. V-bed machines produce garment blanks that require some cutting before assembly; circular machines may be used for producing garment blanks, and also striped fabrics that must be cut carefully to enable stripe matching. The single ply die cutters allow the user to create shaped cutting blades from straight steel knives, and the changeover time is quite short. The operator's task is to load the garment panel to the machine, checking that the alignment is correct. The die press stacks the cut work automatically.

### Laser cutting

A laser produces a beam of light that can be focused into a very small spot (0.25 mm), producing a very high energy density and a rapid, localised increase in temperature. Cutting takes place by burning, melting and vaporisation. A laser beam does not become blunt and need renewing, but it does suffer from limited depth of focus. This limits the depth of fabric it can cut and the best results are achieved when cutting single plies. There is also a risk with thermoplastic fibres that the edges may fuse together.

The system includes a stationary gas laser, a cutting head carrying a system of mirrors which reflect the laser beam to the cutting line, a computer which operates the entire system, and a means of removing cut parts from the conveyor carrying the single ply of fabric. A practical limitation on the speed of cutting is the speed of movement of the carriage bearing the mirrors.

Automatic, single ply, laser cutting is fast compared with automatic multiple ply knife cutters, with speeds of 30–40 m/min being achieved compared with 5–12 m/min quoted already for knife cutting. However, when the cutting of a number of plies is taken into consideration, knife cutters are faster per garment cut, especially with the recent developments towards faster and cheaper equipment for cutting at low and medium ply heights. Such equipment is cheaper to purchase than a laser cutter, and that, combined with its higher cutting speed per garment, has ensured that, for the present, laser cutting seems unlikely to become widespread in the cutting of garments. There are advantages to single ply cutting which relate to the use of information stored in the computer that is controlling it. In principle, this can enable local adjustments to be made to allow for fabric width variation, check matching, avoidance of flaws, and immediate recutting of parts that are flawed. However, most manufacturing units require garments to be transported and presented in some quantity greater than singles, which discourages the use of single ply cutters.

The main disincentives to the use of laser cutters are the quality of the cut edge (which may become charred and, with thermoplastics, may affect the feel of the edge), the possibility of less than 100 per cent efficient cutting (as uncut threads can pull and adversely affect the visual appearance of the fabric), and the requirements to maintain the equipment.

Lasers are not common for cutting garments, but they have been used successfully in home furnishings and in the cutting of sails (where edge fusing is actually desirable). They are growing in use for the production of patterns, labels and appliqués, often in conjunction with embroidery. There is a potential growth area with customised garments, particularly if the concept of mass customisation becomes popular.

### Plasma cutting

Plasma cutting was originally developed to satisfy a demand for high quality cutting on stainless steels and aluminium, but it can also be used to cut textile materials. Cutting is achieved by means of a high velocity jet of high temperature ionised gas (argon). This method has the potential to become the faster cutter of single plies, but there are engineering and cost issues, and the method is affected by the same quality of cut problems as was noted for laser cutting.

### Water jet cutting

A very high velocity, small diameter stream of water is created by applying high pressure water to a nozzle. The high pressure jet acts as a solid tool when it encounters the material to be cut, tearing the fibres on impact. As the jet penetrates successive plies in a spread, the momentum decreases and cutting ability is reduced. The jet spreads out and the cut is wider and rougher at the bottom of the spread. Here the jet of water is normally caught and drained away. There is a danger of wet edges, water spotting and inconsistent cutting quality. The water used must be filtered and de-ionised.

Water jet cutting is most effective with harder sheet materials, including leather and plastic. A complete computer system has been developed for leather in which hides are inspected and blemishes marked, and the hides then scanned into the computer. A marker plan is made in which the pattern pieces are planned on to the hide, allowing for blemishes and for the varying thicknesses that occur in leather; the hide is then cut automatically, in a single layer, by water jet. Capital costs are high and it is difficult to see such systems being taken up by the many small companies in the leather side of the industry. Currently, much leather is cut by hand-held knife blade on a glass surface, with the visual appearance and thickness of the hide being taken into account as every pattern piece is placed. There is no grain direction to be considered.

### Ultrasonic cutting

More recently developed are cutting systems that use an ultrasonically driven knife blade. Vibration frequencies in the 20 kHz range produce 1/20 mm movement in the blade, small enough to remove the need for a bristle base to the cutting table. Disposable knife blades save sharpening time and last for 10 to 14 days. Single ply and very low lays can be cut and low vacuum only is needed.

### Notchers

Many garment parts require that notches are cut into the edges of them to enable alignment during sewing with other garments parts. The previously described methods of cutting can be used to cut notches, but accuracy depends on the operator. Specialised notching equipment provides greater accuracy because a guide lines up the notcher with the cut edge to give consistent depth of notch at a consistent right angle to the edge. A knife notcher is an upright, cylindrical device which cuts the side of a block to a predetermined distance. Both straight notches and V notches are available. An alternative machine, the hot notcher, incorporates a heating element in order that the blade may slightly scorch the fibres adjacent to the notch in order to prevent it fraying and disappearing. This cannot be used with thermoplastic fibres or certain unlined garments. One fabric requiring it may be a loosely woven tweed. A notcher is illustrated in Fig. 2.17.

**Figure 2.17** Hot notcher. (Reproduced by permission of Eastman Machine Co. Ltd.)

## Drills and thread markers

Where reference marks are needed away from the edge of a garment part, such as for the position of pockets, darts and similar features, a hole is often drilled through all the plies of fabric in the lay. The drill mounting includes a motor, a base plate with a hole to allow the drill to pass through, and a spirit level to ensure that the base is horizontal and hence the drill vertical. Figure 2.18 shows the essential features. On many fabrics the drill is used cold and the hole remains visible until the sewing operator comes to use it. On looser weave fabrics, where the hole may close up, a hot drill is used, which will slightly scorch or fuse the edges of the hole. A hypodermic (or dye spot) drill may also be used which leaves a small deposit of paint on each ply of fabric.

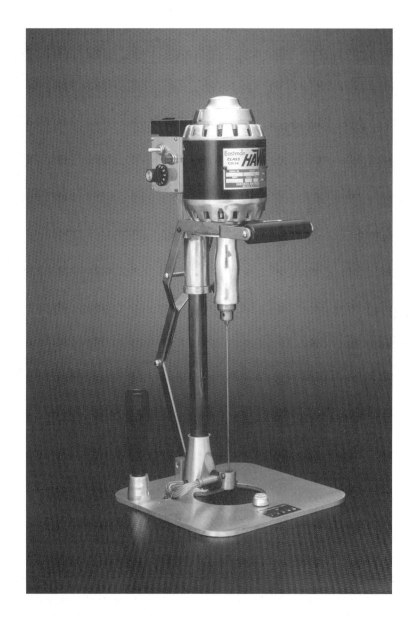

**Figure 2.18** Hot drill. (Reproduced by permission of Eastman Machine Co. Ltd.)

All drill holes must eventually be concealed by the construction of the garment.

With multi-coloured, or loosely woven fabrics, or if it is important that no mark remains on the fabric, a thread marker is used (Fig. 2.19). A long thread may be passed through the lay which is then cut with scissors between each ply, leaving a few centimetres visible on each garment panel.

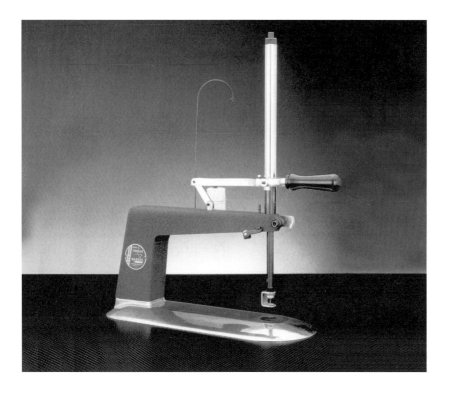

**Figure 2.19** Thread marker. (Reproduced by permission of Eastman Machine Co. Ltd.)

## Preparation of cut work for the sewing room

Some preparatory activities are contemporaneous with cutting, for example notching and drill marking to assist the sewing operation. The most important preparatory activities are bundling, controlling shade separation, indicating the right side of the fabrics, and work ticketing.

### Bundling

Many sewing rooms use the bundle system, whereby small batches of garments move from one workstation to another in a controlled way. Batches may all be the same size (ten units, one dozen, two dozen, etc.), or they may vary depending on the way the fabric has been spread. The task of work preparation is to split the lay (of say 100 plies) into smaller batches in a controlled way.

In order to prepare the cut work, it is necessary for operators to be able to identify each stack. This is the function of the marker, if used, as the style number, the size and the part identification will be part of the plot. If markers are not used (as is possible with computerised cutting), a top-ply labelling system is required.

Many western companies use teamwork systems that eliminate the bundle. In these cases, teams work directly from stacks. The task of work preparation then is to ensure that teams receive all the stacks of cut work needed to make up the garments. Another unit production system involves the use of overhead rails, often powered. Stacks of cut work are fed to a loading station and an operator loads the relevant parts to a specially designed hanger.

## Shade separation control

Variations in colour within dyelots are quite common, and cutting rooms generally maintain checks that the fabric cut is within the tolerance levels set by the customer. Nevertheless, within the batch of fabric cut, there are likely to be shade differences. Some cutting rooms shade-separate by inserting tissue paper between every piece. Others group pieces into batches that have a uniform shade, and instead of say ten shades in the lay, they have only two or three. At the preparation stage, these shades are generally kept separate, to avoid the problem of garments being made up with differently shaded pieces; this is generally the reason for bundles having a variable size.

It might be thought that the answer is to avoid the need to shade-separate by first identifying the top ply of the bundle and then working systematically through the batch. This is, of course, easy to do with the unit production systems, but the bundle system is not a good way of retaining this level of order. Although maintaining the stack sequence is possible, many companies have found that the risks are too high. With quality outerwear garments, it is quite common to give every garment piece a pressure-sensitive adhesive ticket with a ply number. This technique is called soabaring, named after the dominant supplier of the ticketing equipment.

## Indication of the right side of fabrics

Some fabrics have an obvious difference between the front and the back. In such cases, there is no real problem for machinists to identify at a glance how to grasp and manipulate the pieces. Other fabrics are identical on both sides, and again there is no problem. The need for right side identification comes where there is a close similarity between the face and the back of fabrics, and when it is important for the fabric face to be on the outside of the garment. For example, the face may be intentionally slightly glazed, but this cannot be seen easily under factory lighting conditions. Another example relates to some double jersey knitted fabrics that have a slightly different loop appearance on the front than on the back.

Right side identification may use soabar tickets, whereby the ply number is always positioned on the fabric face. Alternatively, an adhesive label is placed on the face of the top ply of a stack, and the machinist then places the stack with the top ply uppermost. The operator can then work through the stack without having to inspect each piece. The latter method does require operators to handle bundles carefully and to ensure the sequencing of plies is not disrupted.

With teamworking or other unit production systems, either the cut paper marker or the top ply label at the top of the stack serves as the identifier.

## Work ticketing

Wherever bundles are used, they are accompanied by work tickets. Tickets provide basic information about the work: the style number, the size of the garment, the number of garments in the bundle, and the date issued. In addition, the operations are often incorporated in the ticket, generally for payment purposes, assisting the control of work, and facilitating quality control.

Work tickets are generally created on site once the outcome of spreading/cutting is known. Computerised management information systems have well-established routines to print the required tickets, which are then linked up with the bundled work.

# Chapter Three
# Sewing

The dominant process in garment assembly is sewing, still the best way of achieving strength and flexibility in the seam as well as flexibility of manufacturing method. Much of the application of technology to clothing manufacture is concerned with the achievement of satisfactorily sewn seams.

It is necessary to define the term 'seam' at an early stage in any discussion because its application is broader than is generally realised. In common parlance, a seam joins two pieces of material. Indeed, this was the essence of the British Standard definition of seams as contained in the 1965 version of BS 3870: *Schedule of Stitches, Seams and Stitchings*. The noun 'stitching' then applied to situations where there was only one piece of fabric, such as when fabric edges were neatened or hems created, and where decorative sewing was involved.

The current BS 3870: Part 2: 1991: *Classification and Terminology of Seam Types*, and the earlier 1983 edition, define a seam as 'the application of a series of stitches or stitch types to one or several thicknesses of material'. Thus the term includes virtually all sewing that goes into garments. Perhaps in the future, the further development of non-sewing methods of seaming will cause this definition to be altered, but the current definition is appropriate to present purposes.

The properties that seams have to achieve can be stated quite simply at an introductory level, but the factors involved in achieving those properties are complex and interrelated. The general properties of sewn seams in garments are discussed in this chapter in order to relate the many relevant factors together as rapidly as possible. The following chapter explores the technical considerations in greater depth by studying the machinery used.

# Properties of seams

The objective of sewing is the construction of seams that combine the required standards of appearance and performance with an appropriate level of economy in production.

Good appearance in a seam normally means smooth fabric joins with no missed or uneven stitches and no damage to the material being sewn. Alternatively it may mean regular gathering to create a style feature or a varying but controlled amount of ease to ensure a good fit to the body. In other cases, fabric may be stretched deliberately to achieve an effect but the amount should still be predetermined and controlled. With the wide variety of fibre types and fabric constructions available, good seam appearance during manufacturing demands varying techniques. Once it has been achieved, it must be maintained throughout the designed lifetime of the garment, despite the additional problems that arise during wearing, washing and dry cleaning processes.

Performance of seams means the achievement of strength, elasticity, durability, security and comfort, and the maintenance of any specialised fabric properties such as waterproofing or flameproofing. Seams must be as strong as the fabric, in directions both parallel to and at right angles to the seam. They must also stretch and recover with the fabric. Stretch fabrics are increasingly being used in garments, both low level 'comfort' stretch as used in stretch corduroy or denim where the amount of stretch may be up to about 30 per cent, and high level 'action' stretch for swimwear and dancewear where 100 per cent or more is normal. Such levels of stretch place very heavy demands on seaming. Seams must also be durable to the kind of abrasion experienced in wearing and washing as well as secure against fraying apart or the unravelling of stitches. A seam in a close-fitting or underwear garment must not present an uncomfortable ridge or roughness to the skin. If a fabric is coated in PVC, neoprene or polyurethane to make it totally waterproof, a simple form of sewn seam joining two sections will leave gaps between those sections, as well as needle holes along the join, and the seam will not be waterproof. According to the nature of the coating, the seam must be welded, taped or 'doped' to seal over the join and block up the needle holes. A fabric used for a child's nightdress, which must by law conform to specified flammability requirements, must be constructed with sewing threads that will not propagate a flame along the seam. Finally, seam performance as well as seam appearance can be spoilt by the fact that damage may occur to the fabric along the stitch line.

The question of economy of seaming in production arises because many seams can be constructed in a variety of ways. Many of the newer machines and stitch types enable shortcuts to be taken in the joining and neatening of seams but the appearance and performance of the seams vary with the different methods. A balance must be achieved when planning garment production between the demands of the end use of the garment, its price and the machinery available for its construction.

Assuming that the fabric is sewable and suitable for garments, the achievement at an economic level of the various requirements of appearance and performance of sewn seams, both initially and during use, is the result of the selection of the correct combination of five factors during manufacturing:

♦ *seam type*, which is a particular configuration of fabric(s)
♦ *stitch type*, which is a particular configuration of thread in the fabric
♦ *sewing machine feeding mechanism*, which moves the fabric past the needle and enables a succession of stitches to be formed
♦ *needle*, which inserts the thread into the fabric
♦ *thread*, which forms the stitch that either holds the fabric together, neatens it or decorates it

These factors are closely interrelated and discussing any of them without reference to at least one of the others is not possible. When dealing with seam types it will be seen that seams drawn as sections of flat or folded fabric(s) with no indication of the position of the stitches holding them together are meaningless. Thus an indication of the position of the needle(s) in the seam is normally given. Similarly, a stitch type and the particular configuration of fabric to which it is applied cannot easily be separated, and diagrams of stitch types inevitably show a variety of seam types. In order to depict fully the construction of sections of a garment, both the type of seam and the type of stitch must be given. The use of a sewing thread is also assumed. It is proposed to begin by describing the basic seam types and their method of representation with only the minimum reference to the types of stitch that would be used on them. Stitch types will then be described in detail, with applications to a wider variety of seam types.

## Seam types

The choice of seam type is determined by aesthetic standards, strength, durability, comfort in wear, convenience in assembly in relation to the machinery available, and cost. BS 3870: Part 2: 1991, referred to above, allows for eight different classes of seam, including some where only one piece of fabric is involved. Examples are the hem of a garment folded up on itself and a raw edge that has been neatened by means of stitches. This alters the traditional concept of a seam as a joint between fabrics.

The British Standard divides stitched seams into eight classes according to the minimum number of parts that make up the seam. These parts can be the main fabrics of the garment or some additional item such as a lace, braid or elastic.

To indicate how the various seam types are formed, several styles of diagram can be used. The one which most clearly relates to garment parts as sewn shows a perspective view of a section of the seam, and, when the various stitch types are being discussed, it is useful to show a section of the reverse side of the stitch. This is shown in Fig. 3.1.

The diagram shows two pieces of fabric laid one on top of the other and sewn close to one edge. The straight lines to the right are the edges that are relevant to the seam being described; the wavy lines to the left represent the rest of the garment parts, of no importance to the seam under consideration. When seam types are being discussed purely as a configuration of fabric, these diagrams are unnecessarily elaborate, especially on complicated seams. Once familiarity with seam types has been established, it is often sufficient to draw the diagrams in a shorthand version which shows a cross-section through the fabric represented by lines, with short lines at right angles showing the point of needle penetration of the stitch. This is shown in Fig. 3.2. Once familiarity with stitch types has also been established, the British Standard stitch number, as given in BS 3870: Part 1: *Classification and Terminology of Stitch Types* can be used.

Certain conventions are observed in depicting the penetration or passage of the needle(s). Thus Fig. 3.2(i) shows the representation when the needle passes through the material, and Fig. 3.2(ii) shows the situation when a stitch type or needle shape is used such that the needle does not pass through the material.

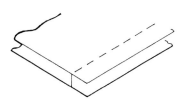 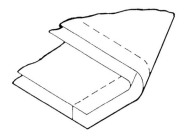

**Figure 3.1** Seam diagrams.

Figure 3.2 Simplified seam diagrams.

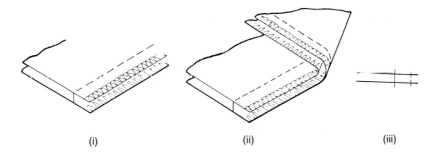

Figure 3.3 Methods of representing seams.

A common seam used on the sides of garments is represented in three different ways in Fig. 3.3. This shows a seam consisting of two pieces of fabric with neatened edges, joined with a further row of stitches. This type of seam can be pressed open. If the third, shorthand diagram is difficult to understand initially, a cast off garment can be examined and, if some of the seams are cut into at right angles with scissors, the layout of the diagram will be more clearly seen.

The British Standard gives an identifying number for each of the hundreds of different seam types which it depicts. Seams are relatively simple to draw and remember, and a great many of them will be encountered. More important than remembering the numerical designation is the ability to relate diagrams to existing or possible garments, as a way of considering the suitability of the seam for its purpose, and the machinery that would be used in its construction. Accordingly, it is not proposed to use the seam type numbers but, if needed, they can be obtained from the British Standard. By contrast, the number of British Standard stitch types in common use is quite small but they are much more complicated to draw and to remember; it will be seen later that it is essential in this case that their identifying numbers are used.

Six seam classes were included in the 1965 British Standard and at that stage they were given names which usefully describe their constructions. Two more classes were added with the publication of the 1983 edition, but without the descriptive names, and the total of eight survives in the 1991 edition. In the following sections these names have been included in brackets. This breakdown of seams into classes is included here as it provides a framework within which seam constructions can initially be explained and an indication given of the variety that exists.

## Class 1: superimposed seam

This is the most common construction seam on garments and the one used in Fig. 3.3 to illustrate the various methods of depicting seam constructions. The simplest seam type within the class is formed by superimposing the edge of one piece of material on another. A variety of stitch types can be used on this type of seam, both for joining the fabrics and for neatening the edges or for achieving both simultaneously.

The seams shown in Figs 3.4(i) and (ii) can be pressed open; that shown in Fig. 3.4(iii) cannot. Not all the seams shown in these diagrams can be sewn in one operation. The diagrams normally show the final version and it should be clear from the positions of the needles and the folding of the fabric if it was constructed in one step or several. An example of this is the type of superimposed seam known as a French seam, which is completed in two stages. This is shown as in Fig. 3.5(i). A similar, and in many cases equally acceptable, seam could be constructed using a folding device and a multi-needle machine, though only on a straight, rather than a curved, fabric edge. This is shown in Fig. 3.5(ii).

An example of a superimposed seam with an additional component would be one that contained an inserted piping, and even here more than one construction is possible, as is shown in Fig. 3.6.

## Class 2: lapped seam

The simplest seam type in this class is formed by lapping two pieces of material as shown in Fig. 3.7. In practice, this simple seam is not

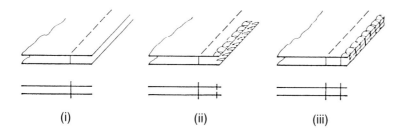

(i)                    (ii)                    (iii)

**Figure 3.4** Superimposed seams.

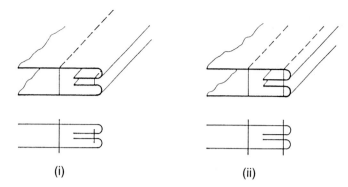

**Figure 3.5** French seams.

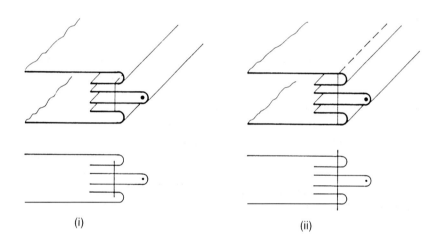

**Figure 3.6** Piped seams.

**Figure 3.7** Lapped seam.

**Figure 3.8** Lap-felled seam.

**Figure 3.9** Welted seam.

common in clothing because it causes problems with raw edges and at least one of the edges must be neatened in a decorative manner. It is more commonly used in the joining of panels in sails where a strong seam is achieved by using two or three rows of zig-zag stitching. Sail fabrics are very finely woven and fray very little.

Much more common on long seams on garments such as jeans and shirts is the so-called lap-felled seam, sewn with two rows of stitches on a twin needle machine equipped with a folding device. This provides a very strong seam in garments that will take a lot of wear, though there is a possibility that the thread on the surface may suffer abrasion in areas such as inside leg seams. The lap-felled seam is illustrated in Fig. 3.8.

The type of raised, topstitched seam often used down skirt panels is also technically a lapped seam, although at the beginning of its construction it appears to be a superimposed seam. It is often referred to as a welted or a raised and welted seam and is shown in Fig. 3.9.

## Class 3: bound seam

In this class, the seam consists of an edge of material bound by another, with the possibility of other components inserted into the binding.

The simplest version of this class is again unusual as it cannot be constructed with self-fabric binding because of the problem of

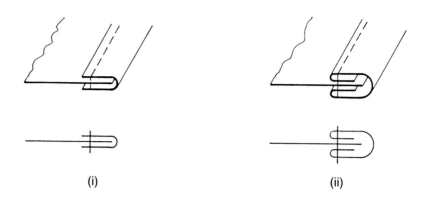

(i)                                        (ii)

**Figure 3.10** Bound seams.

raw edges. It can, however, be made with a binding that has been constructed to a specific width. Figure 3.10(i) shows the simplest bound seam, while part (ii) shows a common version where the garment fabric, or even a contrasting colour of the garment fabric, has been cut into narrow strips. A folding device turns the edges under and wraps the strip over the edge of the main fabric. Bias cut strip would normally be used, unless the fabric had an element of stretch. A bound seam is often used as a decorative edge and the binding may continue off the edge of the garment to provide tie ends.

The types of folding device that can be added to sewing machines to create these bound seams will be discussed further in the next chapter. Their development has given designers the scope to use a wide variety of complicated seam constructions, both functional and decorative. Examples in common use on underwear and leisurewear and on skirts, jeans and ladies' trousers are shown in Fig. 3.11. In part (i) is shown a common finish used on the neck edge of tee shirts, and also on the edges of men's vests and briefs. In Fig. 3.11(ii), there is an insert of another cut strip. This would normally be in a contrasting colour to the garment and both could contrast with the outer binding. In Fig. 3.11(iii), an elastic has been included in a sufficiently stretched state to draw the edge of the garment in to a snug fit. On all these seams, a stitch type would be used which has two needles and incorporates a thread passing between the needle threads on the underside and covering the raw edge of the fabric. Self-fabric in the same or another colour is usually cut into strips for the bindings and the fabrics are normally knitted. In Fig. 3.11(iv), a waistband, usually with an interlining fused to it, is bound on to the top of a skirt, jean or trouser using a folder and twin needle machine. The ends of the waistband require stitching separately.

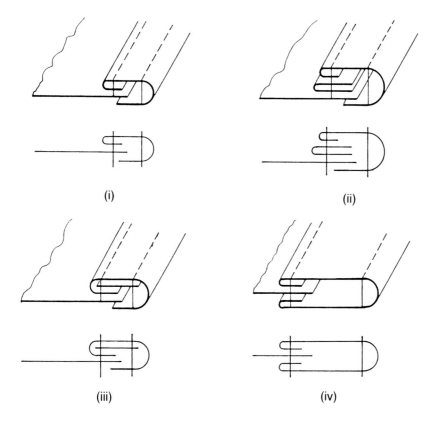

**Figure 3.11** Common bound seams.

## Class 4: flat seam

In this class, seams are referred to as flat seams because the fabric edges do not overlap. They may be butted together without a gap and joined across by a stitch which has two needles sewing into each fabric and covering threads passing back and forth between these needles on both sides of the fabric. Knitted fabrics are most commonly used because the advantage of this seam is that it provides a join that is free from bulk in garments worn close to the skin, such as knitted underwear. The machine trims both fabric edges so that they form a neat join. Alternatively, various zig-zag stitches could sew back and forth between the fabrics which might then have a decorative gap between them. Examples of flat seams are shown in Fig. 3.12.

## Class 5: decorative stitching

This is the first of the two classes of seam which, in the old British Standard, were not regarded as seams at all and were given the name

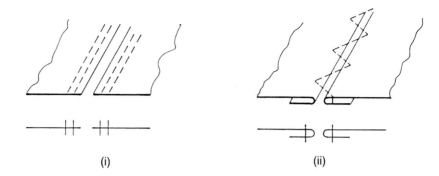

**Figure 3.12** Flat seams.

'stitching'. The main use of the seam is for decorative sewing on garments where single or multiple rows of stitches are sewn through one or more layers of fabric. These several layers can be folds of the same fabric. The simplest seam in the class has decorative stitching across a garment panel. One row would have little effect but multi-needle stitching is common.

Figure 3.13(i) shows twin-needle stitching with a ribbon laid under the stitches while part (ii) shows four rows of stitches. This type of multi-needle stitching has further decorative possibilities if an attachment is added to the machine which lays embroidery threads back and forth under the stitches on the surface of the fabric.

Other possibilities, given the right folding devices, are pin tucks, often sewn in multiples, and channel seams. These are shown in Fig 3.13(iii) and (iv). This type of pin tuck is different from the traditional version, which consists of a fold in the fabric sewn close to the edge. When multiple, parallel tucks are required, the original method is slow and potentially inaccurate. In the version shown here, the folder ensures the tucks are parallel as all the tucks are sewn simultaneously. The tucks must, however, be set to face one way or the other and a decision as to which must be made in relation to the design of the garment.

## Class 6: edge neatening

This is the other seam class that was previously called a stitching. Seam types in this class include those where fabric edges are neatened by means of stitches (as opposed to binding with another or the same fabric), as well as folded hems and edges. The simplest is the fabric edge inside a garment which has been neatened with an overedge stitch, as shown in Fig. 3.14.

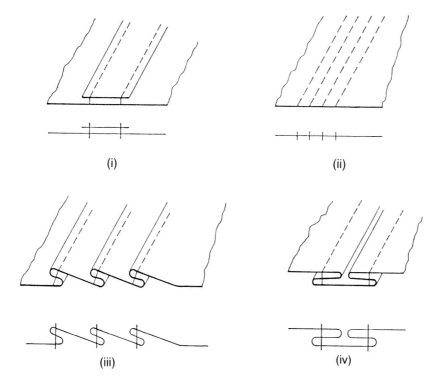

**Figure 3.13** Decorative seams (i) 2 × 301, (ii) 4 × 401, (iii) pin tucks, (iv) channel seam.

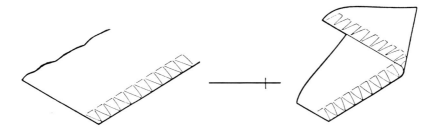

**Figure 3.14** Edge neatening.

In considering hems on the sleeves and lower edges of garments, there are many possibilities when the variety of stitch types that can be used is taken into account. A selection is shown in Fig. 3.15, and at this stage it is assumed that the reader can interpret the construction through the use of the shorthand type of diagram only. The need to know the stitch type used, in order to appreciate fully the construction of the seam, should now become clear. Numbers for stitch types

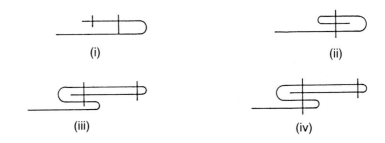

**Figure 3.15** Hemmed edges (i) 504/103, (ii) 301, (iii) 2 × 301, (iv) 2 × 401.

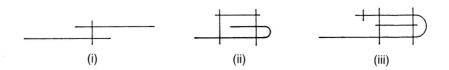

**Figure 3.16** Addition of separate items (i) 304 lace, (ii) 321, (iii) 406/504.

that might be used have been included so that the diagrams can be referred to again later when the reader is familiar with these numbers. In Fig. 3.15, (i) is typical of the hem on a dress or a pair of trousers in a woven fabric, which has been neatened and then sewn up invisibly (blind stitched). In a knitted fabric the neatening might be omitted. In (ii), a folding device is used in the construction of the hem of a shirt or a skirt lining; (iii) and (iv) show a method of folding an edge that is sometimes used on the buttonhole front of a shirt. Two different constructions are possible, the first one requiring the sewing to be done in two stages, the second one requiring a twin-needle machine.

The remaining two seam classes in the 1991 British Standard are an addition to the original standard, added in the 1983 edition, to include seam types commonly seen in modern garment construction. No general descriptive title has been given to either of them.

## Class 7

Seams in this class relate to the addition of separate items to the edge of a garment part. They are similar to the lapped seam except that the added component has a definite edge on both sides. Examples would be a band of lace attached to the lower edge of a slip as in Fig. 3.16(i), elastic braid on the edge of a bra as in (ii), and inserted elastic on the leg of a swimsuit as in (iii).

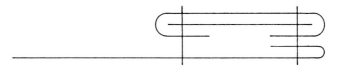

**Figure 3.17** Shirt buttonhole band, 2 × 401.

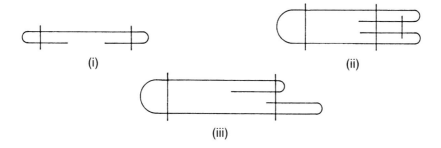

**Figure 3.18** Belt loop and belts (i) 406, (ii) 301, (iii) 301.

An example where the additional item is self-fabric plus interlining is another version of the buttonhole band on a shirt, shown in Fig. 3.17. This is another instance where, by using two folders and a twin-needle machine, a complicated construction can be completed in one step. Without such machinery, achieving a similar, let alone identical, result would be very difficult.

## Class 8

The final seam class in the British Standard is another where only one piece of material need be involved in constructing the seam. The commonest seam type in this class is the belt loop as used on jeans, raincoats, etc. This is shown in Fig. 3.18(i). Also included in this class are belts themselves; two possible constructions for these are shown in Figs 3.18(ii) and (iii).

The use on the belt loop of the stitch type mentioned before, which has two needles and a bottom covering thread, ensures that the raw edges are covered over on the underside while showing two rows of plain stitching on the top. The belt shown in (iii) is quicker and cheaper to construct than the one shown in (ii) but, as always, a special machine attachment is required to fold the fabric.

In this study of seam types, only a selection has been given to demonstrate some of the commoner constructions used in garments.

More will be studied when considering stitch types. It will be seen that many of the seams require complicated folding before sewing while, even the simple ones must be controlled accurately if the sewing is to be neat and the garment the correct size. Sewing machine attachments that fold fabric have already been mentioned; others are available to control or guide fabric and enable a relatively unskilled operator to sew quickly and with a high level of accuracy. However, their use is only justified where considerable quantities of the same sewing operation are to be performed. Small volume production is heavily dependent on skilled operators if the manufacturing quality standards are to be high. These high standards will only be achieved at high cost. Thus, cheaply produced fashion garments tend to be inaccurately sewn. The use of sewing machine attachments will be considered in more detail, along with other aspects of machinery, in the next chapter.

## Stitch types

In discussing seam types it has been necessary to make some mention of stitch types and it should already be evident that a wide variety is required for even the limited number of seam types already demonstrated. There is a need for stitches that join, and stitches that neaten, for machines with more than one needle, and for stitches that form a covering layer over the fabric. Certain stitch types can also aid economical garment production by performing several functions at once such as joining and neatening or by adding decoration at the same time as either of those.

British Standard 3870: Part 1: 1991: *Classification and Terminology of Stitch Types* is the standard reference to the wide range of stitch types now available for use in garment construction. It defines a stitch as 'one unit of conformation resulting from one or more strands or loops of thread intralooping, interlooping or passing into or through material'.

Intralooping is the passing of a loop of thread through another loop formed by the same thread. Interlooping is the passing of a loop of thread through another loop formed by a different thread. Interlacing, a term also used in relation to certain stitches, is the passing of a thread over or around another thread or loop of another thread. These apparently obscure distinctions are illustrated in Fig. 3.19. Their importance in relation to stitch security will become clear as the various stitches are described.

A series of recurring stitches of one configuration is defined as a stitch type. BS 3870 divides the many types available into six classes.

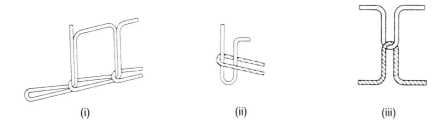

(i)                       (ii)                     (iii)

**Figure 3.19** Stitch formation. (i) Intralooping, (ii) interlooping, (iii) interlacing. The diagrams of stitches used here and the codings are based on BS 3870: 1991: *Schedule of Stitches and Seams Part 1: Classification and Terminology of Stitch Types.* Complete copies of the standard can be obtained by post from BSI, Customer Services, 389 Chiswick High Road, London W4 4AL (website: http://www.bsi-global.com/). British Standard 3870 is identical with ISO 4915: 1991: *Textiles – Stitch Types: Classification and Terminology* published by the International Organisation for Standardisation (ISO).

These cover the demands of joining fabrics together, neatening raw edges, providing decoration, or offering the economy of doing more than one of these at a time.

Of the seventy or so stitch types covered by BS 3870, the number currently in regular use is around twenty. Even that number is only in use at the high volume, bulk production end of the industry where the demands of speed, economy, and high standards of seam performance prevail over flexibility of manufacturing method. In small volume or more traditional production, garments are constructed with two or three stitch types only, and many garments on sale show evidence of having been made by homeworkers with access only to the domestic lockstitch machine or its industrial equivalent.

The diagrams that accompany the following descriptions of stitch types show the stitches as a configuration of thread in the manner used in the British Standard. Stitch diagrams alone can be difficult to relate to the real thing as seen on garments and for this reason they are shown in use in at least one seam type as well.

The six classes of stitch included in the British Standard are as follows:

- ◆ Class 100 chainstitches
- ◆ Class 200 stitches originating as handstitches
- ◆ Class 300 lockstitches
- ◆ Class 400 multi-thread chainstitches
- ◆ Class 500 overedge chainstitches
- ◆ Class 600 covering chainstitches

At the same time as describing the appearance, characteristics and uses of the most important stitch types contained within these classes, it is appropriate to consider how a sewing machine works and in particular how the stitch-forming mechanism works. While the subject of machinery will be dealt with in more detail later, the various parts of the simpler sewing machines and their function will be mentioned many times in the course of the present chapter. Thus, a selection of stitch types will be described in terms of the machines that produce them.

The most common stitch type in use in industry is the lockstitch. It is also the one with which people are initially most familiar since it is almost universally used in domestic machines. For this reason it is the most appropriate to describe first, although it is not the first in the BS classification.

## Class 300: lockstitches

The stitch types in this class are formed with two or more groups of threads, and have for a general characteristic the interlacing of these threads. Loops of one group are passed through the material and are secured by the thread or threads of a second group. One group is normally referred to as the needle threads and the other group as bobbin threads. The interlacing of thread in stitches of this class makes them very secure and difficult to unravel.

Straight lockstitch, 301, with a single needle thread and a single bobbin thread, is still the commonest stitch used in the clothing industry, especially in small volume manufacturing of a variety of garment types. The appearance of the stitch is shown in Fig. 3.20 and the mechanism of stitch formation in Fig. 3.21.

Lockstitch has enough strength for most purposes, provided that suitable thread is used, and enough stretch, when correctly balanced, for conventional and comfort stretch fabrics stretching up to 30% or even more. It has the same appearance on both sides, an advantage denied to virtually all other stitch types, and of significance in the assembly process of garments, especially where topstitching is

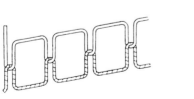

**Figure 3.20** Stitch type 301.

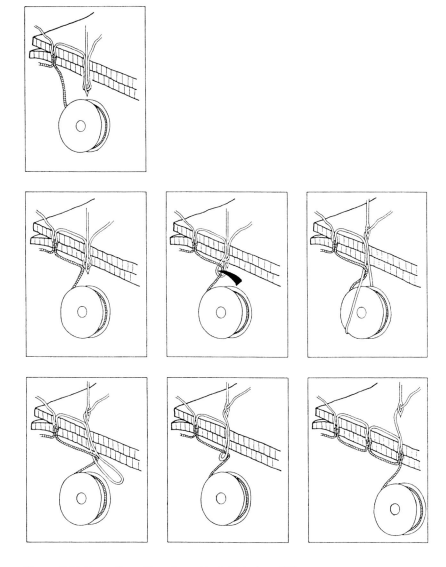

**Figure 3.21** Formation of two-thread lockstitch, type 301.

required. In its straight stitch version, it is also the only stitch type that reliably forms the stitch when it is necessary to sew round a corner by pausing and pivoting on the needle. This is also important in topstitching as well as in seam joining of facings, collars, pockets and many similar garment parts. The stitch is secure because the breaking of one stitch in wear will not cause the whole row to unravel; additionally, the end of a line of stitching can be secured by reversing or 'backtacking'. Alternatively, if the backtack lever is deliberately restricted, a group of small or condensed stitches is formed, which secures the end of the stitching without the machine actually sewing in reverse. The thread in a lockstitch generally beds well into the fabric, which improves abrasion resistance.

In its single throw, zig-zag version, type 304, it is commonly used for attaching trimmings such as lace and elastic where a broad row of stitching but no neatening is needed. In its three-step zig-zag version, type 321, it is commonly used to provide a secure but stretchy stitch for the edges of stretch bras and other corsetry. The single and the three-step zig-zag are also used in two or three parallel rows, in the type of simple lapped seam used for joining the fabric panels in sails. These zig-zag stitches perform a very useful function on seams of the type given here but would not give a good appearance on a super-imposed seam. They are shown in Figs 3.22 and 3.23.

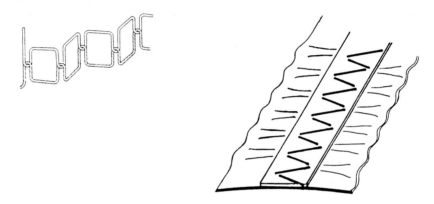

**Figure 3.22** Stitch type 304.

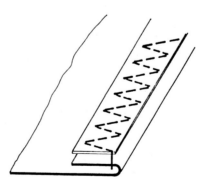

**Figure 3.23** Stitch type 321.

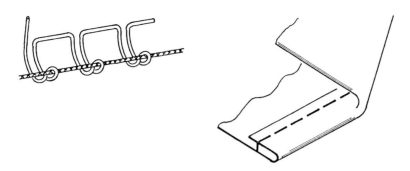

**Figure 3.24** Stitch type 306.

Stitch type 306 provides a lockstitch blind stitch. This is more secure than the traditional 103 which will be discussed shortly, but close study of the stitch construction in Fig. 3.24 will show a straight bobbin thread, which, if caught and broken, can allow sections of the stitching to come undone. It also tends to show pucker on fine fabrics.

The main disadvantage of the lockstitch is that it uses a bobbin to provide the lower thread and this bobbin can contain only a limited length of that thread. Changing bobbins is time consuming in production, as is the unpicking of topstitching when a thread runs out at a point where a join is visually unacceptable. Where garments are sewn with twin or multi-needle machines, especially where complicated fabric folding is involved, the loss of stitching on one row because of one bobbin running out would be a major problem. Multi-needle stitching with many closely spaced needles is not actually possible because of the space that the bobbins would require. Two is the maximum number of needles commonly in use on lockstitch machines.

Optical bobbin run-out detectors, which pick up a reflection from a flat side on the centre of an otherwise round bobbin as the last of the thread begins to run out are being used on some machines, as are automatic counters which stop the machine after a predetermined number of cycles that will leave the bobbin or bobbins almost empty. Even a manual count of the number of garments sewn will tell the operator when another complete seam will not be achieved. On buttonholing, where restitching is possible provided that the hole has not been cut, the machines normally stop without cutting the hole if the bobbin runs out or the needle thread breaks.

The other disadvantages of lockstitch are its limited stretch for today's high-stretch fabrics, and its unsuitability for edge neatening, other than by a simple rolling of the fabric edge or the use of a zigzag, both of which are untidy.

Thus a wide range of additional stitch types replaces the traditional lockstitch in manufacturing situations which allow it. These are primarily situations where large quantities, perhaps thousands, are made of the same style of garment. Small sections only are sewn by each operator who can then use a sewing machine specially suited to the purpose. To a greater or lesser extent, virtually all the stitch types other than 301 are in this category.

Having studied the lockstitch class of stitch as the most common and the one most likely already to be familiar, the other stitch classes will be studied in numerical order, each having its own special contribution to make to garment construction.

## Class 100: chainstitches

The stitch types in this class are formed from one or more needle threads, and are characterised by intralooping. One or more loops of thread are passed through the material and secured by intralooping with a succeeding loop or loops after they are passed through the material. Since each loop is in this way dependent on the succeeding one, stitches in this class are insecure and if the finishing end of thread is not passed through the last loop or separately through the fabric, or if a stitch is broken, it unravels very easily.

One of the simplest of all stitch types is 101, which is formed from a single thread. The appearance of this stitch and the mechanism of stitch formation are shown in Fig. 3.25.

Precisely because of its insecurity, it can be removed easily, and it is used for 'basting' operations in tailored menswear and womenswear garments, using a white, soft cotton thread. It can only be used where the marks of needle penetration close up afterwards in pressing. A basting operation, in positions such as edges, flaps, collars and so on, is a temporary stitch, allowing accurate placement of permanent stitching.

It is too insecure to be used for seams involving the joining of fabrics but it is widely used in multi-needle machines. A range of decorative effects can be achieved using some or all of a bank of closely spaced needles, which may number as many as sixty-five. An additional device can be used to lay embroidery threads back and forward on the surface of the fabric under the needle threads in a variety of patterns to create further decoration. If elastic thread is used in the needles and sewn into the fabric in a stretched state, it then relaxes and draws the fabric in, enabling garment features such as elasticated waists and cuffs to be created. This stitch type is particularly useful in this case as any other stitch which could cope with elastic thread would not use as much and would not enable as much stretch to be included. Multi-needle elastication is illustrated in Fig. 3.26.

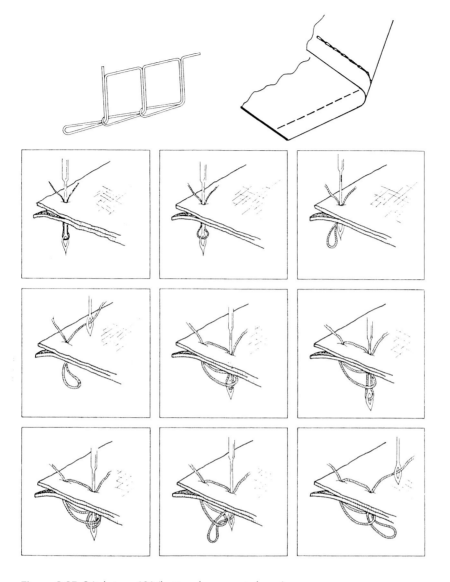

**Figure 3.25** Stitch type 101 (bottom looper not shown).

This stitch type cannot be chained off, i.e. sewn without fabric, nor can the stitching be brought to a halt and the needles removed from the fabric in the middle of a garment part. In the construction of a garment it is necessary to start and finish at a fabric edge, and that edge may need to be a small piece of temporary fabric held to the garment edge by the stitches. The fabric edges must then be joined securely through the ends of the chainstitching in order to prevent

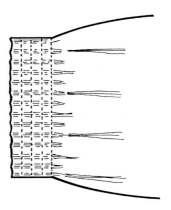

**Figure 3.26** Multi-needle elastication.

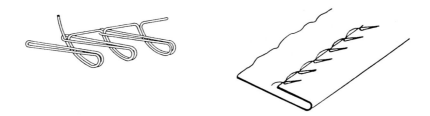

**Figure 3.27** Stitch type 103.

the stitches running back. Where multi-needle stitching is functional rather than solely decorative, stitch type 401, to be described shortly, is increasingly used because of its higher security.

Another common use of class 100 stitches is in the special sewing processes of buttonsewing, buttonholing and blind hemming or felling. The first two hardly merit the description 'seams' but they deserve a mention when considering this particular class of stitch. They utilise the zig-zag version and the machines are fast and require no bobbin, but their use generates a high level of consumer dissatisfaction as the stitching, especially on buttons, often does not last the lifetime of the garment. Careful machine adjustment, along with a small thread tail left at the end is necessary for maximum security.

The blind stitching version, 103, utilises a curved needle in order to successively penetrate partially into the fabric, and then into the hem edge, while showing minimally or not at all on the right side of the garment. If required, the machine can be set to skip stitch, that is, to pick up the fabric on alternate stitches only. This renders it even less visible. The stitch structure is shown in Fig. 3.27.

Again, the level of insecurity is often high but can be improved by the use of slightly hairy rather than smooth sewing threads. Stitch cramming mechanisms are available which condense the stitch length at the beginning and end of seams, though since run-back only occurs from the finishing end it is not really necessary at the beginning. Careful machine adjustment is necessary with all these single thread chainstitches if the garments carrying them are to survive normal wear and tear.

## Class 200: stitches originating as handstitches

The stitch types in this class originated as handstitches and are characterised by a single thread passed through the material as a single line of thread; the stitch is secured by the single line of thread passing in and out of the material.

Handstitching used to be normal practice at the expensive end of garment production. It was thought to be the only way to a perfect finish. Occasionally, it is the only way to achieve a particular sewn effect though it should be said that if a large enough quantity of a garment style is being made, it is frequently possible to engineer the garment so that everything is done by machine.

In some cases, machines have been developed to simulate hand-stitching, the best example being stitch type 209 which is used around the outer edges of tailored jackets. This is referred to as pick stitching and is shown in Fig. 3.28.

A double-pointed, centre-eyed needle sews short lengths of thread in a near-perfect simulation of the hand-sewn version. The machine can be set to show a longer stitch on the top than the bottom or *vice versa*, with instant change-over at the break point of a lapel. Thread ends are trimmed close if the stitch is small or sewn in invisibly by

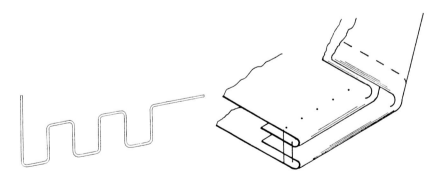

**Figure 3.28** Stitch type 209.

hand. A button sewing version is also available, which both sews the button and wraps the shank.

The machines are not fast by lockstitch standards, achieving a maximum of a few hundred stitches per minute, but this is considerably higher than the rate achieved in hand sewing and a consistently high quality standard is guaranteed.

## Class 400: multi-thread chainstitches

The stitch types in this class are formed with two or more groups of threads, and have for a general characteristic the interlooping of the two groups. Loops of one group of threads are passed through the material and are secured by interlacing and interlooping with loops of another group. One group is normally referred to as the needle threads and the other group as the looper threads.

The simplest version of this class of stitch, 401, is shown in Fig. 3.29. It has the appearance of lockstitch on the top but has a double chain effect formed by a looper thread on the underside. The chain generally lies on the under surface of the material, the needle thread being drawn through to balance the stitch. The mechanism of stitch formation is given in Fig. 3.30.

Stitches in this class are sometimes referred to as 'double-locked' stitches (not to be confused with class 300 lockstitch) because the needle thread is interconnected with two loops of the underthread. Because of the geometry of the stitch, a two-thread chainstitch is stronger than a similar lockstitch, and with no threads interlocking within the fabric it is less likely to cause the type of pucker that arises when closely woven fabrics are distorted by the sewing thread. Its great advantage is that both the threads forming the stitch are run

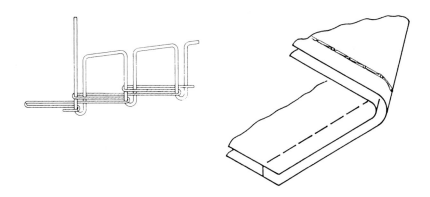

**Figure 3.29** Stitch type 401.

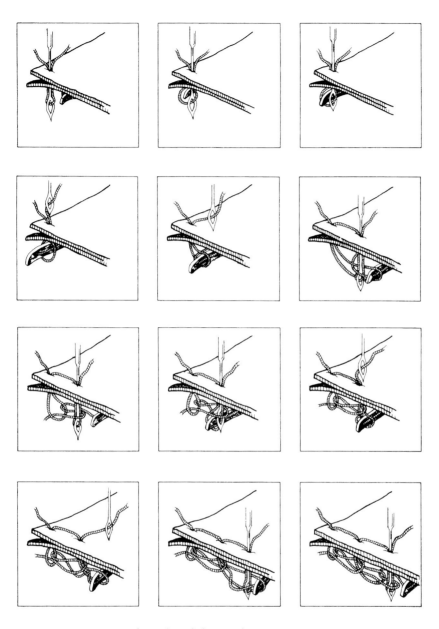

**Figure 3.30** Formation of two-thread chainstitch, type 401.

from large packages on top of the machine so there are no problems with bobbins running out. It is frequently used on long seams in garments such as trousers. On twin-needle folded seams, such as those used on jeans, it is by far the most suitable stitch to use. A bobbin run-out in that situation would be disastrous. It will unravel from the finishing end if broken, but less easily than 101, and provided the machine is correctly adjusted, there should be no problems. If not sewn across at the end in the course of the garment's construction, 1 cm of thread chain should be left. It does not backtack well but the stitches can be condensed.

When adjusted normally, the stretch with this stitch is about the same as with lockstitch, but if a small amount of seam grin is acceptable, the thread tensions can be loosened and a small increase in stretch obtained.

Lower thread tensions are normally used with these machines, compared with lockstitch, and this enables higher machine speeds to be used with less chance of thread breakage. Typical maximum speeds for lockstitch would be 6000 spm whereas with two-thread chainstitch 8000 spm can be achieved. It should be remembered that these are theoretical maxima, and although the machines will run at these speeds, practical garment-making situations rarely allow it. Limitations of seam length and the requirements of operator handling often cause machines to be set to run at lower speeds. Acceleration and braking are often more important than top speed.

Stitch type 401 is often used in combination with an overedge stitch for economy of seam joining and neatening in bulk production. This will be illustrated later.

Another increasingly used stitch in this class is 406, which uses two needles and has a looper thread covering the fabric between them on the underside. It is used for attaching lace and braid trimmings to garments where the edge of the fabric must be neatened, and also for turning up hems where stitching showing on the right side is acceptable. In each case, the raw edge of the fabric can be contained under the cover stitching. It is shown in Fig. 3.31.

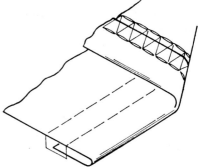

**Figure 3.31** Stitch type 406.

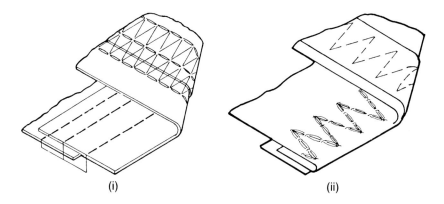

(i)                                                                  (ii)

**Figure 3.32** Stitch types (i) 407, (ii) 411.

Both 406 and the three-needle version, 407, are used for attaching elastic edging to briefs where, in order to achieve a comfortable edge to the garment, a broad band of stitching is needed. Alternatively, a decorative effect can be achieved by folding an edge of the garment and attaching a plain elastic braid by means of the three step zig-zag 411, sewn with the chain showing on the right side of the garment and a contrast thread in the looper. Examples of these uses are shown in Figs 3.32 (i) and (ii). In situations where elastic is attached to garments, the elastic is stretched by a pre-set amount whilst being sewn to the fabric, and on relaxing draws the garment part in to the correct measurement. The methods of achieving this will be described in the next chapter.

The straight or zig-zag version of 401 can be chained off the edge of the fabric and further decorative effects can be created by this means. If 411 is sewn along a garment edge that has previously been neatened or hemmed in some way, and it is sewn with the chain effect to the right side of the garment, an effect similar to a crocheted picot edge can be achieved. With a twin-needle version of the same stitch, sewn with the needles moving in opposition, an openwork join between two folded edges of fabric can be achieved. These effects are shown in Fig. 3.33.

## Class 500: overedge chainstitches

The stitch types in this class are formed with one or more groups of threads, and have as a general characteristic loops from at least one group of threads passing around the edge of the material. The most frequently used of these stitch types have one or two needle threads and one or two looper threads, and they form a narrow band of stitching along the edge of the fabric with threads intersecting at

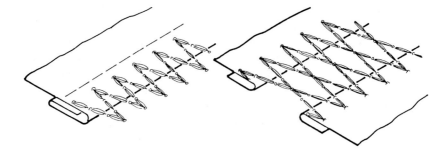

**Figure 3.33** Stitch type 411.

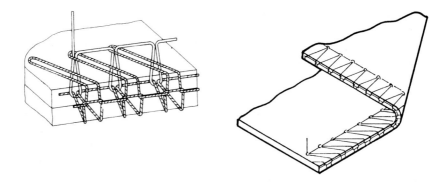

**Figure 3.34** Stitch type 504.

the edge and preventing the fabric from fraying. All have high elasticity, they do not unravel easily, and a trimming knife on the machine ensures a neat edge prior to sewing. This knife can also allow excessive amounts to be trimmed off, thus altering the dimensions of the garment. These stitches are commonly referred to as 'overlocking', although the term derives from a trade mark and is only really correct when used in relation to a particular machine. The correct term is 'overedging'.

Stitch type 504, shown in Fig. 3.34, is formed from one needle thread and two looper threads, and is used for neatening edges and, in knitted fabrics, for joining seams. It has excellent stretch and recovery properties when sewn with suitable threads, but its narrow bight (distance from needle to fabric edge), typically 3–5 mm, does not provide enough strength on fabrics that fray or slip. The bight can be adjusted within these limits to provide satisfactory appearance and an acceptable amount of bulk, according to the nature of the knitted fabric being joined. When joining fabrics with this stitch, a thread chain end must be left and the seam then secured by some means. This may be a cross seam, or if the seam ends on the edge of the garment it may be necessary to secure the thread chain and the seam end by means of a short lockstitch tack or a bar tack, or a short zig-zag of stitching of fixed length. A special machine attachment is available which can 'latchback' the chain end at the starting end of the seam and recently finishing-end attachments have also been developed. The operation of such attachments will be described later.

This stitch type can also be used to provide a decorative neatened edge if sewn with a high stitch density and a narrow bight over an edge which, after the usual trimming, has been rolled under to the width of the stitch, usually 2 mm. A contrasting coloured thread is often used, of a type that spreads out and forms a good cover over the edge. On suitable fabrics, the edge can be stretched while sewing to give a soft frill.

Stitch type 503, formed with one needle thread and only one looper thread, is less versatile and is used mainly for edge neatening, often referred to as serging, especially in menswear. It is particularly suitable for trousers because the two-thread construction is less likely to show an impression of the edge after pressing the legs. The construction is shown in Fig. 3.35. It is not normally used for conventional joining of two pieces of fabric as the stitch opens up when stressed transversely, but there are some situations where this feature can be used to advantage. One such is on tee-shirt hems where careful fabric folding ensures a neatened edge as well as a sewn hem with the minimum of stitching showing on the right side. This process is often called 'over-lock welting' and is illustrated in Fig. 3.36.

Also in this class, and illustrated in Fig. 3.37, are stitch types 512 and 514, which use two needles and a total of four threads. They provide a wider bight than 504 and this, combined with the second

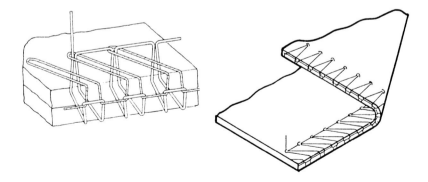

**Figure 3.35** Stitch type 503.

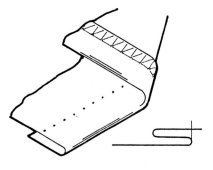

**Figure 3.36** 'Overlock welting' with stitch type 503.

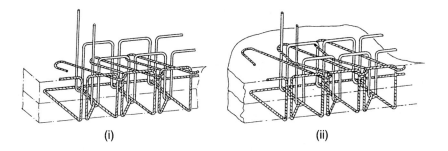

(i)                                    (ii)

**Figure 3.37** Stitch types (i) 512, (ii) 514.

needle, gives a securer seam when fabrics are joined. They are used on light and medium weight woven fabrics, especially lingerie and shirts. They also provide good stretch and recovery when used on knitted fabrics.

As mentioned under type 401, a combination of 401 and 503 or 504 sewn simultaneously on one machine is very common where a joined and neatened seam is required that does not need to be pressed open. It is referred to as safety stitch and provides an economical seam on both woven and low-stretch knitted fabrics. It can be used on the same kind of lightweight fabrics as 512 and 514, as well as on heavier fabrics such as denim and cord for jeans. It is written as (401.503) or (401.504), the dot indicating a combination stitch and the brackets denoting simultaneity of sewing. It has the level of stretch of 401 since that is the stitch that actually holds the seam. For brevity, the US Federal Stitch Type Numbers are often used in the case of these combination stitches and they then become 515 and 516 respectively. Stitch type (401.504) is shown in Fig. 3.38. Because of its similar appearance on one side to safety stitch, stitch type 512 is often referred to as mock safety stitch.

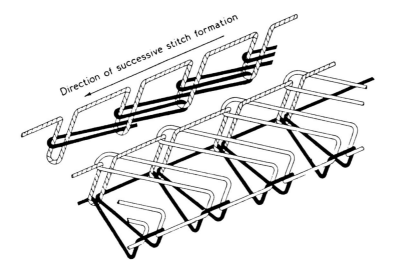

**Figure 3.38** Stitch type (401.504) (US Federal type 516, excerpted from BS 3870: 1965, now withdrawn).

Seam joining with any of the overedge stitches, whether 504, 512 or 514, or a combination stitch, gives a closed seam where the seam allowance must be pressed to one side rather than opened out. The appearance that this gives will not always be acceptable; for example, it is common on youths' trousers but not on men's.

## Class 600: covering chainstitches

With the exception of the very first type, stitch types in this class are formed with three groups of threads. The general characteristic is that two of the groups cover both surfaces of the material. Loops of the first group of threads (the needle threads) are passed through loops of the third group already cast on the surface of the material, and then through the material where they are interlooped with loops of the second group of threads on the underside of the material. The second and third groups are usually referred to as the top cover threads and the bottom cover or looper threads. Stitches in this class are the most complex of all and may have up to nine threads in total including four needle threads. They are used in similar situations to 406 and 407, making a broad, flat, comfortable joining of elastic, braid or binding to the edges of garments such as briefs with the scope for a decorative top cover stitch as well as the functional bottom cover over the raw edge of the garment fabric. Careful study of 602 in Fig. 3.39 will show that it is actually the same as 406 with the addition of the top cover thread.

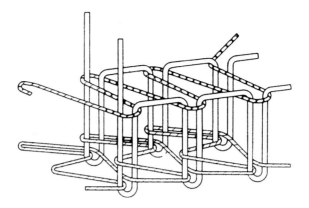

**Figure 3.39** Stitch type 602.

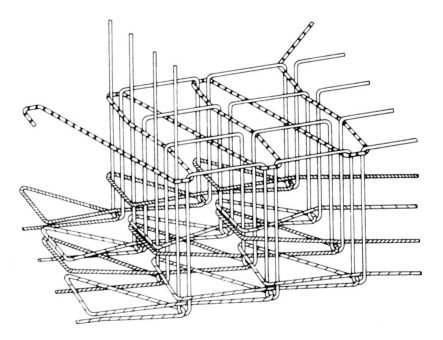

**Figure 3.40** Stitch type 606.

Most types of stitch join fabrics where the two plies are placed one on top of the other, and when the faces of the fabric are opened out the seam is wholly inside the garment. Alternatively, they join fabric to fabric, or fabric to a trim of some kind in a lapped manner as already described. The most complicated stitch type in this class, 606, which is known as flatlock, can be used to join fabrics which are butted together in what used to be called, in the old British Standard, a 'flat seam'. Two trimming knives ensure that neat fabric edges butt together and four needles and nine threads provide a smooth join with good extensibility. It is used on knitted fabrics, especially underwear fabrics, to give a seam with low bulk that can be worn comfortably against the skin. With the top cover thread in a contrast colour, it can be used decoratively on other knitted leisurewear. It is shown in Fig. 3.40. With this class of stitch, a chain end is left at the end of the seam which must be secured if not crossed by another seam.

In this study of stitch types, those currently in common use have been described. New stitches may be developed and the existing ones will come and go in popularity as machines are developed and garment styles and fabrics change. For as long as stitching remains the normal method of joining, neatening and decorating garments, this level of variety of stitch types is likely to be needed.

## Sewing machine feed mechanisms

In achieving the objectives of good appearance and performance in seams, correct and even stitch length is essential, along with fabric joins that are either smooth and unobtrusive or evenly eased or gathered, according to the requirements of fit and style. In the construction of seams and the formation of the stitches that hold them together, these requirements are achieved by means of the mechanism that feeds the fabric(s) past the needle. This can either be a mechanism at the needle point, conventionally referred to as a sewing machine feed system, or some external system of materials control such as is found in certain specialised machines which are part of mechanised workplaces. These latter types will be described in more detail in the next chapter.

The simplest sewing machine feed system, and still the commonest, is known as the *drop feed*; the subject is best introduced by describing the constituent parts of this system and their functions. The limitations of this system will then become clear and the alternatives that aim to overcome these limitations can be considered.

The three sewing machine parts, which together constitute the drop feed mechanism, are the presser foot, the throat plate or needle plate, and the feed dog. These are illustrated in Fig. 3.41.

The throat plate is the most passive of the three parts and its function is to provide a smooth, flat surface over which the fabric passes as successive stitches are formed. It has one or more slots in it which match the sections of the feed dog and it has a hole through which the needle passes as it goes up and down. The needle hole should be only about 30 per cent larger than the size of the needle since, if

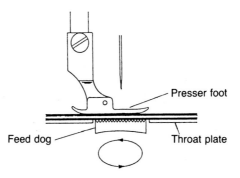

**Figure 3.41** Drop feed system.

this hole is too large, fabric can be pushed into the hole with each penetration of the needle. This is a problem known as 'flagging', which can cause missed stitching and yarn breakage. Most throat plates are made of steel with a polished surface to enable the material to pass freely over it.

The purpose of the feed dog is to move the fabric along by a pre-determined amount between successive stitches. The amount of fabric movement, and thus the stitch length, is controlled by means of a stitch length regulator. The feed dog consists of a toothed surface which rises through the openings in the throat plate, engages the under surface of the fabric, moves that fabric along towards the back of the machine, and drops away again below the throat plate before commencing the whole cycle again. As the feed dog drops below the throat plate, this plate supports the fabric so that it loses contact with the feed dog and is not carried back with it. The motion of the needle in an up and down direction must be synchronised accurately with the elliptical motion of the feed dog so that movement of the fabric takes place only when the needle is out of the fabric. Although the movement of the fabric during sewing appears to be one of continuous motion, it actually happens as a series of discrete steps. If this was not the case, distortion of the fabric and the needle would occur and the stitch might not be formed properly The movement of the fabric after the completion of each stitch aids in setting the stitch and drawing the correct amount of thread into it, as well as positioning it ready for the next stitch.

Even in the simple drop feed, the feed dog can vary in the number and position of the sections comprising it and in the nature of its toothed surface. A single row feed dog has only a small area gripping the fabric and there is a tendency for the fabric to slip to the right or left instead of passing straight through the machine. It is normal in a lockstitch machine to have feed dogs situated both to the right and to the left of the needle hole to ensure that the fabric is fed in a straight line. In an overedge machine, the feed dog is usually mainly to the left of the needle drop point, because it trims and sews the fabric to the right of the needle and because there is a chaining-off finger on the throat plate over which the stitch is formed. Here again the fabric tends to be guided to the left. The problem can be overcome if a machine has a three-row feed dog with one row in front of the needle. This is adequate to prevent sideways feeding. A typical feed dog for an overedge machine is illustrated in Fig. 3.42.

The teeth on the surface of the feed dog can be of different types and sizes but they are generally slanted slightly towards the direction of feeding. For sewing of light to medium weight fabrics, a tooth pitch (distance from peak to peak) of 1.3–1.6mm is normal, with the peaks slightly rounded off if damage occurs on fine fabrics. On very lightweight fabrics, sagging can occur between the teeth and pucker can appear after sewing as a result. Fine-toothed feed dogs with a pitch of only 1.0–1.25mm can be used to prevent this. By contrast, on heavyweight fabrics, a certain amount of sagging is required for satisfactory feeding in order to keep both plies together. In this case, coarser feed dogs of 2.5mm tooth pitch may be needed.

On very delicate fabrics, damage or marking of the fabric may arise against the feed dog, despite rounding off the tops of the teeth. In this case, a rubber-coated feed dog with no sharp teeth at all may be used, although it tends to wear out quickly. Of more importance in preventing damage during feeding is a deliberate mismatch between

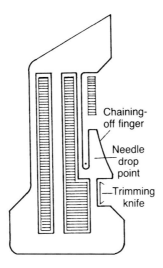

**Figure 3.42** Feed dog on an overedger.

stitch size and feed dog size. If, for example, a seam is sewn at six stitches per centimetre using a feed dog with six teeth per centimetre, then a tooth will repeatedly hit the same section of fabric as it moves past and marking or even damage of the fabric could occur.

The presser foot is required to hold the fabric down firmly against the throat plate, thus preventing the fabric rising and falling with the needle. At the same time, it holds the fabric against the teeth of the feed dog as it rises up to transport the fabric. It is normally held down by spring pressure in order to 'give' slightly whilst the fabric plies are being fed. Minimum pressure should be used consistent with correct feeding of the particular fabric in use. Unfortunately, in high speed sewing there is a tendency for the presser foot to bounce as the feed dog makes contact with it, and this reduces the effective contact between the presser foot and the fabric and thus the control of the fabric.

In the drop feed system, the presser foot remains stationary with the fabric sliding under its sole and this surface must have low friction characteristics. The use of PTFE-coated feet helps reduce friction, though care must be taken not to run the machine without fabric between the PTFE surface and the feed dog or the surface will be damaged.

Presser feet are available in a great many types, both to match the varieties of feed dog which exist and to perform additional functions. The simplest type of general purpose presser foot is spring-hinged to ride over slight variations in fabric thickness and it has two toes so that pressure is maintained on the fabric against the feed dog on both sides of the needle. This type was shown in Fig. 3.41 above.

Even the simplest of presser feet, feed dogs and throat plates must be shaped around whether a particular machine has single or twin needles and whether it sews a straight stitch or a zig-zag. They may also have to be shaped so that a folding device can be situated close in front of the needle to control the folding of fabric right up to the point where it is stitched. An example is shown in Fig. 3.43.

Additional functions that a presser foot can perform, if suitably designed, are guiding stitching a specific distance from a fabric edge or raised seam, positioning a cord, and folding a narrow hem. These will be discussed in the next chapter.

Although this simple drop feed system is still very common in clothing manufacturing, it suffers from a serious limitation in its ability to produce seams of perfect appearance on all types of material. Most seams on garments have to be joined smoothly without any pucker showing in any of the materials. Assuming that two or more thicknesses of fabric are being sewn, regardless of whether they are separate fabrics or folded sections of the same fabric, the problem arises

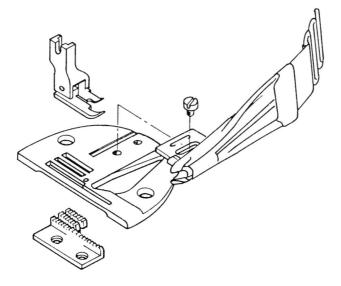

**Figure 3.43** Feed system for use with a folder.

that the friction between the bottom ply and the feed dog is normally greater than that between intervening plies. The tendency is for the lower ply to be taken satisfactorily through the machine by the feed dog and the top ply to be retarded by the presser foot. The problem is variously known as inter-ply shift, differential feeding pucker or just feeding pucker. On a seam that joins two pieces of material together, it causes pucker on the lower ply and spare material left over at the end of the seam on the top ply: spare material which it is tempting to trim away. When pressed, the seam may show a curve because of the excess of the fabric along one side. In sewing a hem, twisting may occur between the layers of material and the problem known as 'roping' will arise. These problems are illustrated in Fig. 3.44.

A well-trained and skilled machinist may be able to minimise the problem by careful handling of all the plies of material both in front of and behind the needle, but is likely to have to work more slowly in order to do so. With the variety of materials that are used in garments, the seam being joined could consist of two layers of slippery, woven polyester, or heavy elastic net and polyester satin, or two layers of a pile fabric such as velvet or corduroy, or a heavy woollen cloth and a viscose lining, or two layers of smooth shirting. All of these can cause difficulty. In addition, the machine may be fitted with a folding device which achieves a particular construction of seam but prevents the operator controlling the exact feeding of the several plies of fabric that are involved. For the sake of both quality and speed in

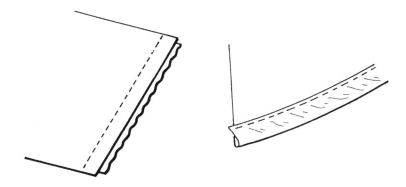

Figure 3.44 Problems of differential feeding.

production, machine feed systems are needed which can be adjusted to enable smooth sewing of any fabric regardless of operator skill or seam type. A variety of these now exists and, in addition to being adjustable to prevent undesirable pucker or easing, some of them can be adjusted so that deliberate, controlled amounts of easing or gathering can be sewn into a seam.

In the drop feed system described previously, the constituent parts of the system are the feed dog, throat plate and presser foot; only the feed dog plays an active part in fabric movement. Thus, successful feeding of more than one ply is dependent on friction holding the plies together. In the more advanced feeding systems, positive fabric control and feeding is achieved by a divided feed dog, which can be adjusted to alter the rate of feeding of the lower ply; by the action of a moving presser foot on the top ply; by a moving needle which assists in holding the fabric plies together; by a roller puller feed behind another feed mechanism controlling both plies; or by a computer-controlled top and bottom belt drive in place of the conventional presser foot and feed dog. All are devices that must be built into the machine during its construction rather than added afterwards; in some machines two or more are used in combination.

*Differential bottom feed* is the name given to a feed dog that consists of two sections, one behind the other. The movement of each section is similar to the movement of the whole feed dog in the drop feed system, but the stroke or movement of each part can be adjusted separately or differentially. In the situation where differential feeding pucker, as described above, is a problem, correct adjustment of this feed system to create slight stretch on the bottom ply will overcome the tendency of the feed dog to take in that ply while the presser foot retards the top ply. The adjustment in this case consists of setting the stroke of the rear section of the feed dog so that it is longer than the

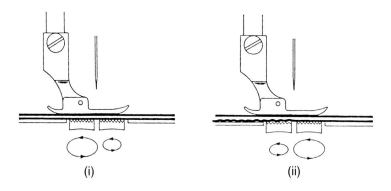

**Figure 3.45** Differential feed systems. (i) Bottom feed set to stretch lower ply. (ii) Bottom feed working fullness into lower ply.

stroke of the front section. It is also possible to deliberately gather the lower ply into the top ply by setting the front section of the feed dog to a longer stroke than the rear section. The correct setting in each case must be achieved by trial and error with a particular fabric. These possibilities are illustrated in Fig. 3.45.

Differential feed is available on chainstitch, overedge and safety stitch machines, as well as on lockstitch machines. When overedge joining soft, knitted underwear fabrics, where there is a high level of friction between the plies, there is a tendency for the presser foot to stretch both plies and thus to sew in some stretch along the seam. A differential feed system can be set to prevent this as in this case the friction between the plies is sufficient for the motion of the split feed dog to be transmitted to both of them.

*Adjustable top feed systems* can take more than one form but all provide positive control of the top fabric ply in a way that allows for adjustment so that the fabric plies will either be fed through exactly together or, if required, the top ply will be gathered on to the bottom ply. The general arrangement of such top feed systems is that the presser foot is in two sections, one holding the fabric in position, while the needle forms the stitch, and the other having teeth on the lower side and moving or 'walking' in such a way that the top ply is taken along positively while the needle is out of the material. All feeding systems with two presser feet can be described using the name 'walking foot'. A total feed system would normally be formed from a combination of an adjustable top feed system and either a non-adjustable drop feed, or a differential bottom feed. Machines are available where the vibrating presser acts in front of the needle, behind it or all around it, and companies would normally purchase machines appropriate to their typical sewing situations. These

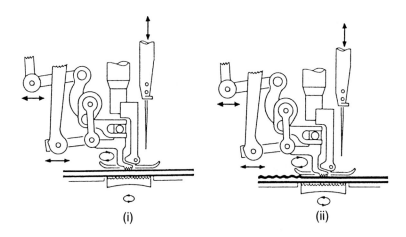

**Figure 3.46** Variable top feed combined with drop feed. (i) To finish even. (ii) To work fullness into top ply.

situations may include sewing of lightweight fabrics without inter-ply shift, marginal stitching to a right or a left fabric edge, the sewing of quilting, the addition of binding to an edge and many other possibilities.

When a variable top feed is combined with a drop feed, there is the opportunity to speed up the movement of the top ply to achieve shift-free sewing, or, by further adjustment of the top feed mechanism, to introduce a deliberate amount of ease or gather to the top ply. This is shown in Fig. 3.46.

When a variable top feed is combined with a differential bottom feed, all possibilities are available for achieving ease or gather in either the top or the bottom ply, and for achieving shift-free sewing. Such a combination of feeding systems, with both the top feed and the bottom feed being independently variable, is the most logical to apply to most seaming situations since it can be adjusted to feed each ply exactly as required in relation to the other. Machines are available on which the required amounts of fullness can be pre-programmed and altered by the action of a finger, knee or foot switch as needed along the length of the seam. Diagrammatic representations of the variable top and bottom feed systems are shown in Fig 3.47.

Overedge machines are also available with differential bottom feed and variable top feed with the top feed able to act in front of or behind the needle in order to give the best effect on a particular fabric. Thus narrow, closed seams can also be obtained free of ply shift or with the correct amount of gathering or stretching incorporated into one ply.

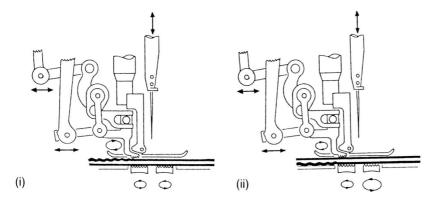

(i)  (ii)

**Figure 3.47** Variable top feed combined with differential feed. (i) To work fullness into top ply. (ii) To work fullness into bottom ply.

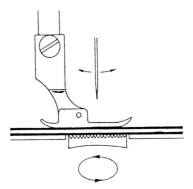

**Figure 3.48** Compound feed system.

*Needle feed* is the name given to the feed system in which the needle itself moves forwards and backwards. Used on its own it tends to produce elongated needle holes in the fabric; to avoid this it is normally combined with a drop feed and given the name *compound feed*. The needle enters the fabric, moves back with it as it is moved along by the feed dog to form one stitch and then rises up and forward again to begin the next stitch. Thus the needle is in the fabric while feeding is taking place and the plies of fabric are held together. It is particularly useful in bulky sewing situations, such as when quilting through fabric and wadding. Exact synchronisation of the movement of the needle and the drop feed is needed. The needle hole is generally within the feed dog. Stitch length adjustment is normal with the needle stroke changing with the stroke of the feed dog. Compound feed is illustrated in Fig. 3.48.

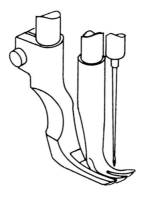

**Figure 3.49** Unison feed system.

*Unison feed* is a further combination of feeding mechanisms which provides needle feed in addition to positive top and bottom feeding. Of the two-part presser foot, shown in Fig. 3.49, the centre part moves with the needle. Its applications are limited because once needle feed is included in a system which also has variable top and bottom feeding, it removes any opportunities for adjusting the amount of feeding in the top and bottom plies by means of the separate upper and under feeds, or by the operator easing in. However, it is valuable in the sewing of certain problem materials, especially those with slippery or tacky surfaces. It can achieve seam joining and edge binding without ply shift.

A *puller feed* is a way of providing positive control of all the plies of fabric as they leave another feeding mechanism such as a drop feed. Two rollers exert a pulling motion on the fabric immediately behind the presser foot or a short distance behind it. Both rollers may be driven, or the top roller only may be driven while the lower one idles. This is shown in Fig. 3.50. Puller feed is particularly useful in multi-needle stitching of parts such as waistbands and it may be set slightly faster than the main machine drop feed to overcome any tendency for the seam to twist. It will be seen later that it can also form the second stage of an elastication system.

In a move away from traditional presser feet and feed dogs, machines are being developed with computer-controlled top and bottom belt drive systems. One that has been developed for the insertion of sleeves on tailored jackets can be programmed to insert different amounts of ease in the different sections of the sleeve head by adjusting the speed of the top belt compared with the bottom belt. A secondary top belt to the right of the main one can move faster on curves and assist in taking in the excess material in the seam allowance

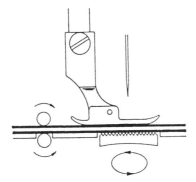

**Figure 3.50** Puller feed system.

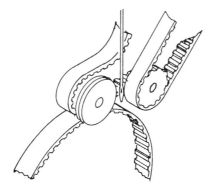

**Figure 3.51** Top and bottom belt feed.

compared with that along the stitch line. The belts have a lifespan of several years provided they are not allowed to run against each other with no fabric between them. This feed system is illustrated in Fig. 3.51.

In the construction of garments it is frequently necessary to ruffle (gather, gauge, ruck – the terms are interchangeable) one fabric on to another fabric intermittently rather than continuously. If the type of machine with programmable adjustment of fullness described above is not available, other methods are possible. In common use on safety stitch machines is a differential feed accompanied by a blade ruffler. For flat joining of two plies, the presser foot holds the material against the rear section of the differential feed only. When a section of the seam is reached where the lower ply is required to be gathered into the top ply, a metal blade is swung into place between the two plies of fabric. This has the effect of extending the presser foot forward and allowing the front section of the differential feed, which has been set to gather, to join in the feeding motion. The lower ply is gathered into the top ply for as long as the blade is left in place. This mechanism is often used in sleeve attachment on dresses and blouses where a section of ruffling is needed over the sleeve head. Notches are cut into the fabric edges during cutting to indicate to the operator where to begin and end the ruffled section. Another option on a safety stitch machine with differential feed is to cancel the operation of the differential feed by means of a lever mechanism. This could be hand operated or controlled by an air cylinder activated by a switch on the treadle. Both these methods of achieving gathers give the pre-set amount of ruffling or nothing, rather than the programmable different amounts of easing or ruffling described earlier.

The simplest ruffling mechanism, and one often used if gathers must be set continuously into a single ply of fabric before attaching it to another in a garment, is a ruffling or gauging foot for use on a lockstitch machine. A small step on the underside of the foot allows fabric to be taken in by the drop feed and it is then drawn back into a small pleat as the stitch is set. The amount of ruffling is controlled by adjusting the stitch size and thread tension or by using a foot with a different height of step. A diagram of the foot is shown in Fig. 3.52(i).

Another special presser foot that can be used in conjunction with a differential feed to ruffle one fabric on to another without any tendency for the top ply to ruffle as well is a split ruffling foot. The top ply misses the front section of the differential feed by passing above a section of the foot; the lower ply passing under it is ruffled by the feed just before being joined to the top ply. This is used for continuous rather than intermittent ruffling and is shown in Fig. 3.52(ii).

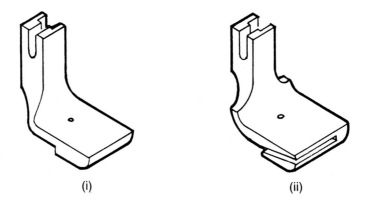

(i)                                    (ii)

**Figure 3.52** (i) Gauging foot. (ii) Split ruffling foot.

In all situations where easing or ruffling must be sewn into a seam, the machine must be set to incorporate the exact amount that has been allowed for on the patterns. In order to take maximum advantage of the types of mechanism that have been described here, pattern cutters must be familiar with their scope and limitations, particularly the need for the same ratio of ruffling across all graded sizes.

It should now be appreciated that a wide variety of feed mechanisms is available in order that materials can be sewn flat or appropriately eased or ruffled, as well as unstretched where there is a tendency for stretch to occur in normal sewing. Such mechanisms are much in evidence in factories which make up a wide variety of fabrics in moderate to large volume and in which high standards of seaming have to be achieved at high speed, often with relatively unskilled labour. Such factories are accustomed to investing in the most suitable machinery for a particular purpose. The shorter run, fashion side of clothing manufacturing has tended to achieve its output on less expensive machines but with a higher dependence on skilled labour and a higher risk of a low quality finish, but even here, such machines are becoming more common.

## Sewing machine needles

The way in which fabric is penetrated by the needle during sewing has a direct effect on seam strength and on garment appearance and wearable life.

The functions of the sewing machine needle in general are to:

♦ produce a hole in the material for the thread to pass through and to do so without causing any damage to the material
♦ carry the needle thread through the material and there form a loop, which can be picked up by the hook on the bobbin case in a lockstitch machine or by the looper or other mechanism in other machines
♦ pass the needle thread through the loop formed by the looper mechanism on machines other than lockstitch

The function of the sewing machine needle in relation to the hook or looper of the machine was described earlier but it is now appropriate to study the details of the separate parts of the needle and their role in satisfactory seam construction and performance. The commonest needle shape, with its various sections labelled, is shown in Fig. 3.53.

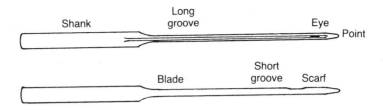

**Figure 3.53** Parts of a sewing machine needle.

The *shank* is the upper part of the needle, which locates within the needle bar. It may be cylindrical or have a flat side, according to how it is secured into the machine. It is the support of the needle as a whole and is usually larger in diameter than the rest of the needle for reasons of strength.

The *shoulder* is the section intermediate between the shank and the *blade*, the latter forming the longest part of the needle down to the eye. The blade is subject to the greatest amount of friction from the material through which the needle passes. In needles designed for use in high-speed sewing machines, the shoulder is often extended into the upper part of the blade to give a thicker cross-section which just enters the material when the needle is at its lowest point on each stitch. This supplementary shank or reinforced blade strengthens the needle and also enlarges the hole in the material when the needle is at its lowest point, thus reducing friction between it and the material during withdrawal after each stitch. Alternatively, the blade can be gradually tapered along its length from shank to tip, as another way of reducing friction. It will be seen later that this friction can create enough heat to cause serious problems when sewing synthetic fibres.

The *long groove* in the blade provides a protective channel in which the thread is drawn down through the material during stitch formation. Sewing thread can suffer considerably from abrasion during sewing as a result of friction against the fabric and a correctly shaped long groove, of a depth matched to the thread diameter, offers considerable protection to the thread.

The *short groove* is on the side of the needle which is towards the hook or looper; it extends a little above and below the eye. It assists in the formation of the loop in the needle thread.

The *eye* of the needle is the hole extending through the blade from the long groove on one side to the short groove on the other. The shape of the inside of the eye at the top is critical both in reducing thread damage as the needle penetrates the material and in producing a good loop formation. On some needles, known as bulged eye needles, the eye area has a larger cross-section than the rest of the blade. This serves a similar purpose to the reinforced shoulder mentioned above in that, as the needle enters the material, it creates a larger hole than is needed by the main part of the blade, thus reducing needle-to-fabric friction. The penalty to be paid for this cooler running needle, however, is a tendency to distortion in fine fabrics, and other methods of reducing needle heating are generally preferred.

The *scarf* or *clearance cut* is a recess across the whole face of the needle just above the eye. Its purpose is to enable a closer setting of the hook or looper to the needle. This ensures that the loop of needle thread will be entered more readily by the point of the hook or looper.

The *point* of the needle is shaped to provide the best penetration of each type of material according to its nature and the appearance that has to be produced. It is also the part of the needle that must be correctly selected in order to prevent damage to the material of the seam being sewn.

The *tip* is the extreme end of the point, which combines with the point in defining the penetration performance.

The features described above are those found on the majority of sewing machine needles but other fundamentally different types do exist. Some overedge and safety stitch machines use curved rather than straight needles. The needles themselves are costly and do not last as long as straight needles but the machine mechanism that makes use of curved needles can achieve higher speeds than that using straight needles. Blind stitching machines, used particularly for felling of hems, also use needles that are curved, but in this case it is to avoid penetration right through the fabric. In the case of single-thread chainstitch felling, the needle penetrates partially through the fabric of the garment and the fabric of the hem edge but re-emerges and forms the stitch with a looper on the same side. Machines that form the simulated hand stitch, type 209, use a double-pointed needle with an eye in the middle, through which is threaded the short length of thread with which this machine sews. In the course of forming the stitches, the needle is passed between a gripper above the throat plate and another gripper below the throat plate. A rotating device catches the loop of thread each time and pulls it right through the fabric. Two of these special needles are shown in Fig. 3.54.

For use in a particular machine, needles must conform to the machine manufacturer's specification as regards shank diameter, length from butt to eye, and total length. In addition, the different needle manufacturers add their own design features as a result of development work to overcome the problems caused by higher machine speeds and the demand for finer needle sizes to reduce

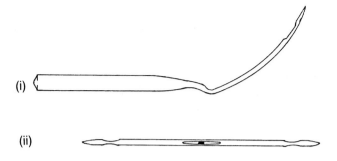

**Figure 3.54** Special needle shapes. (i) Blind stitch needle. (ii) Pick stitch needle.

pucker, fabric damage and needle heating effects. Needle strength must remain adequate despite smaller size. Needle thread loop formation is critical if slip stitching is to be avoided, especially on zig-zag machines where the hook cannot be set as close as on straight-stitch machines.

Needles are available in a wide range of sizes and the choice of size is determined by the fabric and thread combination which is to be sewn. As has already been suggested, correct size is essential to good sewing performance but as fabrics tend to become finer and, in many cases, more densely constructed, the demand is for needles and threads that can be used satisfactorily in smaller sizes.

If the needle is too small for the thread, the thread will neither pass freely through the eye nor fit properly into the long groove and will suffer from excessive abrasion as a result. This can lead to costly thread breakages in production because the machinist must stop to rethread the needle and possibly also to unpick some of the stitching so that a join does not show in an important part of the garment. Even worse, a break in a situation of multi-needle sewing with fabric running through folders could be impossible to repair. The use of too fine a needle when sewing heavy plies of material can lead to the needle being deflected, which can affect the stitch loop pick up and cause slip stitches; it can even lead to needle breakage.

If the needle is too large for the thread, there will be poor control of the loop formation which may cause slipped stitches. There will also be holes in the fabric that are too big for the stitches and give an unattractive seam appearance. An unnecessarily large needle also tends to give rise to damaged fabric along the stitch line and, in closely woven fabrics, pucker along the seam line due to fabric distortion.

Different needle manufacturers use their own nomenclature to describe *needle sizes* but the simplest sizing system is the metric one. The metric size or Nm of a needle is related to the diameter at a point at the middle of the blade above the scarf or short groove but below any reinforced part, as shown in Fig. 3.55. This measurement, in millimetres, multiplied by 100, gives the metric number. Thus a diameter of 0.9 mm is an Nm 90, and a diameter of 1.1 mm is an Nm 110. Typical metric needle sizes are shown in the Table in Fig. 3.56, along with the equivalent sizes in the Singer system, and typical thread sizes, given in the ticket number system for synthetic threads which will be described later.

Selection of needle and thread sizes for a particular seaming situation is a question of achieving a balance between minimum damage

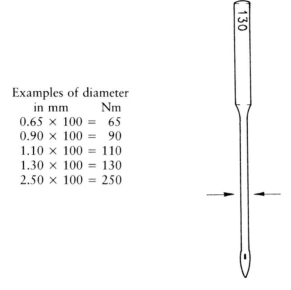

Examples of diameter
in mm      Nm
0.65 × 100 =   65
0.90 × 100 =   90
1.10 × 100 = 110
1.30 × 100 = 130
2.50 × 100 = 250

**Figure 3.55** Metric needle sizing.

| Thread sizes in synthetic ticket numbers | Needle sizes in metric system | Needle sizes in Singer system |
|:---:|:---:|:---:|
| 8 | 180 | 24 |
| 16 | 140 | 22 |
| 30 | 120 | 19 |
| 50 | 110 | 18 |
| 75 | 90 | 14 |
| 120 | 80 | 12 |
| 180 | 70 | 10 |
| 320 | 60 | 8 |

**Figure 3.56** Needle and thread sizes.

and pucker (usually a matter of small needle size and fine thread), and seam strength (which may require a more substantial needle and thread). As will be seen, the answer normally lies in the greater strength for size provided by synthetic rather than cotton sewing threads, especially in the newer versions which, like the needles, provide greater strength for their size than did earlier versions.

So far in this section, needles have been discussed with regard to their various parts, with a brief description of the purpose of each. This must be expanded, particularly in relation to needle points, but first the question of needle quality and condition must be considered. A sewing machine needle is a precision item and if it becomes mis-shapen in any way it will either fail to form the stitch properly or it will damage the material, or both.

A needle that is bent may cause slip stitching if the hook or looper fails to pick up the loop in the needle thread. In a lockstitch this leads to poor appearance and possibly poor strength in the seam. In a chainstitch it can lead to an insecure seam that unravels. The needle can become bent due to faulty operator handling or because the incorrect needle size is used for the fabric being sewn.

A needle with a burred or damaged point will almost certainly cause damage along the stitch line. On a woven material this will cause fibres or whole yarns to become broken, but because of the nature of a woven fabric there is unlikely to be a complete breakdown of the seam unless the damage is very severe. All that will show is a slightly fluffy appearance along the stitch line. On a knitted fabric, the problem is more serious because a damaged yarn is likely to lead to laddering in the fabric, which is very unsightly and could weaken the seam. A yarn in a knitted or a woven fabric can become damaged because it has been broken by the impact of the damaged needle, but in a knitted fabric there is also the possibility that the needle is too large for the size of the knitted loop in the fabric construction and, unless yarn can be quickly drawn into the loop from adjacent loops, it will burst.

Needles can become damaged after striking some part of the machine, usually the throat plate. Occasionally this is a result of the way the operator handles the fabric, but more commonly it arises when the needle becomes deflected during sewing by fabric that is too thick for the size of the needle. Evidence of the cause of the damage may be present in the form of pock marks on the throat plate where the needle has missed the hole. Bevelling out the edge of the hole may help but if the deflection is too severe, a larger size needle may be necessary. Needles can also become damaged as a result of striking a harsh material over a period of time. Material such as the type of denim used for jeans, which is made up in a stiff state and then washed in garment form, can require that the needles sewing it are changed every two hours before they become so damaged that they in turn damage the material.

The problem of materials suffering damage during sewing as a result of using damaged needles must be mentioned before the nature of perfect needle points is discussed because perfect needles can also cause damage in certain circumstances. The question of damaged needles causing damage to fabrics is, in some ways, a straightforward one. It is not surprising that damaged needles cause damage to fabrics and the remedy is simple in that the needle must be changed for an undamaged one, along with an investigation into the cause of the damage to the needle so that it does not continue to happen. The more surprising problem is that a needle with a perfect, undamaged point can cause damage to materials because the point is of an unsuitable shape for the particular material or because the material itself has some inherent problems of sewability. Thus a variety of needle point shapes is needed to sew the various materials that are used and, in addition, steps may sometimes have to be taken to alter the construction or finish of a material in order that it can be sewn without damage.

The basic division of needle points is into *cutting points* and *cloth points*. This division is necessary because of the fundamentally different constructions of the two types of material which must be sewn, namely leathers and plastics, which are essentially sheet materials with no gaps within the structure, and textile fabrics which, whether woven, knitted or made from bonded textile fibres in a non-woven form, have spaces within the structure through which a needle can penetrate. In a sheet material, the needle point must cut a sufficient hole that the needle blade and thread can pass through without excessive friction, but there must be sufficient strength of material left between the holes so that they do not run together, especially when under stress, and cause the garment to split. In a textile material cutting of the fibres is precisely what must be avoided since, depending on the fabric construction, yarns may run back from the hole that is created, causing poor appearance and a weak seam.

Cutting point needles all have sharp tips but they are available with a wide variety of cross-sectional shapes in their points. When sewing leather or plastic, a cutting point needle will modify the set of the stitching and therefore the appearance of the seam. The reason for this is that the other difference between sewing sheet materials and textile materials is that in a sheet material the sewing thread remains essentially in the same position in which it was inserted into the material, because it is held in the cut hole. In a textile material the tension of the sewing thread in relation to the mixture of fibres and spaces allows, in most cases, for a bedding-in effect – a redistribution of the combination of fabric yarns and sewing thread to give a line of straight stitching. This effect is made use of in the sewing of leathers and plastics by having a variety of shapes of needle point. These create particular decorative effects in the way that they cut the hole and insert the thread into the seam, as well as creating seams of the necessary strength. Three examples of cutting points are shown in Fig. 3.57, along with the shape of incision produced when used in a machine with the commonest threading direction, i.e. from the side. In a machine threaded from the front, the direction of the incisions would be at right angles to those shown. An indication of the appearance of the thread in a seam sewn with each needle point shape is also given.

The narrow wedge point cuts at right angles to the seam direction and allows a high stitch density to be achieved while leaving enough material between the needle holes to maintain seam strength. On soft leathers, stitch densities as high as 12 per centimetre are possible. It is the most frequently used point form for stitching uppers in the shoe industry. The thread is raised on the surface of the material.

The narrow reverse twist point produces incisions that lie at 45° to the seam direction, and produces a seam where the sewing thread is turned slightly to the left on the surface of the material. After the wedge point, this is the point form used most frequently. Again, threading direction is important since the narrow twist point, if used instead of narrow reverse twist with the same threading direction, would produce seams where the stitching is relatively straight but not very even. In addition the incisions would not be completely filled by the sewing thread.

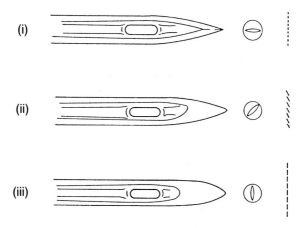

**Figure 3.57** Cutting points. (i) Wedge point. (ii) Narrow reverse twist point. (iii) Cross point.

The narrow cross point creates incisions along the line of the seam and requires a large stitch length with these incisions spaced as far apart as possible if there is not to be total perforation of the leather. Heavy decorative seams can be produced where thick sewing threads are used at large stitch distances. The stitches have a straight appearance.

With points such as these, care must be taken with needle insertion since, if a needle is replaced during sewing, a variation of as little as 5° in the angle of the needle will affect the appearance of the seam. Thread size is also important as a thread that is too small for the holes will give an untidy appearance. Too thick a sewing thread however, although completely filling the incisions, will be subject to excessive friction during sewing, thus causing thread breakage.

A number of other point types are available for the variety of leathers, seams, sewing machines and strength and appearance requirements that arise. These include triangular cross-sections for multi-directional sewing.

The sewing of sheet plastic materials is similar to that of leather but with the added problem of possible damage if the needle becomes hot through friction against the material. If overheating does occur and the edges of the stitch holes become melted, the needle tends to leave a horseshoe-shaped mark corresponding to the shape of the groove in the blade of the needle. Many materials, especially in the synthetic shoe industry, consist of a plastic covering layer on some kind of textile material base. Provided the base is not too densely woven and the yarns are not strongly twisted, they are unlikely to be damaged by a cutting point needle; if the material is sewn with a cloth point needle, excessive friction is likely to occur between the needle and the coating. On closely woven coated fabrics such as are used from time to time for raincoats, the coating is normally sufficiently thin for the material to be sewn with a conventional cloth point needle.

*Cloth point needles*, as their name suggests, are used for sewing textile materials rather than the sheet materials already described. The points have a round cross-section as opposed to the various cutting shapes of the leather needles described previously and the tip at the end of the point can vary in shape to suit the particular material being sewn. The main division in material types which requires different treatment in terms of needle penetration is that between woven and knitted structures.

Knitted fabrics consist of yarns in the form of loops. If a yarn in a knitted fabric is broken, the knitted structure may begin to unravel. This yarn breakage can happen in two ways, either by the needle striking the yarn directly and damaging it, or by the needle entering a knitted loop that is not large enough to accommodate it and where, for reasons of machine speed or lack of movement within the fabric, the loop is not able sufficiently quickly to draw in extra yarn and become large enough to take the needle. This situation is generally referred to as 'needle damage'. It is not the result of the needle being damaged but of the point type and fabric characteristics being incompatible. Thus the requirements in sewing knitted fabrics are for a needle that will deflect the yarns slightly and enter the spaces, but one which is not itself so deflected that it fails to form the stitch properly; a needle of as small a size as possible consistent with needle strength and sewing thread size; and finally a fabric that is lubricated sufficiently such that it has flexibility in relation to the movement of the needle. The shape of the tip of the needle point which best achieves this deflection is a fine ball shape and the needle is referred to as a *light ball point* needle.

Woven fabrics consist of yarns, which can have greater or lesser amounts of twist, interlaced with each other at various degrees of density. Thus woven fabrics may have quite sizeable spaces within the structure if woven loosely from low twist yarns, or they may be extremely dense if high twist yarns have been packed closely together. There is no need for the needle to seek the spaces (if they exist) in the fabric, as there is little difference between the needle going between the fibres of a low-twist yarn or between the fibres of adjacent yarns. What matters is that the needle does not damage the yarns. The tip of the needle point which best achieves this penetration has the shape of a cone. It is usually referred to as a *set point* needle as the tip has been set, or ground, and polished at a broader angle than the main section of the point. This construction strengthens the point and reduces the possibility of damage at the tip.

Both ball and set point needles are available in a number of types, illustrated in Fig. 3.58. If any needle could be regarded as the general purpose needle in no-problem sewing situations, it would be the medium set point. It is used widely for sewing a variety of woven fabrics and in many cases can be used for knits as well. In special cases a very acute set point is needed, for example in blind stitch machines where the curved needle has to hit the fabric almost at a tangent and must pick up a small part of the fabric without bouncing off it. In sewing dense combinations of materials such as shirting fabric and interlining in collars and cuffs, where for the sake of appearance a very straight line of stitching is needed, needles with very acute set points must be used in order to avoid an uneven, wandering seam due to the needle being deflected by the hard yarns in the fabric. The increased danger of damaging the fabric can be minimised by using the smallest possible needle size. At the other extreme, a heavy set point or stub point can be used for buttonsewing so that the button

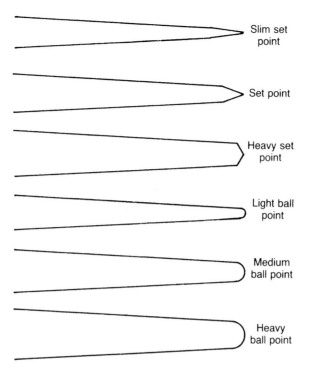

Slim set
point

Set point

Heavy set
point

Light ball
point

Medium
ball point

Heavy
ball point

**Figure 3.58** Cloth points.

can be safely deflected slightly into the correct position so that the needle passes through the holes. However, the use of stub point needles when buttonsewing on some fabrics may lead to fabric damage and it is preferable that operators using buttonsew machines are encouraged to insert the buttons straight rather than crooked in the clamp so that the needle will not strike the button and break either itself or the button.

Ball point needles are available with a light, medium or heavy ball and each of these is available on different sizes of needle. As the needle size decreases, the radius of each ball point decreases proportionately. To maintain the proper tip bluntness, the heavier ball points may be needed for the smaller needle sizes. In general, needle damage is limited by using the smallest possible needle size but there is a limit to the use of thinner needles. They have a higher chance of breaking and are deflected more easily than thicker ones, possibly causing faulty stitches and an irregular seam.

The sewability of knitted fabrics depends on the type and size of yarn, the density, size and regularity of the loops, and the nature of the finish applied. Open-mesh knitted fabrics can usually be sewn without difficulty as the yarns tend to be so thick that they can even be pierced by the needle without being damaged. In these cases medium set point needles are usually sufficient. Materials with very small loops made of a thin yarn are more susceptible to damage and thin needles with light ball points are usually found to be most suitable.

Particular problems of sewing knitted fabrics arise when those fabrics contain elastic yarns, especially the heavy yarns used in corsetry. The elastic threads may be cut or perforated by the needle and the threads then break, weakening the elasticity of the fabric as well as the strength of the seam. Elastic threads come in two types: those with a covering thread wrapped round the elastic and those where it is bare. Where the thread is covered the needle can slide past it and in this case a ball point is normally used. With an uncovered thread, the elastic threads may be pushed out of the fabric by the needle point or twisted or pulled out as a loop by the friction between needle blade and elastic thread. If the needle is too large the friction will be very great. In this instance a very acute set point would be used so that the needle can perforate the threads. The needle must, of course, be as fine as possible so that the elastic thread is not totally cut by it. Occasionally, woven fabrics are used which contain fine elastic yarns and these can also suffer damage during sewing. In this case, ball point needles may have to be used.

Firm guidelines to needle and point sizes are difficult to give but if care is taken to investigate every fabric before a production run to find a combination of needle point type, needle size and fabric finish that gives satisfactory sewing without damage, then few problems should arise in production.

Where dissimilar fabrics are sewn together the problems are even greater, in proportion to the differences between the fabrics. It is sometimes necessary to sew woven corset satin to heavy knitted elastic net. The satin requires a fine, set point needle, while the elastic requires a thicker needle with a heavy ball point. If the combination is sewn with the heavy ball point needle, untidy seams would result on the satin, whereas if sewn with the thin needle it would be deflected too much and possibly cause skip-stitching. There is always a tendency for ball point needles to produce slightly irregular seams because they push the fabric threads aside and in sewing difficult combinations of fabrics, the necessary investigations to determine needle size and point type would have to take place, as always, before production.

The names used here for the various types of needle point, namely cutting point and cloth point, with the latter divided into set point and ball point, are those which best describe the nature of the points and they are the names that are used in many sections of the industry.

It should be pointed out, however, that needle points are sometimes divided up and labelled as cutting points and round points, thus describing their cross-sectional shapes, with the term cloth point used only for the further subdivision that is here called the set point. Since the ball point needle is also used to sew textile materials, i.e. cloth, this seems less logical.

The final feature of a sewing machine needle that can vary is the surface finish given to it. Needles are made from steel and in the final stages of manufacture they are polished, especially in the area of the eye. In many cases they are then electroplated to give corrosion resistance, resistance to mechanical wear, reduction of friction during sewing, and a good overall appearance. The materials used for plating are chromium or nickel. One requirement of the surface finish of needles is that they should not easily pick up any particles of synthetic fabric or synthetic sewing thread which they may have caused to melt as a result of excessive friction-generated heat. It has been found that chromium-plated needles resist the adherence of melted synthetic residues rather better than nickel-plated needles do, despite the fact that chromium-plated needles actually develop higher temperatures during sewing than do non-plated or nickel-plated needles.

## Sewing threads

If seams are to have satisfactory appearance and performance, a prime contributory factor is the sewing thread used. Correct selection of sewing thread requires consideration of its performance properties during sewing as well as its performance in the completed garment under conditions of wear and cleaning. It also requires consideration of its appearance in the sewn seam, which is both its appearance as sewing thread and the effect it has on the appearance of the materials being sewn, the latter being also partly connected with thread performance.

As with other textile materials, sewing threads are composed of a fibre type, a construction and a finish, each of which may influence both the appearance and the performance of the thread. A wide variety of sizes is available; the choice of size relates to the requirements of the materials being sewn, and also determines the size of sewing machine needle used.

### Fibre type, construction and finish

The simplest division of sewing threads is, in terms of materials, into those made from natural fibres, those made from man-made fibres, and those made from a mixture. In terms of construction, threads can be divided into those spun from staple or short fibre lengths, those made from continuous filaments, and those that are a combination of the two.

### Fibre types

A range of natural and man-made fibres is used in the production of sewing threads although some have only limited uses. *Linen* was once used much more than it is now for making strong, rather stiff threads for heavy seaming and also for button sewing, but it has been largely superseded by synthetic threads. *Silk* is available both as the continuous filament extruded by the silkworm and as broken filaments spun into a yarn. It has good appearance and performance but its high cost restricts its use mainly to couture and bespoke tailoring. Its only common use in higher volume manufacturing is as the thread used in short lengths for pick stitching the edges of men's jackets and, in more expensive garments, for machine buttonholes.

The natural fibre used most frequently is *cotton*, spun into yarns from fibres with an average length of 35–40 mm and diameter of 0.02 mm. Untreated cotton fibres have a flattened, ribbon-like appearance with frequent convolutions. Cotton threads in general provide good sewing performance but their strength and abrasion resistance are inferior to synthetic threads of equal thickness. Cotton threads are more stable at higher, dry temperatures than are synthetic threads, and are therefore less affected by hot needles during sewing unless special lubricant precautions are taken with the synthetic threads. In the version sold as soft cotton the fibres receive no other treatment than bleaching or dyeing and the application of a low-friction lubricant. Soft cotton threads generally have a high wet shrinkage, which may cause pucker in seams after washing. In mercerised cotton threads the thread is treated under tension in a solution of caustic soda, which causes the fibres to swell and become rounder in cross-section. The result is a thread with increased lustre and higher tenacity (strength related to thickness). Glacé cotton threads are produced from soft cotton threads that have been consolidated and protected by the application of a special surface coating. This produces a stiffer thread with a smoother surface and better resistance to abrasion than soft cotton. Sewing threads made from cotton used to be by far the commonest in use, for the reasons already given and because they sew well on poorly adjusted machines. In recent years there has been a major decline in demand for cotton threads, and a great upsurge in the use of synthetic or mixture threads which do not rot and which give greater strength for their size and lower shrinkage. However, recent developments in the dyeing of whole garments rather than colour matching the materials separately has recreated a small demand for cotton threads for sewing cotton fabrics.

Under the heading of reconstituted fibres, a limited number of sewing threads are made from *viscose*. They do not have the strength or durability of synthetic fibres and they have low elasticity and low strength when wet, but their great advantage is their high lustre for use in embroidery. Most commonly available in continuous filament form, which has greater lustre than the spun form, their low abrasion resistance and strength is not a major disadvantage in embroidery machines. Garments incorporating them should not undergo repeated washing.

Synthetic sewing threads are made mainly from *polyester* and *polyamide* (nylon) with a small amount of aramid (e.g. Du Pont's Nomex) and polytetrafluoroethylene (PTFE). All synthetic fibres start life as continuous filaments. Various filament sizes are possible according to the size of the spinneret holes from which they are extruded but polyester and polyamide are generally made about twice the diameter of cotton fibres. The filaments are then stretched to orientate the molecules within the material and produce high tenacity filaments. They are processed to ensure low shrinkage in washing at 100°C (between 0 and 1 per cent) and also in dry heat treatments up to 150°C (generally between 0 and 2 per cent). Beyond this, special threads may be needed as polyester and polyamide fibres begin to soften at about 230°C and melt at about 260°C. Low shrinkage is essential to avoid pucker in the seams on minimum care garments.

Synthetic threads are not significantly affected by rot, mildew or bacteria. They have high tenacities, especially in continuous filament form, and also have high resistance to abrasion. Polyester and polyamide possess good resistance to chemicals in general with polyamide being most resistant to alkaline conditions and polyester to acid. Both are degraded in strength by prolonged exposure to sunlight. Polyamide is affected by the visible and the ultraviolet components of sunlight, as also is cotton, but polyester is only sensitive to near ultraviolet light. In tropical sunlight, polyamide may degrade faster than polyester, although it has the higher initial tenacity.

The filaments may be processed to become sewing threads directly or a number of the fibres may be brought together into a tow or rope-like structure which is drawn or crimped to produce a better frictional surface. The tow can then either be cut into a suitable regular staple length or stretch-broken to produce a longer, more variable fibre length. These are then spun together in ways similar to those used with the natural staple fibres to produce yarns. The filaments of both polyester and polyamide used for the production of sewing threads generally have circular cross-sections and a smooth surface, making them more lustrous than natural fibres. Polyester is considered the best fibre for most sewing thread applications, having low cost, high strength, good chemical properties, favourable elastic characteristics and good dye fastness. Polyamide has the high strength to fineness of polyester but less favourable extension characteristics. Its higher elasticity makes it unsuitable as a general purpose sewing thread as it tends to stretch during sewing and relax afterwards, thus causing puckered seams.

All these fibres have been described in terms of being used on their own in a sewing thread but one of the most commonly used threads nowadays consists of a mixture of polyester and cotton in the form of a continuous filament polyester core with cotton fibres spun on the outside. This type will be described further.

Threads made from the *aramid* or aromatic polyamide fibres such as Nomex are expensive but have important uses in fire-resistant garments. They have a high melting point followed by charring rather than dripping like other synthetic fibres. They are combustible but are self-extinguishing when withdrawn from the source of heat. This type of performance is not required by the flammability regulations covering nightwear but in items such as racing drivers' suits where the garment material would also be aramid fibre, such threads are essential so that the garment remains intact for as long as the fabric withstands the heat. PTFE sewing threads are also very expensive but they have a few specialist industrial uses where their complete non-flammability, non-melting property, and high resistance to chemicals makes them important.

*Thread constructions*

The creation of sewing threads from the natural and man-made fibres already described can take a variety of forms. Where the fibres occur naturally in short lengths or have been cut or broken into short lengths, they must be twisted together, initially into a single yarn; that twist must then be balanced by applying a reverse twist as two or three such yarns are combined to form the thread construction. The twist in the single yarn consolidates the strength and flexibility provided by the fibres themselves. Without the reverse twist, known as finishing twist, a conventional thread could not be controlled during sewing. The individual plies would separate during their repeated passages through the needle and over the sewing machine control surfaces. Twist is defined as the number of turns inserted per centimetre of yarn or thread produced. If the twist is too low, the yarns may fray and

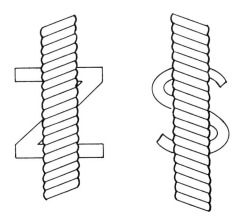

**Figure 3.59** Thread twist.

break; if too high, the resulting liveliness in the thread may cause snarling, loop knots or spillage from the package of thread. There are two possibilities of twist direction, as shown in Fig. 3.59.

The frictional forces acting on a thread during its passage through a sewing machine also tend to insert some twist, predominantly in one direction. In a lockstitch machine, during normal straight sewing, the needle and hook tend to insert some Z twist to the sewing thread. A thread with a correctly balanced finishing twist reaches equilibrium as it resists further tightening up of the twist. A thread with an S twist becomes untwisted by the action of the machine and then frays and breaks. Because the lockstitch machine type is the most severe in its handling of thread, the majority of threads intended for use in machine sewing are constructed with a finishing Z twist. There are only a few machines, such as flatlock, for which this is not suitable and special threads with S finishing twist are available for these. In most sewing threads, two, three or occasionally four component yarns are twisted together to form two-, three- or four-ply thread. Subsequent twisting operations may be used to produce heavier or 'corded' threads, with the direction of twist reversing each time.

The thread construction procedures described so far apply to cotton, and to silk, polyester and polyamide that has been cut or stretch-broken into short lengths. Polyester that has been cut is spun in the same way as cotton. Silk is normally broken and the process of spinning it into a yarn is referred to as Schappe spinning. When polyester is broken rather than cut, the fibres are longer and more variable in length than when they are cut; the yarn produced is also referred to as Schappe spun. Polyamide that has been cut and then spun does not make a general purpose sewing thread because it is highly elastic and is not suitable as a needle thread. It is, however, useful in linking, the joining operation in fully fashioned knitwear, and in other high stretch applications such as bottom threads in sewing swimwear. Threads made from spun yarns have good sewing performance, good dimensional stability and good stitch-locking properties in the seam due to their fibrous surface. Their abrasion resistance varies, depending on the fibre, and is about four times as great for synthetics as for cotton. Abrasion resistance is important in relation to the durability of threads to abrasive forces in the sewing operation.

When threads are made directly from continuous filaments, as in polyester and polyamide, a wide variety of different constructions are possible. The very simplest is hardly a thread at all, being just one filament of polyamide of a larger size than normal. It is called *monofilament* and is of limited use. It is harsh on the machine and rather inflexible because the cross-sectional shape never varies as it would with multifilaments. In addition, the cut ends are harsh on the wearer. It has virtually no seam grip and stitches tend to unravel easily. Its great advantage is a translucency that reduces the need for shade matching and the three tones of natural, light and dark grey adapt to suit the limited range of applications for which the thread is suited. It tends to be used for blind felling and overedging at the lower quality end of clothing manufacturing and for upholstery and household textiles.

More conventional constructions of continuous filament thread are in *multifilament form*, either in *singles* or *plied* or *corded*. Where flexible threads are required, the filament yarns are twisted, set, dyed and lubricated only. Where optimum sewing performance and abrasion resistance are required, the plied threads are treated with synthetic polymer which bonds the individual filaments and yarns together. In polyester, they give higher strength with fineness at a lower price than a similar spun thread, and with good loop-forming properties they give reliable stitch formation. Their fineness enables larger thread packages to be used, thus saving operator time changing them, and in particular they enable more thread to be wound on the bobbin of a lockstitch machine. In polyamide, the bonded threads give the highest strength and abrasion resistance of all the mass-produced threads and for this reason they are popular in the shoe and leather industry. For low fault rates and a consistent, even thread, these multifilament threads are the most satisfactory. They are less expensive than some of the others but there is a limit to the amount of stretch in them because of torque effects and snarling. Care must always be taken to secure the seam ends to prevent run-back.

Other types of thread made from continuous multifilaments of polyester and polyamide are those generally classed as *textured*. Texturing is a term used to describe modifications, obtained by various means, to the appearance and surface characteristics of straight synthetic filament yarns. Depending on the application for which the thread is intended, the degree of crimp rigidity (bulk) can be varied. In fine sizes these threads are useful as needle threads in overedge and chainstitch machines but their commonest use is in larger sizes where their soft handle and spreading properties provide good seam cover when used in the loopers of overedge and covering stitch machines. With appropriate stitch size and thread tensions, almost complete cover of the fabric can be achieved, which adds greatly to comfort in garments worn next to the skin and to appearance in a fabric which frays badly. The degree of stretch in these threads can also be used when a fabric of moderate stretch must be sewn with a lockstitch and in this case they are used in the bobbin. Such threads are commonly referred to as *bulked* though the preferred term is *crimp textured*, their structure having been achieved by twisting, crimping, and untwisting again.

A relatively recent development of general purpose sewing thread is the locked filament polyester, also known as 'air entangled'. Continuous filament yarns are treated by means of air jets to have the characteristics and performance of threads produced by conventional spinning and twisting processes. The threads have high uniformity and freedom from imperfections and suit a variety of uses. An advantage of thread such as this which is constructed without twist is that it has a multi-directional sewing performance and can be used in sewing with the type of automated stitching jigs described later.

It was stated earlier that the sewing action in a lockstitch machine can insert or remove twist from a thread, depending on the twist direction. Z-twist thread is normally used for forward sewing in a single needle machine but problems can arise in twin needle machines equipped with two hooks rotating in the same direction because the thread is pulled off the needles in opposite directions and one untwists and gives a different appearance from the other. Problems can also arise with some automatic machines such as those sewing round jigs where sewing can be in any direction. An untwisted thread would not vary in appearance or performance with varying sewing direction. For inexpensive thread production with very low fault rates, threads made by this process would seem to have great possibilities, although there is some uncertainty about their versatility. For real success they must sew well in high speed lockstitch machines; in particular, they must withstand the high level of abrasion suffered by threads in this situation. Their development may well rest upon the level of price pressure put on the threads at present in common use which give very good sewability.

Yet another fundamentally different type of thread construction is that known as *corespun* where a continuous multifilament core is wrapped around with a sheath of spun fibres, two or three of these yarns then being plied together. This is the construction of the threads referred to earlier that can be a mixture of natural and synthetic fibres, the majority of these corespun threads consisting of a polyester core and a cotton cover. The continuous filament core produces high tenacities and excellent loop-forming characteristics through the sewing machine needle. The thread lubricant is retained well by the surface fibres and, combined with the effect of air carried to the needle during sewing, results in good sewing performance. The thread strength and loop formation are well maintained in multi-directional sewing and on automatic machines. These threads also have a satisfactory amount of stretch and low shrinkage. A major objective was to create a thread that did not suffer damage on contact with a needle heated by friction against the fabric and the cotton cover fulfils this function extremely well. A difficulty with the polyester and cotton combination is that the thread must be dyed twice; this adds to cost.

Developments in thread lubricants in recent years have allowed totally synthetic threads to achieve much greater heat resistance than before, and fewer problems need now be experienced with hot needles against synthetic thread. Accordingly, many of the advantages of the corespun construction are now being achieved in threads that are 'poly poly corespun', i.e. a polyester filament core with a spun polyester covering; these do not need the double dyeing process. There is also a strength contribution from the polyester sheath, which is not obtained with cotton, although with the type of high tenacity polyester used for the cores of these threads, strength is already very high. Sewability remains at least as important as strength and the cotton cover may continue to give this more successfully. Corespun threads in general enable clothing manufacturers to sew with finer threads and still achieve adequate seam strength. This is an important advantage with fine fabrics because the finer the thread, the less it will tend to cause pucker in the fabric. This also matches up with the use of finer needles to reduce needle damage.

From a situation where cotton threads formed a large part of the market a couple of decades ago, the synthetics and corespuns have made great inroads. Polyester/cotton corespun now has over 50 per cent of the market in Britain, especially in high-volume, quality-conscious manufacture where the demands of thread performance in sewing and wearing are great. Spun polyester is the dominant thread in the high volume area of underwear production where large quantities of white are used and it is also used in fashion manufacturing. Spun and corespun threads are illustrated in Fig. 3.60.

(i)                   (ii)

**Figure 3.60** (i) Spun and (ii) corespun threads.

### Thread finishes

The final aspect of thread construction to be studied is that of surface finish, the most important type of finish being *lubrication*. The requirement of a lubricating finish applied to a sewing thread is that it should produce a regular level of friction and that, for synthetic threads in particular, it should provide protection from needle heat. Without a controlled amount of lubrication applied to threads, unacceptable damage would be inflicted on them during the sewing process which would result in thread breaks during sewing and seam breakdown in wear. In a lockstitch machine, for example, each portion of thread may travel at least forty times through the eye of the needle, in repeated cycles of flexing and abrasion, before receiving a last impact from the needle eye as it becomes a stitch. A series of tension peaks occurs as a lockstitch machine goes through its stitch cycle. These occur as the stitch balance is set, as the needle punches the thread through the fabric, as the rotary hook picks up the loop of the needle thread and as the thread is pulled off the rotary hook at its lowest position. Thread must withstand these stresses and, even in fine sizes, retain enough of its initial strength during stitching to give adequate seam strength.

The nature of the lubricating finish is the result of considerable research by the thread companies to fulfil a number of requirements. A lubricant must not clog the needle eye nor cause staining; it must allow the thread to unwind evenly from the package, and it must reduce friction with machine surfaces but without creating too much slippage. It must reduce fibre-to-fibre slippage in spun threads which could lead to loss of strength; it must not react adversely to high temperatures, and it must be relatively inexpensive and easy to apply to the thread during manufacture.

Different threads need different amounts of lubricant according to their end use. Corespun and spun polyester threads must often withstand high temperatures when used as needle threads and thus need a high level of lubricant. A continuous filament thread would not generally need so much to perform well. The type of lubricant would vary between natural and synthetic fibres. Occasionally, where there are still stitching problems with excessive needle heating despite the use of a suitable thread, it may be necessary to add extra lubricant. In certain circumstances, the thread may be run between two felt pads soaked in the correct lubricant in a specially designed box which confines the lubricant to the thread and keeps it from soiling the rest of the machine. This should only be done on the advice of the thread maker as in many cases the problem can be overcome by correct choice of needle and thread, by further investigation of the fabric itself which may be poorly lubricated, and by checks on thread storage in case this is unsuitable and the natural moisture and the lubricant on the thread is becoming dried out. Spraying or soaking the thread package is generally messy and unsuccessful and should be avoided, as should the use of incorrect lubricants such as sewing machine oil.

Despite the discussion of the problems of needle heating given here, and the further discussion which will be included later under the heading Sewing problems (see p. 299), it should be stated that it is by no means as serious a problem today as it was when synthetic fibres were first used in any quantity. There was a time when many factories had needle coolers, in the form of jets of compressed air, attached to virtually all their sewing machines but their use now is far less common. Progress in fabric and thread lubricants, and the use of finer needles, have combined to reduce the problem to more manageable proportions.

Other finishes for sewing threads have been developed for certain threads for particular end uses. Synthetic threads are naturally resistant to *rot* and *mildew* but if cotton threads must be used, especially on items that will be kept in hot and humid conditions, then specially treated threads are available.

Another special demand is for threads with a *water-resistant finish*. Sewing waterproof or water-repellent clothing creates difficulty along the seams, which tend to allow water to enter the garment. Where a garment has to be totally waterproof the seams must be sealed by means of taping or welding over the needle holes; in the more everyday showerproof fabrics, such as those used for raincoats, choice of seam type and positioning of seams in the garment, especially in the shoulder area, will assist in preventing too much water ingress and suitable thread can help in addition. Traditionally, cotton threads were used and the swelling of the fibres when wet helped to block up the needle hole. Unfortunately this swelling also caused a displacement of the fabric yarns which contributed to pucker in the seams and gave a poor appearance. A cotton-covered corespun thread can also achieve the swelling effect but eventually the water begins to wick along the thread and passes rapidly to the inside of the garment. Wicking is the crucial factor in keeping rainwear seams dry, and water-repellent threads are available which reduce the problem. The thread no longer swells to block the needle hole, but this is less necessary when wicking has been reduced; less swelling is also beneficial in terms of reducing pucker. The water-repellent finish must be fast to washing and dry cleaning although if the garment has to be reproofed at any stage this will benefit the thread as well. Lubrication of these threads must be done with care as some lubricants can diminish the effect of the water-repelling agent. The finish tends to darken the thread shade which must be borne in mind when shades are matched. In order to prevent shading of thread within a garment, the whole garment may be sewn with the treated thread.

Another matching of fabric and thread finish which is sometimes needed is in the area of *soil release*. Much workwear fabric is treated with a soil release finish and, unless the thread is similarly treated, the dirt washed off the fabric is redeposited on the seams, thus spoiling the appearance of the garment. A soil release finish is now available on some spun polyester and polyester and cotton corespun threads.

A specific legal requirement is that relating to the Nightwear (Safety) Regulations 1985, which cover the *flammability* requirements of the materials used in children's nightwear and require that seams should come up to the same standard of performance. These requirements are that synthetic nightwear materials should melt before they burn and extinguish themselves by the falling away of any burning, molten material. If a seam in one of these fabrics is sewn with cotton or cotton-covered thread, or even with a totally non-flammable thread such as Nomex, the seam will support the adjacent burning material and even act as a wick to encourage burning.

In sewing flame-retardant fabrics, thermoplastic threads must be used; 100 per cent polyester is the only one recommended as it shrinks away from the flame and does not support combustion. In sewing chemically treated fabric, the seam would probably be extinguished, regardless of its fibre type, by the deoxygenating gases which the fabric releases when burnt, but it would seem sensible to aim for the highest standard of fire resistance possible by using spun polyester thread for sewing all nightwear. In some markets a flame-retardant finish is required, particularly to neutralise any effects of the thread lubricant on the flame resistance of the finished seam, but many difficulties arise in developing satisfactory finishes which will last the lifetime of wearing and washing of the garment. It should be remembered that the choice of stitch and seam type is also important so that no more thread is present than necessary, consistent with good seam performance and satisfactory appearance.

In discussing the requirements of seams it was said that a seam must maintain any particular properties of the material under construction. It can be seen here that a particularly important contribution to most of these properties comes from the sewing thread.

## Thread sizing

Numerous references have been made to fine and heavy threads without, as yet, any indication of these as relative sizes or any indication of the methods or units of measurement. All types of textile yarns can be produced in different thicknesses and the relationship between the length and weight of a specific yarn is known as its yarn count or grist or size. There are many traditional count systems, which are either fixed-weight systems that show the number of unit lengths that give a fixed weight, or fixed-length systems that show the weight of a given length. The latter system is simpler in that it gives a higher figure to a thicker yarn or thread, which is more logical than the other way round, and it is easier to weigh a fixed length than to measure a fixed weight. The systems of measurement in common use for sewing threads in the UK are fixed-weight systems and sewing threads are thus denoted by smaller numbers as they become thicker.

The commonest system and the one used for synthetic and core-spun threads is the *metric ticket number system*. It is derived from the number metric (Nm) yarn count system, which refers to the number of 1000-m hanks that weigh 1 kg, or, effectively, the number of 1-m lengths that weigh 1 g. Thus, a single yarn is labelled as being of count Nm 60/1 if 60 m of it would weigh 1 g. Two singles yarns of this size plied together would be written as Nm 60/2, and in this case 60 m of the yarn would weigh 2 g. Similarly, a thread given as Nm 120/3 would be constructed from three yarns, each of which would weigh 1 g for a 120-m length. 120 m of the complete thread would weigh 3 g. Thus the figures in the metric yarn count system relate to the sizes of the singles yarns used to form the final yarn.

The metric ticket number system for sewing threads is based on a threefold equivalent of the number metric system and relates its number to the finished thread rather than to the single yarns from which it is made. The ticket number is calculated via the resultant count, recalculated into threefold terms whatever the number of plies of yarn twisted together to form the thread. Resultant count is the length of a plied yarn that would weigh 1 g, which means that a thread expressed in number metric system as Nm 120/2 (i.e. 120 m weighs 2 g) would have a resultant count of 60 (i.e. 60 m would weigh 1 g).

The metric ticket number of this thread, based on a threefold equivalent is then three times that, i.e. Tkt. 180. This means that 180 m of this thread would weigh 3 g, and shows that the figure quoted for thread size in the metric ticket number system is the length that would weigh 3 g. The thread could be made from a single yarn or from two, three or more plied yarns. Other examples are: a thread of Nm 80/2 is Tkt. 120; Nm 30/3 is Tkt. 30; Nm 20/1 is Tkt. 60; Nm 60/3 is Tkt. 60; Nm 40/2 is Tkt. 60, etc. This shows that the same ticket number, in this case 60, can be used for three or more different thread constructions but to the user the size of the final thread is the same, i.e. 60-m lengths would weigh 3 g. The inverse nature of this measurement system is demonstrated by the fact that Tkt. 60 is twice as coarse as Tkt. 120.

Cotton sewing threads are sized on the *cotton ticket number system*, which works on the same principle but the figures do not denote the same size in terms of diameter. The basis of it is the cotton count, which is written as, for example, 3/60 Ne, meaning that the thread has three single yarns, each of which would need 60 hanks of 840 yards to weigh 1 lb. The cotton ticket number is the threefold equivalent of the cotton count and is the number of 840-yard hanks that weigh 3 lb. A six-cord construction of cotton yarns of count 60 Ne has a total resultant count of 10 and therefore a Tkt. No. 30 (equals 3 × 10). A construction of three plies of count 60 Ne has a total resultant count of 20 and therefore has Tkt. No. 60. Tkt. No. 30 is twice as coarse as Tkt. No. 60.

To compare thread sizes in the two systems, use the conversion factor where the cotton count is equal to 0.59 times the metric count, i.e. Ne = 0.59 × Nm. The ticket number of a cotton thread that would be roughly equivalent in size to a synthetic thread can be determined by multiplying the synthetic ticket number by 0.6. For example, a Tkt. No. 60 synthetic thread is equivalent in size to a Tkt. No. 36 cotton thread. Conversely, a Tkt. No. 60 cotton thread is equivalent to a Tkt. No. 100 synthetic thread. The comparison relates only to the actual size of threads and does not allow for the greater strength/fineness ratio of synthetic threads which must be taken into account when thread selection is made.

It should be clear from these figures that it is quite wrong to maintain the same ticket number when changing from cotton thread to synthetic. It is not even appropriate when changing from one type of synthetic to another. The choice depends on many factors including seam strength, fabric weight and type, stitch type, seam type, needle size, end use and many others.

The only other system used for sewing threads is the denier system. This is a fixed length system and the denier count or Td is the weight

Spun polyester or polyester/cotton corespun

| Metric Tkt. No. | Typical uses |
| --- | --- |
| 180 & 150 | Neatening and general seaming of lingerie, shirts and blouses |
| 120 & 70 | General seaming of underwear, knitwear, foundationwear, shirts, blouses, dresses, tailoring, jeans, workwear |
| 60 & 15 | Jeans, workwear, decorative stitching, buttonsewing and buttonholing |

Figure 3.61 Typical thread sizes and uses.

in grams of 9000 m of thread. In sewing threads it is generally only applied to polyamide, particularly to monofilaments.

Methods of sizing other than those quoted here are available for use with sewing threads and other yarns. Such systems are the Tex and the related Decitex systems. These systems are described in standard works on textiles and conversion factors exist between all the systems if they are needed.

A particular thread type will be available only in certain discrete sizes, and will cover a size range appropriate to the intended end uses of the thread. While it has already been made clear that a great many factors determine the choice of thread size, it may be helpful at this stage to give a brief indication of the sizes available in the commonest types of thread and their likely end uses. This is given in Fig. 3.61.

## Thread packages

In order that thread should sew well, it must be presented to the machine in a satisfactory way. It must be possible to purchase it in economically large or small quantities, while still having the right number of separate packages available for use on multi-thread machines. It is sold by length rather than by weight, and is available in a variety of types of package appropriate to the thread type and its end use.

*Spools* are the smallest packages and are flanged bobbins, once made in wood but now always made in plastic. Although used to a small extent on slower industrial machines, especially in footwear and leather goods manufacture, they are largely used for domestic sewing. A relatively short length of thread, usually 100 or 500 m, is parallel wound on to the bobbin. Spools are not suitable for delivering thread to high-speed industrial machines, nor for textured threads.

*Cops* are small, cylindrical, flangeless tubes on to which thread is crosswound for stability. The lack of flanges facilitates regular offwinding from the top on industrial sewing machines, mainly lockstitch, their small diameter making them less well suited to the faster thread offtake of machines such as overedgers. They usually contain lengths of 1000–2500 m of thread and are a popular size in fashion manufacturing where production runs in any one colour are short. They are suitable for cotton, spun polyester, spun nylon or corespun threads, but not for glacé finish of fine filament threads where spillage from the package would be a problem.

*Cones* contain 5000 m or more of soft or mercerised cotton, spun polyester or corespun thread, crosswound for stability and good offwinding performance. They give trouble-free thread delivery at intermittent or continuous high speeds and this, combined with their long length capacity, makes them ideal for use on class 400, 500, 600 and combination stitch machines where stops for rethreading need to be minimised. Cones are the ideal package for conventional sewing threads in situations where thread consumption is high and production runs are long with limited shade changes. They are also well suited to automatic machines.

*Vicones* are parallel tubes or low-angled cones with an additional base in the form of a raised flange which may incorporate a small lip. They contain polished or continuous filament thread and are designed to contain any spillage that may occur in offwinding these smooth threads with no snagging or trapping when the slack thread is taken up.

*Large packages* for use on overedge and coverstitch machines can hold in excess of 20 000 m of spun or corespun thread wound on large cones or tubes.

*Containers* are constructed to handle lively monofilament threads that would be difficult to control on standard packages. An exceptionally large spool of thread is held within the container which can incorporate an extra lubricant applicator at the thread draw-off point.

*Cocoons* are self-supporting, i.e. centreless, thread packages, specially designed for insertion in the shuttle of multi-needle quilting machines and some types of embroidery machines.

*Prewound bobbins* are precision-wound thread packages which can replace metal bobbins on a variety of lockstitch machines. Conventional bobbins in these machines are inconvenient and inefficient as time is lost in starting up an empty bobbin on its winder after removing a full one, thread tensions and lengths are variable and faulty build-up of thread on the bobbin may cause jamming in the bobbin case. They also inhibit overspin during stitching, a particular problem on zig-zag machines. Prewound bobbins generally contain more thread and the length is guaranteed. Thus in cases where bobbin runout must be avoided, the number of seams that can be sewn with each bobbin can be determined and the almost empty bobbin changed in time. Bobbin changing time is considerably reduced and smoother unwinding results from the initial precision winding. This improves efficiency and quality of production. A variety of thread types are available prewound and in a variety of sizes to fit most lockstitch machines. From some manufacturers, these packages are self-supporting and have no metal, wood or paper support.

Examples of thread packages are shown in Fig. 3.62. Choice of package is important if sewing is to be trouble-free and thread handling by the operator is to be minimised. Where a number of machines are involved in manufacturing a style and shade of garment, enough thread packages of suitable size must be available without excess stock of thread being required. Thus, a small contract for which only a small quantity of thread is needed may present problems in supplying enough packages to run safety stitch machines which require five threads, especially since thread is normally purchased in boxes of, say, six or ten packages. One answer is for a company to make use of a thread-winding machine, which enables them to rewind cones as smaller cops that can then be spread around more machines, especially when stocks are running low.

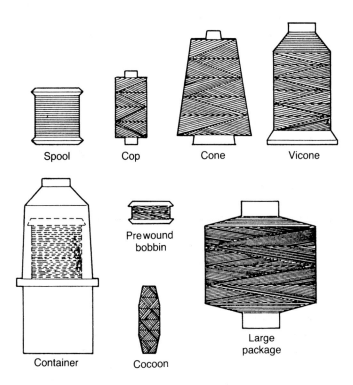

**Figure 3.62** Thread packages (not to scale).

## Thread costs

An important consideration in selecting thread, after performance and appearance have been settled, is the cost. Thread costs represent only a very small proportion of the material cost of an item such as a garment, but manufacturers are nevertheless tempted in some cases to try to cut these costs and use cheap threads. If threads are purchased separately from the other materials used in garment production, the overall thread bill for the year may be studied rather than the cost per garment and in this situation it may be tempting to economise.

Total thread costs are made up of the thread that is actually used in a production run of garments, the thread that is wasted during sewing (e.g. by chaining off excessively on overedge machines), the thread stock that remains unused at the end of a contract, and last, but by no means least, the costs that can arise in production or during the subsequent use of the garment because the thread was faulty. It is these last costs that can increase dramatically if low-quality thread is purchased in an attempt to cut the obvious costs of actual thread purchase.

In the publication *Productivity in Sewing Operations* by Grills and Brown, which demonstrated that only about 20 per cent of an operator's time on a conventional machine was spent in sewing, it was also shown that, on average, about four per cent of the operator's time was spent rethreading the sewing needle after a thread break. This means that about 20 minutes each day is being spent on the unproductive task of making good a fault incurred in the sewing operation. This time could be increased considerably if the operator has to unpick the seam back to the beginning so that a join does not occur in a visible part of the garment, or if working on a multi-needle operation or on a machine where rethreading is a more complex process. It is not difficult to estimate the cost involved here at current labour rates. Estimates from the thread manufacturers suggest that the cost over a day of rethreading a single needle lockstitch machine could be twice the total cost of the thread consumed by that machine in the day. A small increase in the price paid for the thread to obtain more consistent, fault-free thread would be a good investment.

It is possible to estimate the quantity of thread that will be consumed in manufacturing a certain style of garment, either by measuring the seam lengths sewn in each stitch type and calculating the total amount from published rates of thread usage, or by unpicking and measuring the thread used in a sample garment. The latter is more accurate because it allows for fabric thickness and stitch density.

| Stitch type | Thread usage, in cm, per cm of seam |
|---|---|
| 301 locksititch | 2.5 |
| 101 chainstitch | 4.0 |
| 401 two-thread chainstitch | 5.5 |
| 504 three-thread overedge stitch | 14.0 |
| 512 four-thread overedge | 18.0 |
| (401.504) safety stitch | 20.0 |
| 606 flatlock | 32.0 |

**Figure 3.63** Thread consumption rates.

Approximate net thread consumption rates for typical seams sewn in one or two plies of fabric at seven stitches per centimetre are shown in Fig. 3.63.

It will be seen that the more complicated stitch types use large amounts of thread. Tables of likely thread consumption for different types of general garment are also published by the thread manufacturers, based on their experience of actual consumption by customers. These show figures varying from 5 m of thread to make a tie, to 280 m to make a raincoat. In the latter case, thread cost has been estimated at around 22 pence per garment in a raincoat with a wholesale price of about £30. This is a typical order of magnitude of thread cost in relation to total garment cost.

Published estimates of thread consumption by thread suppliers usually include a five per cent allowance for wastage. Some wastage is inevitable, although it can be reduced where machines are fitted with automatic thread trimmers. Extreme situations of thread wastage occur where operators working on overedge or safety stitch machines keep the machine running constantly for long spells as they feed garment parts into them. A long section of thread chain will join the garment parts and where seams are short, e.g. blouse shoulder seams, wastage could easily exceed actual usage. If waste thread is collected and weighed on an accurate balance, some surprising figures may be obtained.

Not only does thread wastage cost money, it may cause a manufacturer to run out of thread before the completion of the contract for which it was purchased. In many areas of clothing manufacturing where long runs of a garment style used to be the norm, styles are changing increasingly rapidly in response to retailing demands. Thread quantities required for these smaller contracts must now be estimated more accurately than before if enough is to be available, in the correct size and number of packages, and if stocks are not to be left over at the end. Lack of control over thread wastage makes such estimates extremely difficult.

# Thread properties and seam performance

Having analysed the general nature of sewing threads, it is appropriate at this stage to summarise their particular properties, most of which have already been introduced, and to consider how they relate to the more general requirements of seams. Although thread is by no means the only factor that determines the value of the properties of seam strength, elasticity, durability, security and comfort (identified at the beginning of this chapter as relevant to seam appearance and performance), or that helps to maintain the special properties of certain fabric types, it is one of the most important ones. The other factors are the type of stitch, seam, needle and feed mechanism, which have now been studied, and the nature of the material being sewn. Thus, in summarising sewing thread properties, it is appropriate to return to the subject of overall seam appearance and performance. The important but purely visual aspect of thread, namely its colour properties, will be discussed in Chapter 5.

## Seam strength

Because of the different natures of woven and knitted fabrics, it is necessary to discuss seam strength separately for each.

When two pieces of woven fabric are joined by a seam, and an increasing force is applied to the assembly at right angles to the seam line, rupture ultimately occurs at or near the seam line and at a load usually less than that required to break the unsewn fabric. Since every seam has two components, namely the fabric and the sewing thread, seam failure must result from the breakage of either the fabric or the thread or, in rare cases, both simultaneously.

In the case of a fabric break, two different mechanisms are possible. The fabric may actually break, perhaps as a result of being weakened by needle damage, and the seam will rupture, but a more common occurrence is the situation where the seam opens up due to the phenomenon known as seam slippage. This happens in fabrics woven from slippery yarns, especially if rather loosely woven, and it is the result of the yarns parallel to a seam, and within the seam allowance, sliding over those at right angles to the seam when the seam is stressed transversely. It shows on the outside of the garment, close to the stressed seam. For a distance of as much as 5 mm from the stitching, there are no yarns in the fabric parallel to the stitching, only the yarns at right angles to the stitching that have pulled out of the seam allowance. It gives an unacceptable appearance long before the seam actually breaks down, which happens when the yarns at right angles to the seam pull completely out and the yarns parallel to the seam in the seam allowance fall off on the inside.

Increasing the seam allowance and neatening the edges may help, especially if there is an additional problem of seam edges fraying, perhaps on the inside of a garment on a lining edge, and an increase in stitch density, up to a certain point, does have a useful effect. A change of seam type from a simple superimposed seam to one such as a lap felled seam can help considerably but only at the expense of a more bulky seam. In practice, many fabrics are unsuitable for making up into tight-fitting garment styles. Examples are fabrics for trousers in a closely fitting style or jackets that are a close fit across the back of the shoulders. Fabrics should be investigated at the garment design stage by means of the standard tests for seam slippage and by wearer trials. Fabrics have on occasions been rejected for garment use without having been worn after trial garments failed at the seams during wash testing for reasons of seam slippage. Garment failure due to fabric breakdown is more common than that due to thread breakdown and it is usually seam slippage that is the cause. In commercial terms, the seam has failed once it has visibly opened up although the seam may still be a long way from complete breakdown.

When woven fabrics are seamed, the absolute seam strength is not, in the majority of cases, of paramount importance, providing it is reasonably high. Knitted fabrics are normally more extensible than woven fabrics and, in some instances, much more extensible. Care is needed in the selection of stitch types so that when a seam in a knitted fabric is extended along its length, the extension limit of the sewing threads is not reached before that of the seam, with seam cracking possibly resulting. Thus, the behaviour of seams under longitudinal, rather than transverse stress is of much greater importance in knitted fabrics than in woven ones. This point will be discussed further.

Seam failure in a woven fabric that is due to thread breakage could be said to be less of a problem than that due to fabric failure because it can at least be repaired, despite causing much consumer dissatisfaction. Several thread properties are connected with seam failure due to thread breakage, most of which have already been introduced.

Tensile strength is the tension at which a thread breaks. It will vary slightly according to the conditions under which the thread is broken, i.e. humidity, temperature, rate of applying the load and the length of thread being tested, and for this reason any testing of it must be carried out in a laboratory in a temperature- and humidity-controlled environment. Tenacity is the relative strength of a fibre, yarn or thread and is obtained by dividing the tensile strength by the thickness. It is obvious that a thick thread will be stronger than a thin thread of the same type, but the usefulness of tenacity or relative strength is that it is independent of thread size and can therefore be used to compare the strengths of various fibres and thread constructions. The conventional measure of linear tensile stength is useful as a quality control check in thread production but bears little resemblance to the breaking point of a thread in a stitch.

The majority of thread-breaks in a seam occur at a looped part of a stitch, and the loop strength of a thread is related more closely to stitch strength than is linear tensile strength. Loop strength is the load required to break a length of thread that is looped through another thread of the same length; it is influenced by stiffness, fibre or filament type, ply and twist construction and the regularity of these factors. The measure of thread strength which most closely relates to stitch strength is minimum loop strength – the strength of the weakest loop in a series, tested in a continuous length of thread. A measurement of this nature is difficult and tedious to do in practice but it has been found that the strength of thread into which has been tied a simple overhand knot or a figure-of-eight knot is very close to the figure for loop strength. The explanation for this behaviour is that the thread is bent sharply round itself and the knot acts as a focus for stress concentration.

For minimum knot strength, a series of knots can be tied in one length of thread, which can then be tested. The work of Burtonwood and Chamberlain demonstrated that it is possible to calculate the strength of a seam under conditions of failure due to thread breakage simply from the stitch density and the minimum knot strength of a thread after sewing into and recovery from a seam. (Measurement of unsewn thread strength would not allow for the loss in strength which occurs inevitably when thread is sewn.) The calculation applies to lockstitch seams, but because chainstitch seams were found to be slightly stronger, the same calculation can be used and a safety margin gained. It applies specifically to simple superimposed seams but it was found that in seams with multiple rows of stitching, the strength increases proportionally to the number of rows of stitching.

Synthetic threads have higher loop strengths than cotton threads and technical developments have increased even these so that finer synthetic threads can now be used with the same strength as coarser threads of a few years ago. The stretch and regularity of the material being sewn influences seam strength, even when it is the stitches that break before the material. For this reason the mean loop strength is only a guide and sample seams should be compared in critical cases.

Other factors affecting seam strength must also be considered. Variations in stitch density affect seam strength, and if other factors remain unchanged, seam strength normally increases with stitch density up to a point where the concentration of needle holes starts to weaken the material. After this, a stronger thread should be used at a lower stitch density. This will require a larger needle size with all the attendant problems of possible needle damage, emphasising again the need to use the strongest possible type of thread so that the finest size of thread and consequently of needle can be used, consistent with other sewing properties. The effect of stitch type on seam strength relates to the greater loss in strength that affects needle threads, especially in lockstitch machines, during the sewing process, and to the stitch geometry that puts more strain on the needle thread in a lockstitch than in a chainstitch or overedge stitch. Thus chainstitch 401 and overedge 504 are slightly stronger than lockstitch 301, though 504 is limited in its uses because of its narrow bight. Variations in seam type can also affect seam strength with improved strength obtained in some of the lapped seams which have additional rows of stitching. For the full benefit to be achieved, care must be taken to set the thread tensions the same in each row.

### Seam elasticity

When knitted fabrics are being considered, the questions of seam strength and seam elasticity are difficult to separate because the majority of problems of seam breakdown arise from thread breakage when a seam is stressed longitudinally and stretches in excess of the amount that the stitch type and the stretch in the sewing thread can accommodate. With comfort stretch fabrics stretching up to 30 per cent and action stretch fabrics stretching 100 per cent or more, it is necessary to create seams that will stretch and recover in excess of this so that they do not restrict the flexibility of the garment or break at their limiting extension.

Choice of stitch and seam type is very important. Both lockstitch 301 and chainstitch 401, if adjusted carefully, will give adequate stretch for sewing comfort stretch fabrics when used with superimposed or lapped seams. In experimental conditions, figures as high as 80 per cent have been obtained for seam stretch. With lockstitch, there is a limit to the extent to which the stitch tensions can be loosened to increase stretch and still obtain a satisfactory stitch formation. With chainstitch 401 it is possible to set the stitch looser but only at the expense of an increase in seam 'grinning', a temporary appearance of the stitch opening up in the seam when stressed transversely. A small amount of grin is normally acceptable and 401 stitch can thus be used where a little more stretch is needed. This feature has given 401 the reputation of having higher stretch than 301 but it must be remembered that this is only in circumstances of increased grinning.

To achieve maximum stretch with this stitch, a ratio of needle thread to looper thread length in the seam should be of the order of 1:3. Seam grinning can itself cause problems since each time the seam gapes in wear, the sewing threads themselves are pulled through the fabric as it distorts in the neighbourhood of the stitch. They return again when the strain is removed but this sawing to and fro of the sewing threads must eventually tend to cut through the yarns in the fabric and lead to seam breakdown.

For action stretch fabrics and for cut-and-sew knitwear, it is not possible to achieve high enough stretch in a seam using stitch types 301 or 401. Fortunately in many garments a class 500 overedge stitch is acceptable, despite the bulky seam it inevitably produces. The 504 three thread overedge stitch provides the maximum attainable extensibility. The length of the looper threads in the class 500 stitches, together with the compressibility of the enclosed fabric edges, enables these seams to extend to over 100 per cent without cracking. In garments such as corsetry and swimwear, use is made of lockstitch zig-zag stitches to give high stretch as well as high seam security but, as was shown previously, limited seam constructions are then available. In appropriate fabrics, class 600 covering stitches can also be used to sew flat seams with high stretch and low bulk. Since the stitching shows on the surface of the garment, this is generally used on underwear garments or where the seam can be used as a decorative feature.

Increasing stitch density helps to increase seam stretch but only up to a certain point. In lockstitch seams, an increase in stitch density actually reduces the proportion of thread lying on the surface of the fabric and available for direct extension with the seam, unless thread tension is adjusted at the same time as the stitch is shortened. If the tension is adjusted so that the amount of grin with the higher stitch rate is the same as with the lower stitch rate, instead of being less, the expected increase in stretch with a higher stitch density will be achieved. It is these kinds of adjustment that are necessary in order to produce stretch figures in lockstitch seams of 70 to 80 per cent. Stitch densities of at least eight stitches per centimetre are needed. With overedge stitches, increasing stitch density will increase seam stretch but a limit is reached when the fabric becomes jammed between the crowded stitches. The seam extension is then limited and the fabric edge cannot relax completely after stretching. Too many stitches may also weaken the fabric and cause failure under transverse stresses.

Thread extensibility has a part to play in achieving seam extensibility but with conventional needle threads it is not the overriding factor. Cotton threads typically have extensions at break of 6–8 per cent; with many synthetics threads the equivalent figure is 15–20 per cent. This extra extensibility of synthetic threads will only increase seam stretch by ten per cent over what can be achieved with cotton threads. If a dramatic increase is required, use can be made of spun polyamide threads, which have extensions up to 30 per cent. However, because of their specially engineered high stretch properties, none of these can be sewn as efficiently as needle threads. When 401 chainstitch is stressed, it is the needle thread that breaks first because of the greater amount of looper thread present in the seam, but the use of a high stretch thread in the needle would just result in poor sewing perform-ance. When used in the loopers of chainstitch or overedge machines, with standard synthetic sewing thread in the needles, these more elastic threads stretch first, allowing the maximum extension to be obtained from the needle threads to suit the most demanding situa-tions. An improvement in the stretch performance of a lockstitch seam can also be achieved by a similar combination of threads provided the stitch is unbalanced. A balanced stitch is normally required to give maximum stretch, but with a highly extensible thread in the bobbin the sewing tension can be adjusted to hold the needle thread loop under the fabric as in a chainstitch. The bobbin thread should also be wound with the minimum tension so that it is relaxed as it comes off the bobbin. This helps to realise the full stretch potential of the seam and prevent creep-back and pucker.

### Seam durability

This is the third aspect of seam performance originally identified as necessary to satisfactory seaming. The length of life of a seam in a garment should be as long as that of the other materials and both should be appropriate to the required end use of the garment. The seam can be considered to have failed in durability terms if either the thread or the fabric in the seam fails at an early stage. (An immediate failure of the thread would be regarded as a failure of seam strength or extensibility.) Jeans and workwear garments, underwear, school-wear, etc. all suffer considerable abrasion in wear and seams must be designed to resist this abrasion as effectively as possible.

The first abrasive act to be overcome is that of the act of sewing itself and the problem of loss of strength in needle threads during sewing has already been discussed. The durability of a thread in a seam depends on a number of factors, including the stitch type, stitch balance, stitch tightness, seam type, thread type and the nature of the material being sewn. The critical factor is the extent to which the thread beds into the material. Investigations by thread manufacturers have shown that the exposed surface of a balanced lockstitch has much better abrasion resistance than the exposed underside of a chainstitch and seams sewn at high tensions are much less susceptible to damage than those which are sewn at low tensions. Also, the life of the looper threads in a chainstitch increases if the stitch balance is adjusted so that the needle thread to looper thread ratio is approximately 1 : 1. This is because the stitch loops are spaced out instead of being concentrated at each stitch hole. All these effects are concerned with the improved bedding in of the thread into the material, affording a degree of protection.

As would be expected, seams sewn in a densely woven or coated material cannot bed in and are therefore more quickly abraded than those sewn into softer materials. A typical area of a garment where abrasion may be experienced is on the inside leg seams of denim jeans. The traditional strong jeans seams consisting of a lap felled seam with two rows of 401 chainstitch does not always perform well in this position because the stitching suffers considerable abrasion, a heavily built wearer adding to the problem. Superimposed seams sewn with safety stitch are more commonly used, preferably sewn such that the needle side of the chainstitch row is worn against the skin with the chain underside protected by the seam allowance.

A different problem of seam durability and abrasion can arise with denim jeans when they are subjected to stonewashing. In this process they are severely abraded to produce a worn and faded look. Careful thread selection is required to prevent damage to seams requiring immediate repair, or damage which shows later and shortens the life of the garment. A satisfactory result can be obtained with polyester/cotton corespun thread and an even better result with the new type of locked filament polyester thread, although the latter has poorer initial sewability.

A stitched component of a garment that is both functional and decorative and is subject to much abrasion is the buttonhole, especially when the button is being undone. Synthetic threads give greatly superior performance to cotton threads and spun polyester and cotton- or polyester-covered corespun give both good durability and good appearance. Of relevance to the life of a buttonhole is the thread with which the button is sewn and this should also be a spun thread. The use of continuous filament button thread may significantly shorten the life of a spun fibre buttonhole thread by its abrasion.

### Seam security

This is another important seam performance factor but at this point it will become clear that these various factors are not independent. If seam security is regarded as including seams that do not break down as a result of thread or fabric breakdown or seam slippage, then all the factors discussed above are important in this context. Seam security has further implications, though, such as those of stitch security due to stitch type and due to stitching quality in an individual case. In earlier discussions on stitch types, three possible ways were given for threads to pass each other in a stitch, namely interlacing, interlooping and intralooping, and it was said that this has an effect on stitch security. Particular stitch types were also described as having various levels of security.

The securest of stitches, lockstitch, is formed, as its name implies, by the interlocking of the threads together. If a thread breaks in a lockstitch seam, the stitches may run back for a short distance, depending on the longitudinal and transverse stress applied to the seam, the stretch in the fabric and the surface nature of the thread used. There is, however, no tendency for the stitch to continue undoing along the seam, nor any loops of thread that can be snagged and pull the stitches undone further. Additionally, the stitches can be backtacked at the end of the seam, which makes the seam even more secure.

The least secure stitches are the single thread chainstitches in class 100. This is because they are formed by intralooping where each loop of the thread is secured by the succeeding loop of the same thread. Such a simple construction contains very little friction within it, especially in the blind felling 103 version which is often sewn with a fine multi-filament thread for minimum visibility. If the last stitch is not properly locked, if a thread is broken, or if a stitch slips because the machine is improperly adjusted or it sews over a thicker section of fabric, it will run undone very easily. In the case of slip-stitching, a loop of thread is left which is particularly likely to become pulled. Because much of the blind felling, buttonsewing, buttonholing and multi-needle stitching that is used on bulk production garments today makes use of this stitch, and because it is inherently insecure, there is much customer dissatisfaction with garments where the stitching fails to last the lifetime of the garment. However, the machines are fast and there are many of them in use. They could be replaced with other, more modern machines using different stitch types but only at considerable expense in capital investment and slower production. Other modern machinery goes part of the way to improving the situation by automatic condensation of stitches at the ends of seams on stitches which cannot be backtacked. Careful thread selection can also increase friction within each stitch and reduce the tendency to run back. As consumers generally become more quality- and performance-conscious, they are likely to become more aware of the problem of seam insecurity. They may be willing to pay more for more secure stitching but unfortunately this willingness is not normally transmitted to those who purchase machinery.

Intermediate in security are the chainstitches in classes 400, 500 and 600. Here the threads are interlooped – i.e. needle threads are looped through one or more loops of one or more other threads. Although run-back is still possible, the greatly increased friction within each stitch, subject as always to smoothness of thread surface, ensures that in many cases tangling of the thread in the stitch occurs before it has run very far. The most likely to run is the simplest, 401, and as with 101 just described, it can run from the end, from a break in the thread, or because there is a slip-stitch at some point along the stitching. The latter leaves a loop of thread which is easily caught and pulled.

In dealing with insecure ends of stitching, careful thought must be given to the overall method of construction of a garment and particularly to the sequence of the various stages, to ensure that weak ends of seams are not left and those where sewing across is necessary do actually receive it. In many cases, there is no alternative but to bar-tack the chain end of thread back into the seam.

Where seams become insecure because of thread breaks, the problems are usually those of seam strength and stretch described earlier. Thus the stitch type used influences the initial likelihood of a thread breaking in a seam and also the extent to which the stitching will further unravel. The type of seam break familiar to many consumers is the hem that comes undone as a result of catching in it the heel of a shoe or the zip tag of a knee-high boot. Most of these problems can be avoided by care on the part of the wearer but, nevertheless, the garment tends to be given the blame.

Slip-stitching arises as a result of a failure of the bobbin hook or the looper to pick up the loop in the needle thread. Thread elongation and recovery properties are very important in determining the thread loopforming properties. Threads that form large, consistent loops are much more safely picked up by the looper, even if the timing is imperfect or the needle is badly deflected in passing through heavy material. Other causes of slip-stitching are bent needles, incorrect needle size or type for the thread size or type, incorrect thread tensions or poor material control arising from a large throat plate hole or poor presser foot control. If presser foot and needle hole clearances are too great the fabric may move up and down with the needle. This keeps the sewing thread taut in the needle instead of it being held by the fabric as the needle rises, thus allowing the loop to form. A typical needle deflection problem can arise on a jeans waistband, commonly attached with 401 chainstitch, where there are belt loops and zip tapes to be sewn across in addition to the thickness of the body of the garment and its waistband.

*Comfort*

This is the last of the five seam performance factors previously introduced. Comfort is rarely a conscious sensation but discomfort certainly is. Seams may be locally tight against the body, they may present a ridge or roughness to the skin because of an unsuitable choice of stitch, seam or thread, or there may be local discomfort because of things such as thread ends or label corners. All may be aggravated by poor garment fit.

If a seam is tight against the body, it suggests that the extension in the fabric is greater than that in the seam which in turn suggests that seam cracking is a strong possibility. An alternative stitch type may be more suitable. If a seam forms an uncomfortable ridge it is likely to be because it is a closed overedged or safety stitched seam which is more bulky than an open seam would be. Unfortunately the alternative open seam is considerably more expensive to make and the stitch types that can be used on it may have insufficient stretch. Any seam that is likely to be rough against the skin can be softened by the use of a crimp textured thread in the loopers of the overedging or cover stitching that is used to neaten the raw edges. Particular problems of discomfort are associated with the use of monofilament polyamide threads. If used in places such as hems, the long ends that must be left to prevent unravelling, along with the cut or melted end of a rather substantial filament, can cause considerable discomfort.

Investigations into comfort sensations of garments in general have recently shown that there is a high level of complaint as a result of the types of labels used in many garments and the methods of attaching them. Many of the less expensive labels are printed on fabric made from thermoplastic fibre and cut and sealed to narrow widths. They may then be cut and sealed again to the short length that is needed to insert into the garment. For economy, many labels are simply folded and inserted into a row of overedging or even just lockstitched close to the sealed edge. Sharp corners abound and while a lockstitch-attached label might be easily removed (though possibly with the loss of any care instructions), labels inserted under overedging or cover stitching must be regarded as permanent. This might not appear to be a problem of seam performance but it is certainly a common cause of dissatisfaction with garments. Greater care in choosing label positions, in deciding how to sew the seam which attaches them, and in covering over the cut edges with a textured thread, will produce more satisfactory garments.

The other seam properties mentioned earlier relate to the maintenance of specialised properties of a fabric. Those that can be spoiled by incorrect choice of seaming are the properties of waterproofing and water resistance and of flame retardance. These have been discussed when considering sewing thread finishes.

## Sewing problems

These are addressed in Chapter 10.

## Classification of sewing machines

The sewing machines used in clothing manufacture can be classified into the following levels, with the quantity of machines in commercial use decreasing rapidly from the first level to the last.

### Basic sewing machines

These are of the types already studied under the subject of stitch formation. They consist of several elements: a stand, table, electric motor, a head normally offering one stitch type, a bed of various shapes and the means for the operator to control the speed of sewing and stitch density, and presser foot position. A large number of additions are available for these machines, such as work aids to relieve the operator of some of the handling associated with sewing operations. Microprocessor systems are increasingly being applied to these machines to enable such things as presser foot lift, backtack, thread trim, fullness and numbers of stitches to be pre-set and controlled automatically.

### Simple automatics

Here the machine is usually cam-controlled, producing only one configuration of sewing. Examples are buttonholers, buttonsewers, bar tack machines, and label sewers. The shape of the sewing line is determined by the machine, hence achieving consistency, but the operator must still carry out all the handling both before and after sewing.

Automated workstations

These carry out many complex functions in addition to sewing. They make use of electric, electronic and pneumatic control, and incorporate sophisticated conveyor and clamp technology. Examples are patch pocket setting on jeans and shirts, run stitching collars or flaps, long seam joining, making jetted pockets, serging trousers and sequential buttonholing. The operator still loads the machine and may remove the garment part after sewing, but the machine controls the rest of the handling and all of the sewing. The operator is able to undertake various handling activities, depending on the type of machine, during the sewing cycle. Thus handling time is incorporated into sewing time and the machine utilisation can rise from the 20 per cent that is typical of a basic sewing machine to as much as 80 per cent. Each machine carries out one basic conformation of sewing, but size or shape of, for example, collar or patch pocket, can be altered for different sizes and styles.

Reprogrammable automated systems

Here garment parts are loaded and a series of machines carries out a series of operations to a section of a garment. For example, one system utilises robotic handling to assemble a three-part jeans pocket. This level of automation, apart from sophisticated handling devices, requires extreme consistency of material characteristics and shape, and extreme reliability of operation by the machines in the line. Reprogrammable automated systems have been the subject of extensive research, but are not yet in commercial use for clothing operations.

Each succeeding level in the classification means a large increase in capital cost, hence a large increase in the output necessary to sustain it. It also means a corresponding decrease in flexibility, because the machines produce one basic form of stitching with few variations. The more variations, the higher the cost.

Basic sewing machines and associated work aids

The sewing mechanism of the lockstitch machine has already been discussed, along with the actual stitch formation of lockstitch and single- and two-thread chainstitch in their simplest forms. The extent to which the operator is responsible for everything the machine does and the quality of the work it produces has also been stated, along with the unacceptably low figure of 20 per cent as the average time one of these machines is actually sewing during a working day. The main purpose of this section is to study the variations that exist in the machines and the types of additions that can be made to them in order to speed up production and control quality standards.

## Sewing machine shapes

In fashion manufacture the machines are still predominantly used in their basic forms, but for more specialised garments and those made in higher volume, variations in machine shape are available that enable easier movement of the materials around the machine. These variations primarily affect the shape of the bed of the machine, i.e. the part on which the materials rest. The best known version is the flat bed; the main alternatives are cylinder bed, post bed and feed-off-the-arm. The blind felling machine sewing stitch type 103 is also a special shape, as are the overedge machines which have no fabric space to the right of the needle. These are illustrated in Fig. 4.1: shapes (i), (ii) and (iii) occur in lockstitch and chainstitch machines, while (iv) normally occurs only in chainstitch.

The flat bed is used in the majority of sewing where a large and open garment part can be handled easily past the needle. It provides a suitable surface for much flat sewing and also facilitates the use of markers to control the position of garment parts, for example a patch pocket on a shirt front. Cylinder and post bed are used where the parts to be sewn are small, curved or otherwise awkward in shape, a particularly common situation in sewing footwear. The feed-off-the-arm machine is used where a lapped seam has to be closed in such a way that the garment part becomes a tube. They are common in jeans production where the outside leg seam is normally the type known as lap-felled and it is joined after the inside leg seam in the sequence of construction. The operator wraps the part to be sewn around the machine bed and it is fed away from the operator, off the end of the bed, as he or she sews.

## Requirements for work aids

The additions that can be made to basic sewing machines are many and they come under the general term *work aids*. The typical sewing operation has been analysed into the stages of separate and pick up, orientate, mate, control through sewing and dispose. The term 'handling' is normally used to describe those elements that are not sewing and it is this handling, along with that of dealing with garment bundles where they exist, plus various aspects of machine attention and personal needs, that make up 80 per cent of the time spent working by most sewing machinists. In the search for improvements in the ratio

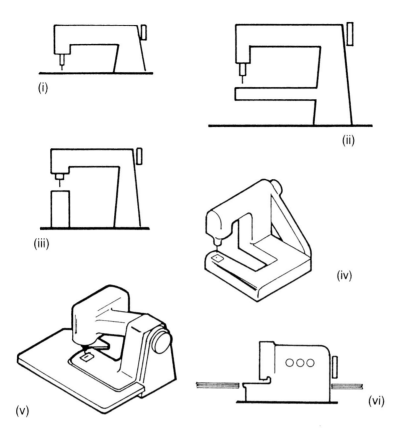

**Figure 4.1** Machine bed types. (i) Flat bed. (ii) Cylinder bed. (iii) Post bed. (iv) Feed-off-the-arm. (v) Blind stitch. (vi) Overedge.

of time spent sewing to time spent handling, some elements of the sewing operation offer more scope than others. Thus the nature of clothing materials makes the stage of separate and pick up difficult because the materials are limp and they slip or cling. In this case, what is difficult for a machinist is also difficult to mechanise. Orientate, mate and control through sewing are slowed greatly in some operations because of the need to pause repeatedly to realign the parts or to fold them into position. Disposal may include severing the sewing thread as well as stacking the garment part. Sometimes threads must be cut close for neatness while on other occasions a stitch type requires an end to be left. The stacking of completed parts by one operator not only takes time but may affect the next operator as well.

Slowness, however, is not the only problem. While machinists are matching up fabric edges in order to sew them together to the correct width or turning up double rolled hems, not only are they working slowly but they are also trying to achieve the required quality standard in their work. Depending on the standards required in relation to the operators' skill levels and the nature of the fabric and the sewing operation, this will in some cases be very difficult. Achieving accurately controlled stitching at speed with operators without a high level of skill is greatly desired. A further drive for economy arises from the fact that there are some seam constructions where the final effect can be achieved in more than one way, typically in several stages of sewing with perhaps some pressing in between, or in just one stage by using a device that folds the fabric, along with a multi-needle machine. Finally, in this justification of machinery development, machinists are required to change the operation that they do from time to time, and it is in the interests of efficient production that they are quickly able to gain proficiency in the new operation. Thus machinery is needed which will minimise the training time required on a new operation but without that machinery being too restricted in its flexibility.

All these factors point to the need for work aids in as many applications as possible in relation to the use of conventional sewing machines. Work aids are devices built into machines, added to them afterwards, attached alongside or made use of in whatever ways a resourceful engineer can devise to improve productivity, improve or maintain quality standards, reduce training time and minimise fatigue for the operator. In some cases it is difficult to distinguish a work aid defined in this way from aspects of machinery that are an accepted part of modern development such as microprocessor control. It is not proposed to be too pedantic in this matter, simply to indicate the opportunities that are available for the application of technology. If a broad enough definition of work aid is used, it will be seen later that certain types of interlinings can even be included, rather than it being a name reserved solely for machinery. It will probably long remain the case that garments made for the fashion market will be made with the minimum of additions to the basic sewing machine so as to maintain maximum flexibility of style, while those made in high volume in limited styles will make use of every device available.

## Types of work aids

The work aids that are used during sewing operations can be categorised in a number of different ways and they vary in the aspects of their overall purpose that they emphasise. Some offer greatly increased speed of working in a situation where quality is already satisfactory. Others give very little improvement in productivity but great accuracy of sewing. In terms of their function the commonest ones are used for guiding or folding materials, for trimming threads and other components from garments, and for stacking the work after sewing. Least common are those that assist the initial picking up of the parts to be sewn. In terms of their method of working, some are purely mechanical, some operate pneumatically, some are photo-electric and some are electronic. Some are built into the machine such as a special motor, some are a variation of a normal machine part such as a special presser foot, and some are a completely separate added part.

*Guides* are used where sewing must take place in a certain position on a garment, usually a certain distance from a raw edge as in a conventional superimposed seam, where a narrow item such as a lace or braid must be correctly positioned on a garment and where one garment part must be correctly placed on another such as a patch pocket on a shirt, skirt or pair of trousers.

In their simplest form they are *edge guides*, forming some kind of physical barrier to the edges of the fabric being joined together. Instead of the operator having to match two fabric edges together and sew the correct distance from that edge by eye, an upright section of metal is screwed to the machine bed and each of the fabric edges is butted up to it. For accuracy on a sharply curved seam the edge guide can also be curved. Examples are shown in Fig. 4.2.

Edge guides enable seams of accurate width to be sewn, giving more accurate garment sizing and allowing the operator to work faster. On an overedge machine an edge guide can be set so that the amount trimmed off by the trimming knife is that intended by the pattern cutter rather than an amount that will cause the garment to be too large or too small. In some sewing situations it is important for the neatness of the finished garment that the seam turnings contained within it are uniform in width and without frayed edges. An example would be the outer edge of a tailored jacket, where the facing is

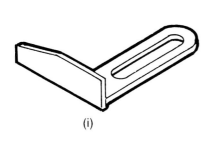
(i)

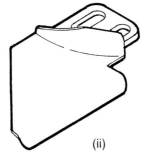
(ii)

**Figure 4.2** Edge guides. (i) Straight. (ii) Curved.

joined to the main garment. Such neatness may not be achievable by an edge guide alone if the edges have frayed during handling of the garment parts. Lockstitch machines are available with a trimming knife attached which trims the seam turning during sewing to an even width which is narrower than could be sewn but which will give the correct amount of bulk in the finished garment.

The function of edge guiding can be performed in some circumstances by a special presser foot called a *compensating foot*. In general, presser feet can be used as specialised work aids, in addition to their normal function of holding the materials against the feed dog, when the scale of the situation is within the small size of the foot. Thus an edge guide to give a line of stitches 2 cm from a fabric edge can only be a separate guide attached to the machine bed. Where the requirement is to sew at 1 or 2 or 5 mm from an edge, such as when topstitching a shirt collar, the guide can be contained within the presser foot which is able to carry out its normal function as well. The compensating foot comes in a variety of forms according to the configuration being sewn and the width of stitching needed but the basic principle is of one or more fixed toes and one or more which can move up and down vertically on a spring. Two types are illustrated in Fig. 4.3: (i) could be used for topstitching a shirt collar 5 mm from the edge, and (ii) for stitching 1 mm from the edge.

A compensating foot can be used in any situation where there is a difference in height to the left and right of an edge and stitching is required a specific distance from that edge. Thus they are not only used for topstitching around garment edges, where there is fabric to one side only of the edge, but they are also used for attaching and for topstitching patch pockets and topstitching raised seams that have been created by turning the seam allowance to one side. These could be things such as topstitching a lengthwise seam on a skirt or pair of

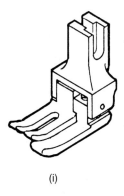
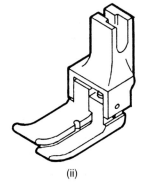

(i)                                                    (ii)

**Figure 4.3** Compensating feet.

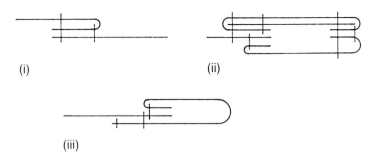

(i)

(ii)

(iii)

**Figure 4.4** Applications of compensating feet. (i) Topstitching a seam. (ii) Closing down a shirt collar. (iii) Sink stitching to close a waistband.

trousers or the lower edge of a waistband. A conventional edge guide cannot be used in these circumstances as there is no exposed edge of garment for it to run up against. In addition they are used for closing seams such as the inside of a shirt collar or the lower edge of a waistband where sink stitching is required. Diagrams of these seams are shown in Fig. 4.4.

The stitching known as sink stitching is shown in Fig. 4.4(iii). As its name implies, it is stitching that sinks in under a turned edge of fabric. It is also referred to as stitching in the seam shadow. Accurately sewn, sink stitching is almost invisible.

In some circumstances an operator can make use of a combination of a compensating foot and an edge guide. When a garment style requires two rows of topstitching round the edges, such as on a raincoat sewn at 1mm and 6mm from the edge, this could be done on a twin-needle machine. However, if there are any corners to be turned the machine must be equipped with a split needle bar whereby, at the touch of a lever, the two needles are separated and the outside one sews round the corner while the inside one remains stationary until they are level again. This machine would use a compensating foot on its own but if a twin-needle machine in the split needle bar version is not available, the sewing would have to be done in two stages, using a compensating foot for the outside row and an ordinary edge guide for the row further from the edge.

In all these instances, the operator is able to work quickly and accurately as far as the actual sewing is concerned and skill can be concentrated on aspects of the job that are less easy to mechanise. If a particular sewing operation includes some stitching where there is not any difference in height to the right and left of an edge, the presence of the compensating foot does not present any problems since the spring on the lower toe enables it to be used equally well with all the toes on the same level.

Other types of *specialised presser feet* can also be used in guiding situations. If a piping has to be attached to a garment in the manner shown in Fig. 3.6, a specially shaped foot will control the position of the piping in relation to the needle so that the stitching is always close to the piping. When sewing zips into garments, the stitching must often be closer to the teeth of the zip than a standard presser foot would allow. A half foot enables this to happen, or alternatively two very narrow toes give the same result but with improved fabric control. These feet are illustrated in Fig. 4.5.

In the special case of setting an invisible zip used frequently in ladies' wear to give a neat and unobtrusive fastening, a specially shaped presser foot is essential. On these zips the teeth are turned inwards and join together on the inside of the garment. If the seam is not to gape on the outside the fabric must be sewn very close to these teeth. The zip is attached unfastened from the inside and the special foot rolls the teeth upright as shown in Fig. 4.6, giving the seam type indicated. The stitching can only go as far as the opened slider at the bottom of the zip and the zip is sewn in before the seam

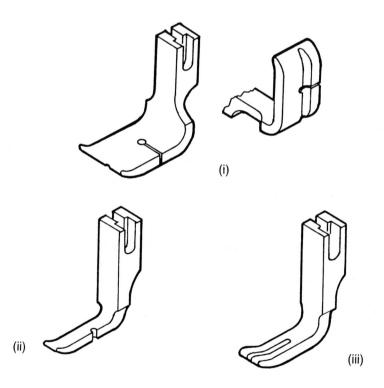

**Figure 4.5** Special presser feet. (i) Piping foot. (ii) Half zip foot. (iii) Narrow toed zip foot.

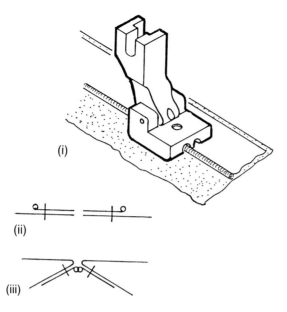

**Figure 4.6** Invisible zips. (i) Presser foot for invisible zips. (ii) Seam diagram as sewn. (iii) Seam diagram as worn.

is joined. When the seam is joined at a later stage, the stitching overlaps the zip stitching by about 1cm and a half foot is used so that the stitching can be as close in as possible. Since the zip cannot be sewn in right to the bottom, and the stitching of the seam then overlaps this stitching, there is a loss in operating length of these zips and they must be at least 2cm longer than conventional zips. The spare length of zip at the lower end is secured by sewing the zip tape to the seam turning on each side. The advantage of invisible zips lies not just in their appearance but in the simpler handling and hence lower level of skill required to attach them compared with a conventional zip.

Yet another type of edge guide can be used to ensure an accurate stitch line in relation to an edge of fused interlining in a garment part. In the sewing of shirt collars, an accurate collar shape is required and the best appearance is obtained if the stitch line is uniformly close to the edge of the interlining without actually sewing through it. Interlinings can be cut very accurately using dies and the use of the outer edge of the interlining as a stitching guide gives the correct sewing line. The device that enables this to be done is a small toothed wheel alongside the presser foot with which the operator follows the edge of the interlining.

Another type of work aid in wide use where accurate stitching lines are required is the *stitching jig*. Using an edge guide to achieve accurate sewing assumes accurate cutting and for many garment parts this cannot be adequately achieved. Collars must have two identical points; patch pockets, cuffs and other small items such as epaulettes and tabs must be perfect pairs; and reverse and front edges of formal jackets and raincoats must match. The only way to ensure this where die cutting is not possible is to control the sewing line in relation to the pattern shape of the garment rather than the edge of the cut material and this is what stitching jigs achieve. The simplest type is illustrated in Fig. 4.7. It shows a jig for sewing a pair of pocket flaps.

The jig consists of two layers of a rigid material such as aluminium or plastic which are joined together by a hinge. A slot is cut out of both layers of material which conforms to the exact sewing line of the garment part and the bottom layer carries a shaped guide close to the hinge to which the edges of the garment parts are aligned. This would be the neck edge in the case of a collar. The lower section is normally also covered with a non-slip material so that the fabric plies are firmly held. The two pieces of the garment part are laid into the jig, along with the interlining if a sew-in interlining is being used, and the jig is closed to hold them firmly. If fullness is needed on the top ply to give a piped effect on a part such as a pocket flap, a fulling bar would be included in the jig between the two plies. This ensures the inclusion of extra length in the top ply so that the lining cannot show on the right side of the finished part. The operator then sews round the slot on a machine with a specially adapted presser foot and feed dog. There is no conventional feeding system as the operator needs to move the jig in every direction while sewing. The lack of a feeding

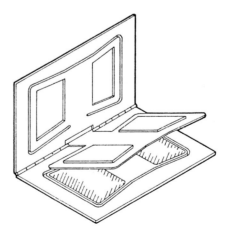

**Figure 4.7** Stitching jig for sewing a pair of pocket flaps.

system also means that there is no control over stitch size other than the rate at which the operator handles the jig past the needle.

Careful training and control are required if stitches on the longer edges of a garment part must be no longer than 5 mm. Another disadvantage of the jig as a work aid is that a larger seam allowance around the outside of the garment part is needed so that the fabric edge does not become pushed down into the stitching slot but remains firmly held during sewing. This extra fabric is costly and it must be trimmed off, often by hand, afterwards. An advantage may be that the outer edge of the collar need not be accurately cut. The use of hand-controlled stitching jigs such as those described here achieves quality rather than productivity. Separate jigs are needed for every style and size and consequently they are only used for long production runs. A minor change of pattern shape can require a costly new set of jigs. As will be seen later, the process can be automated fully to give greater improvements in productivity as well as quality.

Another situation where a guide is needed is when a lace or braid or binding is attached to a garment part. It is not usually satisfactory for the operator to unroll the reel on which the material is wound and then lay the material freehand on to the garment as it would be impossible to position it accurately. In this instance a guiding system known as a *rack guide* is needed in addition to the edge guide which will still be needed to obtain the correct position for the fabric. The rack guide ensures that a material of narrow width is presented flat to the needle and in a position such that the stitching will be in the correct place on it. It usually consists of a series of linked bars the width of the trim to be attached and, if the trim is being attached on top of the garment fabric, it is mounted above the presser foot and carries the trim downwards from a reel mounted above the machine. If the trim is being attached below the garment fabric, the reel would be mounted below the machine table and then carried up on to the machine table and through a series of bars to the presser foot. Where bias trim in the form of a binding is attached to a garment, it is normally fed in at right angles in the manner shown in Fig. 3.43. If a ribbon is being attached to a garment it is likely that a twin-needle machine, either lockstitch or chainstitch, would be used and the guide would ensure that the ribbon was presented centrally between the needles. If a lace is being attached by means of a 406 bottom cover stitch, the lace would be guided such that the edge of it projected just above the left-hand needle and the use of an edge guide as well for the cut edge of the garment part would ensure that the raw edge was maintained between the two needles of the stitch.

The third situation described above where a guide is needed is when one garment part is positioned on to another. When a patch pocket is added to a shirt front there are several ways of ensuring that it is in the correct position but some of them are slow or inaccurate. One method is to drill holes for the pocket corner positions when the material is cut, but drill holes frequently occur out of position. Even if they are in the correct position there may be problems in covering them with the pocket corner and its stitching. Another method of positioning pockets is to lay a pattern-shaped template over the garment part and mark the required position with tailor's chalk, which melts when pressed, or with special ink that shows up under an ultra-violet light placed over the machinist's work area. This kind of marking is extremely time-consuming but virtually unavoidable in circumstances, such as the positioning of buttons and buttonholes on double-breasted garments.

For a shirt front, a skirt panel or a trouser back where the pocket is normally attached to the flat garment part, guides can be set up on the machine bed for the position of the part to which the pocket is being attached. These are really edge guides, though often far removed from the needle, and at least two would be needed so that the part is correctly positioned in two dimensions. The guides are made of a material such as Perspex and are a few millimetres thick, enough to form a barrier edge to the fabric but not so high as to be in the way of the rest of the sewing. Once the garment panel has been positioned, the pocket is placed correctly by putting the top right-hand corner under the point of the needle.

If the pocket is being sewn parallel to a garment edge, as it would be on a shirt, it is usually possible for the operator to set the pocket straight by eye. If there is no such reference, as there would not be on the back of a pair of jeans, there can be a further guide on the bed of the machine which the operator can feel through the thickness of the fabric and match up with the centre back seam. The machine would be fitted with a compensating foot to determine the stitching width on the pocket itself. A guide system for a shirt pocket is shown in Fig. 4.8.

Once a flexible attitude is developed towards the use of guides, a great variety of possibilities can be seen in a variety of sewing situations, especially where positioning is needed well away from the garment edge. To give just one more example, if a seam is being joined in which an opening of the correct length must be left for the insertion of a zip, a guide placed the correct distance behind the needle, to which the edges of the garment part are put, will ensure that sewing commences the necessary distance down the garment. A second edge guide will, of course, also be needed to ensure correct seam width.

Where garment parts must be positioned without reference to outside edges, increasing use is being made of *lights as guiding*

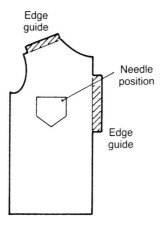

**Figure 4.8** Guides for positioning a shirt pocket.

*systems.* On both sewing and pressing equipment, narrow-beam light sources can be set up so that the garment part is positioned with a seam or a dart aligned with the light markings. For very accurate location, fibre optics can give very fine points of light. In some cases where the marking of garments using a template is unavoidable to ensure correct positioning of such things as double-breasted fastenings, if pencil or other visible marks are used they often remain visible on the finished garment. Markers are available which are invisible in ordinary light but which show up under ultraviolet light and such a light over the needle enables the operator to see the position needed.

*Folders* are used, as their name implies, in situations where fabric must be folded before sewing. They vary from the simple fold that can be achieved by an operator alone, though only slowly and perhaps untidily, through to extremely complex combinations of folds that enable constructions to be achieved in a fraction of the number of stages that it would take without the folders, and indeed enable some to be achieved that would not otherwise be possible at all. In most cases they are separate devices attached to the machine; where the scale of the folding job is very small, the folder can be contained within the presser foot. Folders are frequently used on machines with more than one needle.

Folders enable great increases in productivity to be achieved along with a high standard of control over the quality of the finish obtained. They are made from highly polished metal over which the material will pass smoothly and they can either be purchased from specialist suppliers or made by skilled factory engineers. They must be made to take particular materials so that they are held firmly enough to remain under control but not so firmly that there is a risk of them jamming. The demand for folders in a company will depend to a large extent on the type of garment they make: lingerie, corsetry and children's dresses offer particular scope for combining economy with decorative effects by their use. Their use is justified only in moderate- and high-volume production, and they bring their own limitations. Although some folders are easily loaded with fabric and must be loaded afresh with each garment, many add another section of material or trim to the garment and are much more quickly used if that section is in continuous form rather than short lengths. Where self-fabric is involved, this means that enough garments must be made to make it worth cutting fabric into straight or bias-cut strip on a long roll. It also means that control of colour must be good enough between pieces of cloth that the use of such strip will not introduce shading into garments. The sequence of construction of the garment may also have to be altered since a section of a continuous strip can only be applied from an edge to an edge and not in a circle.

Folders are of many types but can be divided roughly into those which *fold a part of a garment piece*, commonly an edge in a seam of class 6 but not always so, those which *join garment sections together*, and those which *add a section of self-fabric or other material to a garment*. The latter type usually create bound seams of class 3 or seams of class 7. In addition many class 8 seams require folders.

Examples of folders that operate on a garment part without any additional materials are shown in Fig. 4.9. The *narrow hem folder* makes a double rolled hem of the type used on scarves and handkerchiefs; a folder to make a hem as narrow as this is contained easily within the space of a presser foot. Indeed, since it is a requirement of folders that they keep the materials being sewn under control right up to the needle point, it would be difficult to site a separate folder close enough that such a small hem did not become unrolled before it was sewn. Once a hem as wide as 5 mm is required, a *separate folder* would be needed and this could look like that shown in Fig. 4.9(ii). Many widths of hem can be sewn, up to at least 40 mm but a different folder is needed for each. They can be used on items such as dresses, shirts, skirts and linings; the stitch used is usually either 301 lockstitch or 103 chainstitch. The use of 401 chainstitch requires that the hem be folded down rather than up which, though possible, is less easy to handle. The nature of the hem may also require backtacking. On more expensive garments the bulk of a double rolled hem may be unacceptable; in this case the edge is neatened with overedging, and the hem folded up only once. A folder would probably still be used in this situation although with some materials the operator might handle the garment sufficiently quickly and accurately freehand.

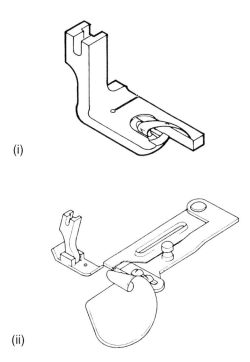

(i)

(ii)

**Figure 4.9** Hem folders. (i) Narrow hem folder. (ii) Wider hem folder. (Not to the same scale.)

The main concern is that hems often develop a roping or ringing appearance as the fabric twists on being sewn down. This tends to be worse if the hem is wide and particularly if the garment is very flared as there is then more hem edge than the length of garment it is being sewn to and the grain direction changes as the operator sews around the hem. Folders are a great help in achieving good quality hems, especially when used in conjunction with specialised machine feed systems, but in a double rolled hem it may only be possible to obtain a high enough standard if the hem is very narrow. Where a single turned hem such as on a dress is used it may be helpful to ease the fabric slightly on to the overedging by means of a suitable feeding system before blind felling, so that there is no extra length of fabric in the edge of the hem compared to the part of the garment to which it is being sewn.

Where the garment is open at each end of the hem, a fixed folder can be used and the fabric can be introduced to the folder at the beginning and run right through to the end. On many garments, such as shirts and dresses, the beginning and end of the hem is bulky because of the presence of a placket front of some kind. In this case the start of the hem might need to be turned up freehand and a swing out folder of the type shown in Fig. 4.9(ii) swung into place after that section had been stitched. This type of folder would also be used where an item such as a lining hem had already been joined into a complete circle by the time the hem was sewn, the starting and finishing points of the hem again being made freehand.

Other hem-type effects that require folders are shown in Fig. 3.15(iii) and (iv). The first one requires a second row of stitches after being sewn with the folder; the second one is done in one step with a folder and a twin-needle machine. It is common on the buttonhole side of men's shirt fronts but would not be suitable for garments in more bulky materials because of the difference in thickness between the two sides of the placket effect.

Another situation where folders are increasingly being used is in the production of shirt collars that give an appearance of being a two-piece collar when they are actually only one-piece. Shirt collars were traditionally constructed from a separate neck band and collar and the additional curvature that could be put into the collar compared with the neck band allowed an extra good fit to be achieved. Such collars are more expensive to construct and are rarely seen nowadays. The joining of the curved shapes is difficult to automate but equipment does exist to join a collar and separate neck band without additional shape along the seam and this is in common use in the production of men's shirts because it still gives a higher quality appearance than a one-piece collar. Women's shirts rarely have a genuine two-piece collar and it is here that the mock two-piece is often seen. The use of special fusible interlinings enables a sewn down pleat, giving the appearance of a seam, to be incorporated into the top collar only. Two types of fusible can be used. One has lines of adhesive resin along the fold lines, the other has slots cut out. Either reduces bulk and enables the collar to be folded easily by the operator where required, to create the pleat. The collar does not, of course, have the shape advantage of a genuine two-piece collar but a good break-line is achieved at moderate cost. The construction is shown in Fig. 4.10.

Of the folders that join major garment parts together, the commonest one is that already mentioned for jeans construction, the *lap fell folder* shown in Fig. 4.11. As stated previously, twin-needle 401 machines are used for this seam to avoid problems of bobbin run out. The folder is used on a flat bed machine or a feed-off-the-arm machine, depending on the configuration of the part of the garment being sewn.

Many folders are available which add further items of self-fabric or other material to a garment; many of these come into the category known as *binders*. Fabric edges are frequently bound, either as a means of edge neatening or to create a decorative effect, or both.

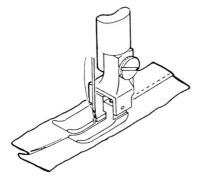

**Figure 4.10** Construction of mock two-piece shirt collar.

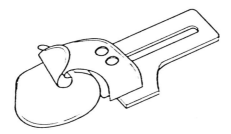

**Figure 4.11** Lap fell seam folder.

Indeed, one of the great advantages of the use of this type of work aid is the scope that is offered for modifying the methods of garment construction so that stitching, which is a necessary part of the garment, also provides the decorative effects.

The simplest bound seams can be constructed only with a material such as a braid which does not have raw edges; a double fold is necessary where self-fabric is used. A folder of this type is shown in Fig. 3.43, along with its associated rack guide. Most situations require the binding to lie smoothly round a curved fabric edge and for this reason bias cut binding is used most often. While straight cut binding is easy to make, requiring only that a roll of cloth is sectioned off to the required width with a power saw, bias cut strip is initially made by unrolling the cloth, folding it in half and seaming it into a tube. The open end of the tube is then rotated past a knife blade which cuts through one ply at 45 degrees to the grain direction, the bias fabric thus created emerging from the machine at 45 degrees to the original fabric direction to be re-rolled. The re-rolled cloth can then be sliced through to the required width. A result of this procedure is that bias stripping always has joins in it at intervals and there may be problems over the acceptability of these joins, depending upon where they appear on the garment and the requirements of the market for which the garment is being made.

As always, it is necessary that the folder maintains total control of the fabric right up to the point of sewing and with many folders a conventional presser foot would not allow for this. Accordingly, the presser foot and also the feed dog can be cut away to enable better positioning of the folder; these three items together make a package which is needed to sew that particular bound seam. On concave curves the binding is stretched slightly as it is sewn on; on convex curves it is fulled or eased. In all cases the garment part must be fed fully into the folder or the binding may slip off it.

A wider, straight grain version of the type of binding shown in Fig. 3.43 is used for waistbands on jeans and on some trousers and skirts. A twin-needle machine is used and the seam type achieved is that shown in Fig. 3.11(iv). The fabric for the waistband normally has an interlining fused to it; it is cut longer than required and a number are joined in a long length, often by fusing them to a continuous strip of interlining, to avoid repeatedly loading the folder. Twin-needle 401 chainstitching attaches and topstitches the waistband, but the speed and quality advantages of this method of construction are offset to some extent by the fact that the ends must be turned in and sewn down separately. This separate operation can be facilitated by a compressed air jet which can be activated during the binding operation to blow the needle thread away from the looper so that there is a short gap in the stitching at each end of the waistband. Without this extra work aid, the stitching must be unpicked sufficiently to allow the ends to be tucked in. Apart from the time this would take, it could lead to insecure stitching at the finishing end.

Other common types of bound seam are those shown in Figs 3.11(i), (ii) and (iii) when discussing seam constructions. These also require fabric to be cut into long strips but as they are always constructed in knitted fabrics for underwear type garments, the fabric has adequate stretch when cut straight across in the course direction. More than one folder may have to be put together to achieve these seams.

The type of fabric folding that the bias binder achieves is similar to that used on single sections of fabric to make items such as belts. Two possibilities for belts were shown in Figs 3.18(ii) and (iii). In (ii), the belt must be seamed inside out with a space left in the stitching for it to be turned through to the right side. Pressing it is then slow and difficult and following that it must be topstitched. If the seam is offset slightly as in (iii), the main part of the belt can be run through a folder after the ends have been bagged out. A swing out folder would be needed. Not only is this quicker to sew but the pressing of the finished and topstitched belt is quick and easy compared with one that has been totally bagged out. If the topstitching is not to be on the edge of the belt, the seam must be offset. If there are to be four rows of stitching on the belt the seam could remain on the edge. With lower-priced garments, it may be acceptable to make a belt where the ends are not bagged out but are just turned back and sewn down. The belt could then be run through the folder from end to end.

A commonly used seam from class 8 is the lengthwise fold of fabric that makes a belt loop for jeans, raincoats etc. Folders are available for use on stitch type 406 bottom cover machines which not only fold the fabric to the required shape but which can accept scrap pieces of fabric of various shapes and widths. A pair of cutting knives in front of the folder trim off waste fabric so that the folder is presented with the correct width. The operator feeds successive pieces of fabric into the folder with a small overlap when a join is needed. When the belt loops have been cut to length, any containing a join are thrown away.

The examples given here of folders, combined with machines of particular stitch types and numbers of needles, are just a sample of the opportunities available to construct garments quickly and accurately, provided enough of the style is to be made to justify the purchase of the necessary equipment. In small-volume manufacturing, garments will be made in many more stages with many separate rows of sewing and a need for much more pressing. Thus the actual methods of construction of apparently similar garments may vary a great deal according to the quantity of a style that is made.

## Slack feeding and elastication

The work aids described so far are static, mechanical devices. The only movement that occurs is the simple motion of the swing out folder, moved by the operator as needed. Most of the other work aids to be studied are dynamic, e.g. those that help supply materials to the needle point. Rack guides have already been mentioned but supplying lace or braid in a flat state to the needle or a folder is not the only requirement. Many braids are slightly stretchy and in order to roll them on to some kind of reel they will have been put under some tension. If this tension is not allowed to relax, it will be sewn into the garment, relax and cause pucker later. Such materials are often just pulled off the reel and left to relax but tension may again be introduced into them as they are pulled by the machine or the operator into a rack guide.

The device known as a slack feeder enables narrow materials to be presented to the needle point in a completely relaxed state. The device consists of a small motor and a set of rollers through which the material passes. From the rollers, the material hangs in a long, slack loop down to the sewing machine. A small tension on this loop, such as occurs when all the slack has been sewn on to the garment, causes the motor to drive a further section of material through the rollers and this then hangs in a relaxed state ready to be sewn.

Many other items are added which are deliberately highly elastic such as the stretch braids, laces and plain elastics used in lingerie and corsetry. Although in the past elastic was inserted into a casing sewn to the garment, nowadays it is almost always sewn to the fabric in a stretched state, all along its length, giving uniform gathering all round the garment. A method must be adopted to stretch the elastic by just the right amount so that the garment part will have the correct relaxed and stretched sizes. Several different ways are available to generate this stretch. The simplest is by means of a screw-down bar which clamps the elastic a short distance before it arrives at the needle. It is held stretched from the clamp to the point of sewing, and relaxes and draws up the garment immediately behind the needle. The screws are adjusted until the correct measurements, both stretched and relaxed, of the garment part being sewn are achieved.

Another method consists of a set of metering rollers in front of the needle, driven from the machine and metering out the right amount of elastic for each revolution of the machine, with a puller feed behind. The elastic is maintained in a stretched state between the rollers and the puller feed and the fabric is sewn flat to it while it is in this state. This method is used frequently for wide elastics sewn down with four needles such as are used in the waists of pyjama trousers and short, casual jackets. Fabric can be folded around the elastic by means of a folder if necessary.

The methods described so far for stretching elastic can only provide the same amount of stretch all along and can be used only when sewing from one edge of a garment to another rather than round in a circle. Computer-controlled methods are available now which allow both intermittent elastication and sewing in a circle, thus allowing much greater flexibility of both design and construction methods of garments. For intermittent elastication, an electronic motor is used which can be either pre-programmed or operated by the machinist using a knee press. When elastication is required, the motor meters the elastic to give the right amount of stretch. When a flat section, i.e. no elastication, is required the motor speeds up and runs in enough of the elastic material so there is no stretch in it. A typical use would be in the waistband of sports shorts; in the non-elasticated sections, the unstretched elastic would act like an ordinary waistband interlining.

It should be noted that nearly all the mechanisms for feeding forward elastic material have no feedback sensor to adjust the tension. The feed mechanisms are pre-set and there is no real-time adjustment. While this is acceptable for most cases, problems do occur, and they are associated with the variable Young's Modulus of the elastic material. Quality variations mean that the same force will produce different extensions of what is nominally the same material. Feedback mechanisms can be devised and fitted, but they add cost, and in a price-conscious industry, there is little demand for them. Technologists, however, should be alert to this potential problem.

## Cutting of threads, elastic and tapes

When the sewing of a seam has been completed, the machinist needs some means of separating the work from the machine, preferably without the time-consuming act of picking up a pair of scissors and cutting it away. In a limited number of instances, the operator 'chains off' the parts, i.e. sews continuously from one to the next and leaves them joined by the thread, to be cut apart later with scissors or even presented to the next operator in a ready-to-sew form. In the majority of cases, however, the threads must either be cut close (normally the case with lockstitch sewing) so that the garment is neatly finished and thread ends are not sewn into subsequent stitching, or a safe length of end must be left, usually at least 1cm in the case of the various chainstitches. In many factories thread ends are left on all the stitching at the time of sewing and those that have not been subsequently sewn across and trimmed off by the time the garment is finished will be hand-trimmed at final inspection. This is time-consuming and some of the ends may be visible but difficult to remove; given that the machinist has to separate the material from the machine anyway, it is better if it can be done in the minimum of time and with the correct length of thread left.

A simple method that may be used on lockstitch machines is a metal edge behind the needle bar which is sufficiently sharp that a thread pulled tight across it by the machinist will be cut. It is quicker to use than scissors but the thread ends will vary in length. In would not be suitable for use with chainstitching as the pull that is required to sever the threads would be too great and might cause them to unravel.

Among the more complex systems are those that provide a knife to cut the thread behind the presser foot; these are available for most machine types. The actual knife operation is pneumatic, i.e. by means of compressed air, the use of which will be described later. The differences between them are largely in their methods of activation, which can be a knee press operated by the machinist when the material has passed beyond the knife or a photo-electric or infrared detector that senses the presence or absence of fabric. During the time that the material is being sewn, the sensor on the bed of the machine is covered and the knife is inactive. When the edge of the garment part is reached, the sensor is uncovered and the knife cuts the thread. Suitable knives can be used to cut through reinforcing tape, elastic or other materials if necessary. Such cutters, often known as impact cutters, save not only time but also materials.

On lockstitch machines, the most satisfactory thread trimming mechanism is the underbed thread trimmer, which is usually combined with a needle positioner motor. The underbed thread trimmer severs the threads below the machine throat plate and no thread ends show on the top side of the stitching. It is activated by the operator 'heeling back' on the treadle controlling the machine. The needle positioner motor operates such that each time the machinist stops without activating the thread cutter, the machine stops with the needle in the down position. This enables corners to be turned or work to be read-justed before continuing sewing. When the thread cutter is activated, the needle is automatically raised. The savings in time for the sewing operator are considerable and there are no threads to be trimmed at a later stage. Machines must be purchased with the needle position-ing and underbed thread trimming facility already fitted but the extra cost is well worth it and they are increasingly common in all sections of the industry.

It is perhaps appropriate at this stage to mention another time-saving device related to thread trimming – the *latch-back device* used on overedge machines (such as the one illustrated in Fig. 4.12). In the construction of leisurewear and underwear made from lightweight knitted fabrics that can be overedged together, it is not always possi-ble to sew across every seam to secure the chain end of thread from that seam. They cannot be trimmed close or the seam will unravel and in many cases there is no alternative to a separate lockstitch tack or bar tack securing the thread chain to the seam turning just before the end of the seam. This is time-consuming and could be avoided if the thread chain could be secured as part of the seam. A device known as a latch-back is available to secure the thread at the starting end of the seam. More than one version exists and they begin operation at the end of the previous piece of sewn work.

At the same time as a chain end is left on the end of the previous seam that was sewn, one is also left extending away from the operator from the chaining off finger on the machine. This will be the starting-end chain end on the new seam. In one system, a jet of compressed air blows the chain towards the operator and, as he or she begins to sew the new seam, the thread chain is laid along under the looper

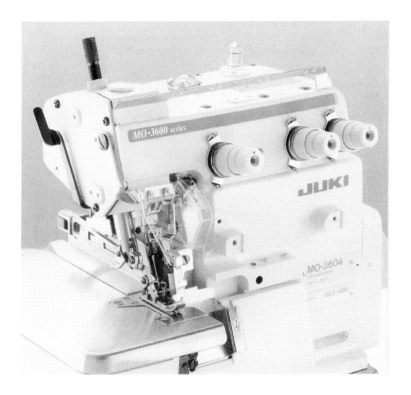

**Figure 4.12** Overedge machine, suitable for producing stitch type 504. (Reproduced by permission of Eastman Machine Co. Ltd.)

threads of the new seam. This is sufficiently secure and no further tack is needed. In many cases the sequence of construction of a garment can be arranged so that all seam ends are either latched-back or sewn across. An example is a tee shirt where the side seam and the sleeve seam are each sewn from the hem edge, which can then be latch-backed and the setting of the sleeve on the round used to secure the other end of both seams.

Latch-back devices for the starting ends of seams have been available for some time but more recently it has become possible to latch-back the finishing end as well. In this case an accurate sensing device detects the end of the seam and stops the machine immediately. The operator turns the garment part over and sews a short distance back along the seam. Correctly set up, no loop of thread is left at the turn. The appearance of the starting and finishing latch-back on an over-edged seam is shown in Fig. 4.13.

Another work aid of the cutting variety is that used to cut items such as belt loops to the required length. Separate machines have long been available which can take a reel of any such narrow material and

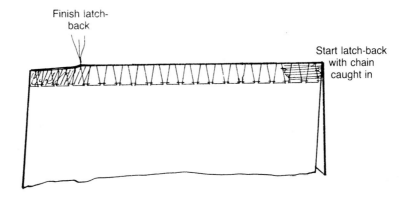

Figure 4.13 Start and finish latch-back on an overedged seam, stitch type 504.

cut it into the necessary short lengths, heat-sealing the ends where appropriate on a synthetic material. More recently developed is the means to determine the lengths of sewn seam by microprocessor-controlled stitch counting rather than physically measuring the length. In a machine such as the one described earlier, where random pieces of denim are fed past trimming knives to a folder making belt loops for jeans, it is possible to equip the machine with a *stitch counter operating an impact cutter*, which cuts the sewn strip to the required length.

Although very useful in this last situation, stitch counting is not universally applicable for measuring sewn distances. Over lengths greater than a few centimetres, and especially on a fabric with any stretch in it, inherent limitations of the feeding mechanisms can cause the length measured by stitch counting to vary considerably. The solution to such measuring problems is to combine the use of stitch counting with photo-electric or infrared sensing. For example, in topstitching a shirt collar, it is possible to programme in a number of stitches to give the correct size for the stitching at the end of the collar band, along with photo-electric or infrared detection of the collar point so as to stop the machine at the right position, with the needle down for long enough for the turn to be made. These sensors can also detect different thicknesses of materials such as occur between a patch pocket and the garment panel it is being attached to. Thus the machine can be set to stop automatically at the pocket corner for the operator to move the garment around.

Other tasks that the machinist must do as part of the sewing job are raising the presser foot and, on a lockstitch machine, backtacking at the end of a seam. These activities can also be programmed into a microprocessor-controlled machine, along with needle positioning and thread cutting, so that the operator has only to depress the foot pedal for the initially required cycle – raise presser foot to allow insertion of material, lower presser foot, commence sewing with a backtack, and sew forward – to occur. A similar cycle is activated at the end of the sewing cycle by heeling back on the foot control.

These programmable machines are often referred to as integrated sewing units (ISUs). The various facilities described above, including details such as how many stitches a backtack will consist of, are entered by pressing buttons on a box on top of the machine, the result being visually displayed. Different levels of facility are available at different cost but the advantages to the operator in a typical short-cycle, repetitive sewing operation of just the backtack, needle position and thread-cut facility are considerable. Once the programme has been set for a particular operation, such as attaching a rectangular label or top-stitching on a patch pocket, all aspects of the stitching cycle are operated by the foot control, leaving the operator free to concentrate on the amount of handling that unavoidably remains.

*Compressed air* can be an effective work aid, assisting the quantity and quality of a machinist's work. One such application overcomes the problem of single jersey fabrics which curl at the edges, especially when given a light pull as they are handled through the machine. If two plies are being joined on an overedge machine, the amount of the edge that curls is just that which should be under the stitching; if attempts are made to sew inside the curl it will result in excess fabric being trimmed off by the knife on the machine. Often, the two edges are curling away from each other and a jet of compressed air above and below the fabrics will flatten them sufficiently so that they can be joined with the correct trim-off. Another rather similar use of compressed air overcomes the untidy effect often associated with sewing hems on fabrics that fray badly. Where hems are double rolled and lockstitched up on garments such as blouses, the edge has often frayed considerably by the time the garment reaches that stage in its construction. The frayed ends often remain partly out of the seam even when it has been sewn with a folder. A jet of compressed air can be directed towards these ends and into the fold of the hem so that they are secured tidily inside.

The applications of compressed air in clothing manufacture have become so widespread that it is impossible to describe them all. A brief description of how it works should give an idea of the possibilities. When introduced in the early 1970s, it was expected to provide a wide range of low cost automation. In practice, the applications have generally been restricted to two main areas: where a company already uses compressed air to operate pressing machinery and has already accepted the capital costs of the system, and where bulk staple manufacture gives opportunities for considerable workplace engineering.

The air is normally supplied at a pressure of 5.5 bars. The main features of a compressed air system are the compressor, a storage vessel to act as a reservoir, an air cooler to maintain a constant temperature (because changes in temperature affect pressure), a main air filter to clean the air, pipework (usually in the form of a ring main to provide constant pressure), drains in the pipe to remove moisture, and flexible tubing to carry the air to individual workplaces. Clean, dry compressed air at each workplace is produced by a filter to clean the air, a regulator to maintain pressure and a lubricator. As has been described, a jet of air can be used alone for moving fabric edges and for cooling overheated sewing machine needles, but its main use is as the power source to move machine parts or ancillary equipment. At the point of application, a valve, opened by an electric signal from a switch or sensor on the operator's machine, admits air to a cylinder. This drives a piston to the end of the cylinder. The movement of the piston carries out the work required, which may be to depress an impact cutter behind the presser foot to cut threads or tapes, to raise the presser foot or to operate a stacker.

## Stackers

The work required for an operator to dispose of the garment at the end of the sewing cycle depends to a great extent on the size of the garment or part, and on the method of handling of the garments or parts between operators.

In many factories, garments are transported in tied bundles or boxes, and they must be formed into some kind of stack as they are worked on. Where small parts such as collars and cuffs are being sewn, off-loading devices are available where each part is passed off the machine table into a box which will confine all of them in a stack and which adjusts its height so that the top of the stack is always level with the machine table surface. When sewing larger garment parts, the operator passes the piece off the back of the machine over the horizontal bar of a stacker. Pneumatic operation then moves this bar away from the machine so that the garment part falls astride it and the bar then returns to its former position to await the next garment.

In companies where hanging transport systems are used, there are many sewing operations where the machinist does no more than reach sideways for the garment without taking it from its hanger or clip. When the section of the work is completed the garment is released and returns to its hanging position. The operator pushes a button on the machine table which moves this garment on and presents another one ready for work. There is a considerable saving in handling time, as well as a reduced amount of capital tied up in bundles of partly assembled garments in the line, but the capital cost of the installation is high. The requirement for pick up or stacking devices is nil but other work aids, as described, would still be used.

In more recent developments in production organisation and garment handling, a style of team working has been introduced where the operators in a production line work standing up at machines on higher pedestals. Each operator is multi-skilled and can do several operations in the sequence of construction of the garment. Thus they move along several machines, taking a single garment through these several operations, until they meet another operator ready for work, when they pass the garment on and return to an earlier machine to begin working on another garment. Again, no pick-up or disposal mechanisms are required, and in this case there is no investment in garment handling equipment between operations, but investment in sewing machines may be higher because the production line usually contains more machines than operators. There is very little work in progress and throughput is very fast. This is the main aim of the system as it enables a fast response to be made to demands for style change but it also improves skill levels amongst operators and gives opportunity for greater job satisfaction. Machines are specialised to each operation, with all appropriate work aids, and are generally slowed down to improve machine reliability and the operators' control of their work.

## Simple automatics

There are machines that sew a short, automatic cycle such as a buttonhole, bar tack, buttonsew or label. The machine sews only one stitch type and changes in the stitching configuration are limited. As is the case with the plain machines described previously, more possibilities are available with the advent of microprocessor control.

### Buttonhole machines

These come in a variety of types according to the type of buttonhole needed on the garment. The simplest buttonholes are used on shirts, blouses and other lightweight garments; more complex buttonholes are used on heavier tailored garments. An example of a buttonhole machine is in Fig. 4.14. The variables in buttonhole machines are the form and size of the buttonhole, the stitch type (lockstitch or single- or two-thread chainstitch), the stitch bight, the stitch density, whether the buttonhole is cut before or after sewing, and the presence or absence of a gimp.

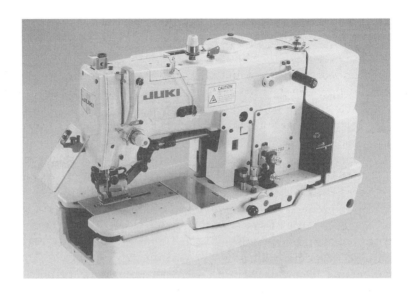

**Figure 4.14** Buttonhole machine. (Reproduced by permission of Eastman Machine Co. Ltd.)

Buttonhole machines may form a simple circle, where the stitches radiate from the centre of an eyelet hole; two legs on either side of a straight cut with a bar tack at both ends as in a shirt or blouse; a continuous line of sewing up one leg, round the end and down the other without a cut, as in the sham buttonholes on the cuffs of jackets; a buttonhole similar in form but larger in length and bight, with the hole partially or wholly cut and a separate bar tack closing off the end as on the lapels of jackets; a buttonhole with two legs and an eyelet hole at one end, with a separate bar tack closing off the other end, as on the fronts of jackets and overcoats; a variation in which the second leg is sewn over the first stitches of the first leg to close off the end, as frequently on knitwear; and an eyelet ended or lapel type buttonhole, the edges of which are lightly oversewn, known as 'cut and serge', which does no more than provide a firm edge to receive a hand-sewn buttonhole, now increasingly rare.

The choice between cut-before and cut-after machines applies principally to buttonholes in tailored outerwear. The advantage of cut-before buttonholes is a neat appearance with the thread covering the raw edges of the hole effectively. The disadvantages are that once the sewing cycle has begun, the position of the hole cannot be altered and that with the fabric flagging slightly at the edge of the hole the regularity of stitch formation may vary (which tends to restrict cut-before buttonholes to relatively densely woven, well-milled fabrics). The advantages of cut-after buttonholes are that the edge of the fabric gives some protection to the thread, the fabric is more stable during sewing, and repositioning is possible after the machine cycle begins if an error is detected. The main disadvantage relates to the finished appearance of the buttonhole, with the cut ends of fibres protruding between the stitches; the worst appearance is on the fronts of jackets with a dark coloured outer fabric and a light coloured inter-lining. This style of buttonhole is also used on denim jackets and jeans that are laundered before sale to give a worn look. In this case the cut-before buttonhole is preferable as the severity of the laundering process causes a very untidy appearance on cut-after buttonholes.

Gimp is a stiff thread positioned at the edge of the buttonhole under the stitching when the finished buttonhole requires reinforce-ment to preserve its shape and bulk to raise the purl effect of the stitch proud of the surrounding fabric.

The choice between lockstitch and chainstitch is affected by the security requirements of the hole, the finished appearance required and the relative costs involved (both capital and operating costs). In general, buttonholes on tailored outerwear make use of a two-thread chainstitch of the 400 class, the chain effect giving an attractive purl appearance to the buttonhole. The simpler shape of a buttonhole on shirts and other lightweight garments is often sewn with single thread chainstitch, and in some cases the sewing is done inside out on the garment so that the purl side of the back of the stitch is on the right side. Increasing use is being made of lockstitch buttonhole sewing to give greater security on these types of garment. For shirts, where the garment shape remains the same and the fronts can be buttonholed before assembly, sequential machines are available which sew all the buttonholes on the front, moving the garment part along by the correct amount between each and stacking it at the end. These will be referred to again when describing automatic machines.

## Buttonsew machines

The variables in buttonsew machines are the size and shape of the button that determines the design of the button clamp, the number and disposition of the holes, the form of stitching where there are four holes (this may be crossover or parallel – known as 'swiss kiss'), whether the button has a sewn shank or neck, the stitch type (lock-stitch or single thread chainstitch), and the number of stitches. Buttons may be flat with two or four holes or they may have a shank on the back. Where they are flat, a thread shank may be required so that there is space behind the button for the thickness of the garment when fastened. This can be created by means of a spacing 'finger' over the button during sewing. In the case of the shank button, it is clamped on its side during sewing and the needle passes alternately into the garment and then into the hole in the shank and into the garment. The advantage of lockstitch buttonsewing is security but its disadvantage is an untidy look to the stitching on the other side of the fabric from the button. A chainstitch buttonsewer gives a cleaner appearance at the back but less security.

For tailored garments, machines are available sewing stitch type 209 and giving the appearance of a hand-sewn button. The machine sews the button, wraps the thread shank, and secures the stitching by passing the last few stitches through the thread of the shank. The front edge of the garment is presented folded to the needle so that the minimum amount of stitching appears on the reverse side. This increases security.

On the basic machines sewing two- or four-hole buttons with lockstitch or chainstitch, the requirement for the operator to position the button in the clamp can be avoided, where long runs justify it, by using a hopper feed which automatically feeds the buttons to the clamp at the needle point. For standard garments such as shirts, the same type of sequential machines are available for sewing buttons as were described for buttonholing.

## Bar tack machines

These machines sew a number of stitches across the point to be reinforced and then sew covering stitches over and at right angles to the first stitches. The variables are the number of tacking stitches and the number of covering stitches. Typical uses are closing the ends of buttonholes, reinforcing the ends of pocket openings and the bottoms of flies, and sewing on belt loops.

## Label sewers

A variety of label sewers are available, from those sewing simple zig-zag stitches to a predetermined length on one or two edges of a label, to programmable profile stitchers that can sew round a wide range of shapes and sizes of label. A specially shaped cylinder bed machine is available over which the inside pocket of a jacket can be passed, enabling jackets to be labelled with a retailer's label after manufacture.

A variety of other short-cycle machines are available for attaching hooks, bars, metal badges, motifs and many other decorative and functional garment parts. These increasingly take the form of programmable machines that can sew a variety of items provided an appropriate clamp is attached.

# Automated workstations

These are sewing systems that can be described as fully automatic and which offer the opportunity to raise dramatically the proportion of a sewing machine operator's productive time. In all the machinery that has been discussed so far, the operator must still undertake a significant amount of the handling. Despite the application of a wide range of work aids, the operator's pattern of activity is still handle – sew – handle – sew – handle, etc.

The material must still be loaded into the machine and removed at the end and however much the section in between has been made more efficient it normally involves the operator waiting while it happens. An operator's activities may vary from constant handling and attention to the job in the attachment of a complicated collar, to intermittent spells of activity while a machine sews round a button-hole. In each case, the productivity is low.

The principle behind automated workstations is that the operator is able to undertake further useful handling while the machine is sewing and at least some of the handling time is incorporated into the sewing time. Such workstations always contain a sewing machine, but in many cases it is surrounded by other parts of the total system and is barely visible. The machine is normally equipped with any necessary folders and thread cutters, the latter being operated automatically, but in addition the workstation has sophisticated positioning and guiding equipment operating before and during sewing, and stackers that operate afterwards. Combinations of pneumatic and mechanical handling achieve the wide variety of fabric movements that are needed, and consumption of services such as compressed air can be high. The space required may be the equivalent of several ordinary machines. The workplaces are relatively expensive, but are justified primarily on their productivity and quality characteristics.

The complex automatics are available in a variety of types to achieve particular sewing operations. Their modes of working can be roughly classified as follows:

(a)  The machine sews continuously while the operator keeps it supplied with garments. An example would be a machine that turns up the cuffs on short sleeved casual shirts. The operator can pick up and position a garment part during the time the machine takes to sew the previous part. The parts are normally positioned on to a conveyor which takes them past the sewing head. Only a short space is left between parts and the machine automatically cuts the thread between each part after sewing and stacks them at the end. Thus the machine, in this case a lockstitch or a chainstitch, is utilised for a large part of the time (allowing for the short gaps between parts) until the operator has to stop and deal with a completed bundle and organise another one. The average utilisation of these machines is about 75 per cent.

Other operations that can be done by this type of workstation are attaching interlining to the front edge of blouses by means of an overedge stitch, with the interlining feeding from a roll cut to the correct width, and constructing the placket on the buttonhole front of a man's shirt. In the latter case, if the placket is constructed by folding the edge of the shirt front, a folder is built into the workstation and the operator has only to load the front into the machine. If a separate strip is used to make the placket, the operator has to load the strips and the fronts, and the machine pauses between fronts while this is done. A photo-electric device detects the end of one shirt front and stops the machine. Even allowing for these pauses, a utilisation of 65 per cent is achievable with these workstations. Unfortunately, lack of uniformity of shade of fabric frequently prevents continuous strips of fabric being used for these plackets.

If H and S are taken to represent operator handling and machine sewing respectively, and – to indicate continuous operation, the operation of this type of machine can be represented diagrammatically:

Operator   H – H – H – H – H – H deal with bundle
Machine       S – S – S – S – S – S  pause

A large number of garments would normally be sewn before a pause would be necessary.

(b)   The machine sews an automatic cycle, which includes the handling during sewing that would normally be done by the operator. During the cycle the operator performs the considerable amount of handling that is needed to prepare for the next cycle of automatic sewing. An example is the automated version of the stitching jigs described earlier. In this situation the machine, once loaded with a jig and started, controls the speed and direction of sewing around that jig. It stops automatically at the end, whereupon the operator removes the jig and replaces it with a new one, which was loaded with garment parts during the previous sewing cycle. There is thus an overlap between the handling (unavoidably the operator's), unloading and reloading the jigs and presenting them to the sewing head, and controlling the speed and accuracy of the stitching. As well as the sewing of small parts such as collars, cuffs and tabs, which can be sewn more slowly with the hand-held jig, the automatic jigs can also be used for large garment parts such as jacket and raincoat fronts. The additional seam turning that is necessary when using jigs is trimmed off by a knife immediately after sewing as the jig moves around. Utilisation with these machines is about 75 per cent.

Another example of this type of operation is the workstation that makes gauntlet openings in shirt sleeves, traditionally an expensive part of shirt production. Only one sewing head is required but two loading stations are needed, which separately create the type of fold used on a left and a right sleeve. One side of the opening in the sleeve is pre-hemmed and the operator then loads the sleeve and the gauntlet patch piece into the loading station for that side while the machine is sewing the previously loaded sleeve for the other side. Manually constructed gauntlet openings usually have a square end to the gauntlet section rather than the pointed end which is regarded as more desirable. The automatic machine is able to make the pointed shape, which is actually easier for a mechanical folding device than the square shape. A representation of the operation of this type of machine would be as follows, the colon (:) indicating a brief pause on the part of the operator and the machine as each reaches the end of its cycle of loading or sewing.

Operator   H : H : H : H : H : H deal with bundle
Machine      S : S : S : S : S : S   pause

(c)   The machine sews an automatic cycle in which a difficult sewing job is achieved very quickly and accurately, but the operator is not able to do much during the cycle time. Examples are the construction of a jetted pocket in a tailored jacket or the attaching of a patch pocket to a shirt front or a pair of jeans. Several parts have to be loaded into the machine but the sewing cycle is then short and of perfect quality. The utilisation with these machines is about 80 per cent.

In the attachment of patch pockets, the workstation incorporates a folding device which folds the side and lower edges on a pocket that has been hemmed at the top edge. The operator loads the pocket into the folder and the garment part on to the machine. The pocket is folded, placed on the garment part and sewn round. The stitching includes the required shape of reinforcement at the top, often a triangle. There is normally provision for the operator to intervene in the placing of the pocket so that, in the case of checked or striped shirts, the pattern can be matched. An example of such a mechanised workplace for attaching jeans pockets is shown in Fig. 4.15(i). It includes a milling machine with which to make new pocket creases when the pocket shape changes.

In the construction of jetted pockets, the jacket front, the fabric that forms the jetts, and if appropriate one side of the pocket bag are

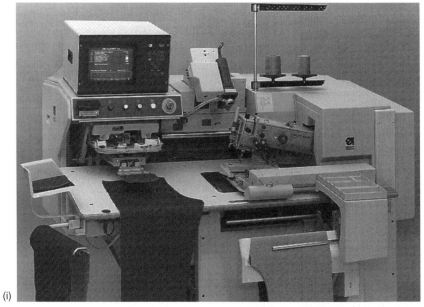

(i)

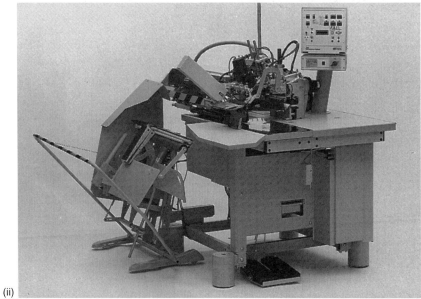

(ii)

**Figure 4.15** Mechanised workplaces. (i) For attaching patch pockets on trousers and jeans. (ii) For making jett, welt and flap pockets on tailored jackets and trousers.

loaded into the machine. The sewing head sews two parallel rows of stitching of the correct spacing and length, a knife slashes the fabric along the middle and two further mitre knives slash into the corners. The pocket is completed by turning the jetts through to the wrong side, tacking the triangular sections left at the corners to the ends of the jetts, and attaching the pocket bag sections. A pre-made pocket flap can be incorporated if necessary. The machines will normally also do a single rather than a double jett. The size of pocket is easily adjusted. An example of this workplace is shown in Fig. 4.15(ii).

A representation of the operation of this type of machine would be as follows, w indicating that the operator is waiting for the machine.

```
Operator   H w H w H w H w H w H deal with bundle
Machine       S : S : S : S : S : S   pause
```

The workplace shown in Fig. 4.15(ii) is available in several different levels, at different prices; at the highest level, the operator waiting time has been largely eliminated by clamp technology, which allows the operator to begin loading jetts and flaps while the previous cycle of sewing is taking place.

(d)   The machine sews a fairly long automatic cycle during which the operator is idle between loading and unloading. To avoid this, more than one machine is operated, perhaps even three or four. An example is the buttonhole and buttonsew machines referred to as sequential, which can move the garment part, normally a shirt front not yet attached to the rest of the shirt, by the correct amount between each buttonhole or button until the complete set has been sewn. Automatic button feeding would, of course, be included. The sewing of six buttonholes on a shirt front can take around 0.35 minutes and in this time the operator can easily load another machine and then another. The sewing of six buttons takes slightly less time but still offers scope for multiple machine operation. Balanced combinations of several buttonholers and buttonsewers are possible with very little sign of hurry on the part of the operator. Indeed, since the machines are large, a constraint can be the time it takes for the operator to move from one to the other.

Another workstation type in this category hems tee shirts and underwear. The type of hem previously referred to as overlock welted, used frequently on lightweight knitted garments such as tee shirts, is extremely difficult to sew and operators require long training. On the automatic machine, the operator loads the lower edge of the garment, already joined into a circle on to guides that move apart to place the garment under the correct tension. The edge is inserted into a folder and the complete hem is sewn automatically. While this is happening the operator can operate a second machine.

Yet another example is the automatic serging machine often used on men's trousers. A machine can be set to sew three sides of a leg panel with automatic turning at the corners; during this time the operator can unload and reload two or three other machines. A representation of the operation of three machines could be as follows. The cycle time of each of the machines does not have to be the same.

```
Operator   H(1)  :  H(2)  :  H(3)  :  ....
Machine 1       S(1) .......
Machine 2                 S(2) .......
Machine 3                           S(3) ...............
```

The operation of the machine for overlock welting described above is the only one mentioned that sews a garment in three dimensions rather than working on flat parts. Although there are some mechanised workstations that automatically sew these types of construction, they are few and far between because the control systems needed to handle fabric in three dimensions are very much more complicated than those needed for flat fabric. The limp nature of textile materials makes automatic handling difficult and the frequency of style change in most sections of the industry means that any automated systems built for them must be easily adaptable. This is not always easy.

The result of these constraints is that most of the fully automatic sewing equipment available has been developed for assembling the types of garment that are made in very large quantities with minimum style change, and which have within their design a number of parts that can be sewn with the materials in a flat state. These garments are primarily shirts and men's jackets and trousers. On formal shirts, the operations of collar and cuff assembly and topstitching, label attachment to yoke, yoke attachment to body, folding of front edges, buttonholing and buttonsewing of fronts, patch pocket attachment and attachment of gauntlet openings to sleeves can all be achieved with mechanised workstations where the operator only loads the machine. When these stages have been completed, however, the ensuing three-dimensional activities of attaching sleeves to body, closing side seams, attaching collar and cuffs, and turning up the hem have to be undertaken by operators at more conventional machines, albeit fitted with appropriate work aids and programmable facilities. On men's jackets and trousers, the main opportunities for automation are in the construction of the varied jett, welt and flap pockets that most styles include, and in the serging and joining of leg panels.

Some generalisations can be made. Automated workstations have achieved productivity improvements by:

♦ increasing speeds of machines
♦ numerically-controlled (NC) features, often combined with sensors
♦ attachments and work aids, generally requiring the operator to load and unload only
♦ enhancing reliability and thereby reducing downtime
♦ quick changeovers, thereby reducing downtime

## Reprogrammable automated systems

Throughout the 1970s and 1980s, the vision of sewing system automation was held up as the way for developed countries to compete in clothing manufacturing. This section presents the case for systems automation and considers research designed to achieve it.

Reference has been made many times to the labour-intensive nature of the sewing process and to the small proportion of a sewing machinist's time that is actually spent sewing; it is the sewing area of garment manufacture that has long been expected to offer the widest scope for imaginative research and development.

The term 'operation' has been used loosely throughout this book to denote some stage in the manufacturing process. Operations are the divisions of the total work content of garments. Each operation consists of a work cycle, which is the sequence of elements of cutting or sewing, fusing or pressing, required to perform a job or yield a unit of production. Operations define the work done by people in a factory.

In the sewing room, the breakdown of the total work content of a garment into operations has traditionally included long, medium and short operations, the actual length being influenced by the amount of work content in the garment, the predicted quantity of output of an individual style, and the number employed in the company manufacturing it, with the consequent potential for specialisation among its operators and managers. In this case an operation was the amount of the work content of a garment that was undertaken by one operator.

On this principle, a garment manufactured in small lots or as individual garments in a small company would tend to have long operations, if not a form of make-through organisation, where an operator constructs virtually the whole of the garment. The throughput time for a garment in this case would be the actual making time for the garment.

By contrast, the operation length would be short for garments manufactured in volume in a large company with a large workforce, and with specialist managers as industrial engineers who would plan the best utilisation of people and machinery. The organisation of production in this case would be that of a *progressive bundle system* or PBS, with the successive operations on the garment performed by different operators, and with considerable quantities of partly made garments working their way through the production line. The throughput time for a garment in this case could be days or even weeks.

Thus this operation or unit of work undertaken repetitively by an operator could vary in size from perhaps hours for a handmade bespoke jacket to fractions of a minute for the bulk production of briefs. Between the two extremes lie all possible variations.

Traditionally, two themes in the design of operations vie with one another. These are the technical requirements of the process and the managerial requirements of planning a production line. The production line itself could take several forms, varying gradually between the make-through and the PBS described above. Make-through methods were, and still are, used for the very small volume couture or bespoke garments and also for runs of perhaps a few hundred of a style for the high fashion retail sector. Technologically, they require garments to be assembled by very simple methods, predominantly lockstitch with overlocking if available. Typically much of this work is undertaken by homeworkers who have access only to a lockstitch machine with no work aids of any kind. If overlocking is essential, it may be done before despatch to the homeworker or when the garments are returned to the organising company. Garments made by the latter route tend to be very untidy. Whilst virtually any fabric, unless it has high stretch, can be assembled entirely on a lockstitch machine with an overedger used for neatening, it is almost certainly the case that it could be assembled to higher standards of appearance and performance, and at a more competitive price, if it could be assembled using the wide range of machines and attachments that have previously been described. This is only possible if construction is as a sequence of operations, with the most appropriate machinery used for each one; this was one reason for the widespread development and use of the PBS as a production system.

The other apparent advantage of assembling a garment as a sequence of operations, each undertaken by a different operator, was the opportunity to motivate operators to high rates of work by individual financial incentive schemes. These determined a further technical requirement of the design of operations, in addition to the use of a particular machine and attachments, which was that an operation should encompass only one basic skill, and preferably only one level of that skill. Thus pressers would not normally sew, and sewing operators would not be making the best use of their sewing skills if they were pressing, trimming or doing any other job requiring less training time than sewing. In addition, operators trained on lockstitch machines would not be using their skills to the full if employed on a buttonhole machine which requires minimal handling skills, and an operator skilled enough to attach collars to shirts would not be best employed sewing darts.

A final technical requirement in the design of operations is that there is often a necessary sequence of construction. One seam may have to be sewn before another. A seam must be sewn before it is pressed open, though it may not have to be pressed open immediately after sewing. A number of seams may be sewn before all are pressed together.

The managerial requirements of operation design in the PBS relate to the need for operators to be highly trained on the specific tasks that form the sequence of operations in the assembly of a particular garment style, and for the flow of work through these operators to be tightly controlled and well balanced. Longer operations need longer training times since rates of repetition are lower. Short operations are quicker to learn but can result in a disproportionate amount of time being spent organising the bundle of garments that is presented to the operator. The pressure is on operators to develop limited skills to a high level. This maximises production for the company and earning levels for the operator who is working on a payment-by-results system. In terms of the flow of work through the sequence of operators, there is a need to balance the work content of operations so that there is the right flow of work for every member of the production sequence, as well as the right total amount of work to fill each operator's working day. This has to be achieved despite variations in operators' rates of working and a tendency to a high level of absenteeism. Inevitable unevenness is smoothed out by high levels of buffer stocks between operators. The achievement of this high level of training and smooth line balance is dependent on long runs of the same style of garment, on sophisticated management skills in industrial engineering, and on the availability of capital to invest in the variety of machinery that is required.

Through the 1970s it appeared that production runs of most styles were set to become longer and longer and the answer to economical production was to mechanise the processes of assembly that were being used and refine the methods used in operator incentive schemes. These schemes are heavily dependent on sufficiently long runs, preferably many weeks, of the same style of garment so that operators can reach a steady rate of working and a suitable rate can be set for the job. In the 1980s the trend towards longer production runs began to reverse and in many sectors of the industry the demand changed to more and more varied styles in ever smaller quantities. These variations result from the increasingly market-driven nature of clothing retailing and now affect much of the 'middle market' that forms a large part of the UK clothing industry and that hitherto could rely on continuity of demand for its products.

This sector of the industry has considered how it can organise its production so that garments are made efficiently and to a satisfactory quality standard but with as short a throughput time as possible. This has generated an increasing requirement for flexible machinery, multi-skilled operators and lateral thinking about the actual methods of assembly that are used for garments.

Having considered the nature of sewing operations within the organisation of garment assembly, it is now possible to return to the theme of the way forward for the clothing industry in terms of likely technological developments.

As has been noted, there has been a considerable amount of automatic machinery developed for the earlier, two-dimensional stages of the assembly of items such as shirts and men's suits, and for two- and three-dimensional operations on underwear, where high-volume production continues to be the case and where the limited style and fabric changes that do occur have little effect on the machinery used. However, this machinery is only automatic in the sense of handling materials whilst they are being sewn, and in most cases still requires loading by a human operator. It is also available only for a few of the assembly operations for each type of garment, the rest of the garment being assembled by operators working at machines of less specialised types, in the same way that is used for all other, less high-volume types of garments. Figures of up to 80 per cent machine utilisation have been achieved for the fully automatic or mechanised workplaces described here, but for the rest of garment assembly the amount of the operator's time actually spent sewing is, as has already been stated, typically around 20 per cent. It is worth considering this breakdown of time further.

The analysis of typical sewing machinists' activities from which this figure of 20 per cent is taken was carried out by Grills and Brown (1975) for the Shirley Institute; it is likely that in many companies the picture they found has not changed radically since then. An abstract from their table of results in Fig. 4.16 shows the percentage of time spent on each category of activity for four machine types (eight were studied).

The authors point out that 'differences in percentages among different machine categories for similar activities are due to sampling error and real differences in the operations carried out, the latter

| Activity | Single needle lockstitch without thread trimmer and needle positioner | Single needle lockstitch with thread trimmer and needle positioner | Overlock machine without chain cutter | Overlock machine with chain cutter | All machines average |
|---|---|---|---|---|---|
| Bundle handling | 5.6 | 4.2 | 6.0 | 14.9 | 5.7 |
| Work docket | 2.4 | 2.1 | 2.3 | 2.6 | 2.4 |
| Present work to machine | 18.4 | 17.4 | 24.8 | 15.6 | 20.1 |
| Sew | 19.5 | 22.2 | 22.1 | 33.0 | 20.2 |
| Realign | 14.8 | 17.9 | 12.4 | 5.0 | 14.2 |
| Remove and aside | 3.6 | 4.7 | 5.3 | 7.2 | 4.4 |
| Trim threads | 6.7 | 2.7 | 6.7 | – | 6.0 |
| Needle position | 3.5 | 0.8 | – | – | 2.4 |
| Relaxation | 7.9 | 7.9 | 8.0 | 10.1 | 7.8 |
| Talk to supervisor | 2.0 | 3.4 | 2.1 | 1.1 | 2.3 |
| Change thread | 0.9 | 0.8 | 1.3 | 1.9 | 1.0 |
| Rethread needle | 4.5 | 3.8 | 3.0 | 5.2 | 4.3 |
| Machine repairs | 1.2 | 1.5 | 1.3 | 0.2 | 1.3 |
| Miscellaneous fabric handle | 6.8 | 7.0 | 3.5 | 1.8 | 5.7 |
| Other | 2.2 | 3.6 | 1.2 | 1.4 | 2.2 |
| | 100.0 | 100.0 | 100.0 | 100.0 | 100.0 |
| Work stations observed | 366 | 50 | 97 | 9 | 605 |

**Figure 4.16** Table of sewing machinists' activities. (Excerpted and reproduced by permission of the Shirley Institute.)

being the more important cause'. An explanation of the non-sewing activities may be helpful and will also show the areas where the recent trends in the organisation of production described above may alter the figures.

*Bundle handling* signifies untying and laying out the bundled parts before the operation as well as reassembling and retying after the operation. This relates specifically to the progressive bundle type of production system and is reduced substantially in either a unit production system or a team system.

*Work dockets* signifies the cutting of a 'coupon payment ticket', as a record of work done, for payment purposes. Even in PBS systems this is being replaced increasingly by simpler or automatic methods of recording the work done by individual operators, where there is computer processing of pay and other information. In a UPS, the computer control of the system is such that individual work flow is recorded. In a team system it is commonly the case that the team is paid as a group and the record of workflow is simply a record of the number of garments completed compared with the target number.

*Present work to machine* involves separating and picking up the parts, matching plies, and orienting the needle for further sewing.

*Sew*, *Realign*, and *Remove and aside* are self-explanatory.

*Trim threads* and *Needle position* mean cutting the thread chain from the needle to the workpiece after sewing and adjusting the needle position before that. Here, the quantity of lockstitch machines with thread trimmers and needle positioners, and those without, is today likely to be reversed.

*Relaxation*, *Talk to supervisor*, *Change thread*, *Rethread needle* and *Machine repairs* are self-explanatory.

*Miscellaneous fabric handle* includes turning out, especially points and corners, cutting, notching and trimming.

*Other* means rewinding bobbin spools and similar activities.

Changes in equipment and handling will alter the details, but since a great deal of the industry still works on bundle systems, the average will not have changed much.

In the study, the proportion of time spent on sewing actually varied from as little as 3 per cent to as much as 45 per cent. Those showing less than 10 per cent were sewing short seams requiring great accuracy and change of direction. Work handling amounted to 44 per cent of the total time, and if 'Miscellaneous fabric handle' is included, 50 per cent. Twenty per cent of the total was presenting work to the machine.

The industry has considered three basic approaches to improving the non-sewing parts of sewing operations:

1. An analysis of the psychomotor skills used by operators, leading to improved methods of training operators.
2. A study of the methods the operator uses at the workplace, to develop both equipment and new methods step by step which will bring about a gradual but continuous reduction in the work content of operations.
3. The development of robotics to transfer the manual elements to a dedicated but flexible computer-controlled machine.

## Analysis of psychomotor skills

This analysis breaks down conveniently into three sections:

♦ effector processes (the motor system), i.e. the visible part of skill, the organised movement of hands, feet, and other parts of the body;
♦ receptor processes, i.e. how the senses take in and transmit information from the environment;

♦ central activities taking place in the cerebral cortex, which link and organise the other two processes.

Regarding *effector processes*, it is predominantly the skills of hands and fingers that govern clothing production, resulting in the rapid, highly dextrous manual movements of the sewing machinist. Skilled performance is most evident where movements of different limbs are co-ordinated, as in the movements of the foot, the knee and the two hands of the machinist, who on completing a line of sewing, stops the machine and operates the underbed thread trimmer with the foot, raises the presser foot by means of the knee lift, and removes the sewn fabric parts in a smooth and continuous process.

Regarding *receptor processes*, the sewing machinist uses principally three or four to transmit information. Vision is used to recognise shapes and profiles, sometimes in unusual attitudes, to discriminate between the right and wrong side of the fabric, to assess when two edges of a seam will not fit, to gauge distances and to provide a continuous series of cues about the matching of parts being sewn, the orientation of edges to the needle and the appearance of work completed.

One of the most important and often unrecognised senses a machinist depends on is the kinaesthetic sense which provides information about the position of limbs and the pressures they exert. It provides the means for control of movement, both gross and delicate, from deep-seated nerve endings in muscles, tendons and joints. To enable the operator's eyes to concentrate on the area in front of the needle point, the position of the foot pedal, and hence the speed of stitching, is sensed kinaesthetically. Similarly, the tensioning of the two plies of fabric being joined is sensed kinaesthetically in the fingers. Such sensations are seldom at the level of consciousness in an experienced machinist, but have been 'internalised' during the training process.

The sense of touch is used to gain information about fabric surfaces and the force of grip required to manipulate them.

From time to time, the sense of hearing will come into play to signal a defect in the running of the sewing machine.

Regarding the *central activities*, a skilled performance is partly based in the conditioning of reflexes, but appears to be more complex than that. Each response to a stimulus grows out of those that have preceded it in a continuous stream. The complex co-ordination of senses and movements, and the precise timing and rapid rate of decison-making below the surface of consciousness indicate that the level of skill achieved by sewing machinists can be very high.

The procedures of training require an analysis of the range of activities in the operations to be learnt, not only in terms of the result desired but also in terms of the movements required and the perceptual cues necessary for its accomplishment. The basic skill components can then be isolated and taught separately before the complex co-ordinations of actual operations are attempted. Clearly, control of machine speed with accurate stopping, and fabric control before, during and after sewing, are components of the total skill requirement built up through practice on appropriately designed exercises and finally on operations themselves.

## A study of the methods used

The methods the operator uses can be analysed by looking in more detail at the Grills and Brown (1975) research in conjunction with the different stages of sewing operations that have been identified. These can be grouped into five phases as shown in Fig. 4.17.

*Phases 1* and *5* are concerned with transport of materials into and out of the workplace, changing thread and dealing with the work docket. The first principle is that the operator should not be diverted from a task by having to fetch work from a remote location. The second is that the work should be presented to the operator between hip and shoulder height. The third is that the work should require the minimum manipulation before and after sewing. In a progressive bundle unit this might be achieved by presenting operators with larger bundles, but there is not always scope for this since bundle size is determined largely by a combination of the piece length of the cloth and the length of the marker. In a unit production system all three principles are adhered to simply because it is the designed purpose of the system to present each operator with single garments in the correct position for working on them. In a team system, interoperation handling is reduced greatly as the garments are either taken through a succession of operations by the same operator or handed directly to the next operator in the team.

*Phases 2* and *4* are concerned with presenting work to the needle, involving separating and picking up parts, matching plies and orienting the parts to the needle ready for sewing, realignment and trimming threads and disposal within the workplace after sewing (50 per cent of time). This involves a number of principles, to be applied where appropriate:

♦ Separating and picking up the two plies to be sewn simultaneously using opposite symmetrical motions.
♦ Positioning parts to be picked up as near to the operator as possible, and planning storage of parts within the workplace in three dimensions.

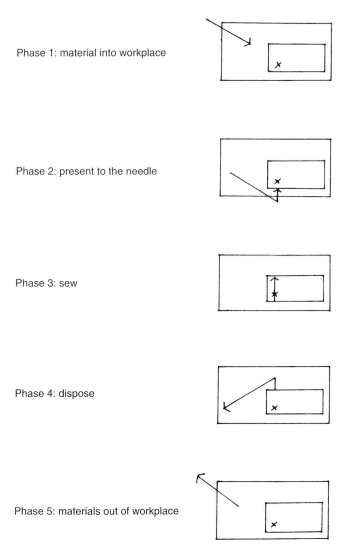

Phase 1: material into workplace

Phase 2: present to the needle

Phase 3: sew

Phase 4: dispose

Phase 5: materials out of workplace

**Figure 4.17** Five phases of a sewing operation.

- Providing a defined and fixed place for all tools and materials.
- Designing the sequence of activity to provide for continuous, smooth and rhythmic motions, which are easier to control and more accurate than intermittent motions, for example, in the sequence from sewing to disposal.
- Designing a larger table surface which normally avoids parts of the garment hanging over the edge to the left of the

needle, thus encouraging free movement of the garment
during presentation to the needle and realignment.

♦ Assessing the most effective distance from needle point to
the front edge of the table (this is commonly fixed at 15 cm
or so, but might be varied to accommodate longer runs of
sewing).

♦ Distributing work among different limbs to relieve the
hands. This is increasingly easy to achieve by using
programmable machines so that the activities of backtack,
thread trim and foot lift become foot-controlled instead of
hand-controlled.

♦ Ergonomic factors such as seating, lighting and temperature.

*Phase 3* is concerned with sewing (20 per cent of time) and the
needle point engineering that makes it easier and more accurate, as
well as rethreading the machine (4.3 per cent of time). Sewing machine
manufacturers have in the past invested a great deal in the development of higher speeds for sewing machines. Beyond a certain point,
the objectives of this investment were largely irrelevant to reducing
the work content of operations. The first reason is that higher machine
speeds affect only 20 per cent of the average operation time. The
second reason is the time taken by the foot to depress the pedal, and
the effects of acceleration at the beginning of the sewing run and
deceleration at the end. The result of these two factors is that increasing the machine speed from 5000 to 6000 stitches per minute on a
typical fairly short sewing operation would reduce overall time for the
operation by less than two per cent. It is also the case that at a given
level of accuracy of stitching, the limit of speed in sewing together
two pieces of fabric is about 10 metres per minute, i.e. 4000 stitches
per minute with a stitch length of 2.5 mm. This limit depends on the
human operator, not on the machine. Speed of sewing might be
increased if the tolerances on the seam could be increased, but this
may not produce acceptable quality. It is relevant to note here that
typical speeds of machines used in team systems, where operators
are required to be multi-skilled and often work standing up, are no
higher than this.

Another reason for limiting machine speed was demonstrated by
investigations into the effects of machine speed on the regularity of
stitch density. It was found that when sewing a seam at low speeds,
the presser foot pressure must be reduced to achieve a particular
stitch density, since at low speeds higher presser foot pressures cause
compression and stretch of the fabric and the stitches fall too close
together. However, as the machine speeds increase to 5000 stitches
per minute, a high foot pressure is required. This is because, with low

foot pressures, there is little contact between fabric and presser foot due to the effect of the feed dog inducing bounce in the presser foot. At speeds in excess of 5000 stitches per minute, even under maximum presser foot pressure conditions, the presser foot may not be serving its purpose, and irregular, inconsistent results may be obtained. This result is a consequence of basic sewing machine construction. The designs of the 1850s, running at approximately 200 stitches per minute, had hardly changed by the 1970s, but were then expected to run at 7000 stitches per minute. A fundamental redesign of the hinged, spring-loaded presser foot is required if it is to be efficient above a point somewhere between 3000 and 5000 stitches per minute.

Much more fruitful sources of reduction in work content are other aspects of needle point engineering such as the specialised presser feet, special purpose feeds, folders, tape feeds, edge trimming knives and multi-needle machines that were described in previous chapters. These all contribute, not only to more consistent quality, but also to shorter working time.

One area that has not until recently attracted much attention is the figure found by Grills and Brown (1975) for rethreading the needle following thread breaks (4.3 per cent of total time on average). This is an aspect of the unreliability of the sewing machine which is important in operator-controlled operations but is crucial in automatic, machine-controlled operations. Some of the cause can be found with the sewing thread and thread manufacturers are increasingly aiming towards knot-free thread as an aid to solving the problem.

## Development of robotics

In 1965, Arthur D. Little Inc. published a report to the Apparel Research Foundation in the USA. The study was entitled 'State of the Art Investigation of Automated Handling of Limp Fabrics', and was at least as significant as the subsequent second volume describing an experimental programme leading to the building of demonstration 'Rink' equipment. The study divided automation into five consecutive elements:

*Separation and pick up* The researchers state: 'In order to quantify by ranking the difficulty of accomplishing any of these steps, we applied, from judgment, a difficulty factor. The higher this difficulty factor, the more difficult the task is to automate from a technical as well as a possibly economic standpoint. These difficulty factors are assigned in the values of 1 to 5. One is the easiest; 5 is the most difficult. For other elements of automation, difficulty factors go as high as 25'. They considered three conditions:

- An aligned stack straight from cutting and undisturbed, with each ply within plus or minus 1/32" of any other ply. This condition could apply only to the first operation following cutting. (Difficulty Factor 1.)
- A non-aligned stack in a flat stack with each ply aligned within 1/4" of another ply. (Difficulty Factor 2.)
- A non-aligned stack of three-dimensional pieces, with tolerance limits as above and in which two or more individual pieces have been sewn together. (Difficulty Factor 5.)

*Orientation of piece in direction and plane* Again three conditions were considered:

- A piece of irregular shape but with one straight edge that can be detected and oriented by a simple three point sensing system such as three photocells. (Difficulty Factor 2.)
- A flat, irregularly shaped piece without a straight edge is far more difficult to orientate, requiring recognition of the total shape. (Difficulty Factor 4.)
- A piece of irregular shape in three dimensions requires a matrix of sensors, detecting pitch and yaw on at least two axes out of three. (Difficulty Factor 10.)

*Mating* Mating is defined as bringing two or more plies or pieces under proper orientation with each other in plane and rotation. Three conditions were considered:

- Aligning two flat pieces, one on top of the other by the straight edges common to both, which would then be joined by sewing, is the simplest. (Difficulty Factor 2.)
- A more difficult case involves aligning two pieces of irregular shape with no straight edge. (Difficulty Factor 4.)
- The most difficult case involves aligning two pieces both of which have an irregular three-dimensional shape, such as mating a shirt sleeve to the body of the shirt. (Difficulty Factor 10.)

These cases are by no means exhaustive and, for instance, do not include aligning more than two pieces, matching checks or the insertion of fullness.

*Control through the work point*

- The simplest is where two mated pieces require the application of a fastener, such as a stud, through the two plies. (Difficulty Factor 1.)

- The next order of difficulty involves sewing along the straight edge of two mated plies. (Difficulty Factor 2.)
- More difficult again is the sewing of an irregularly shaped edge on two flat plies mated together. (Difficulty Factor 4.)
- Most difficult is the sewing of mated, irregular, three-dimensional shapes. (Difficulty Factor 25.)

One difficulty mentioned is the likelihood that complete mating cannot be achieved before sewing and therefore the need for breaking a sewing operation into sections with a sew – mate – sew sequence.

*Accurate stacking so that subsequent operations can be performed on the combined piece* Again the same type of analysis emerges:

- A flat piece with a straight edge. (Difficulty Factor 1.)
- A flat piece with an irregular shape. (Difficulty Factor 2.)
- A three-dimensional irregular piece. (Difficulty Factor 5.)

Even though the orders of difficulty quoted are achieved by judgment and are therefore to some extent subjective, this is a remarkable analysis, taking the understanding of what takes place in sewing operations a lot further than hitherto. It is clear that as sewing operations move away from an aligned stack, straight edges and two dimensions, the difficulties are compounded (in other words as sewing operations move away from cutting and progress along the line). The 'Rink' demonstration device actually constructed involved no order of difficulty higher than 2. The researchers then ranked a proposed automated series of operations for the manufacture of shirts and of work trousers. Operations such as set collar, close collar, set sleeve and hem bottom on the shirt were ranked as high as 285, and some operations on the flies of trousers as high as 212.

Another major research project, funded by the Pfaff Company, was the transfer street, designed to carry out all operations on a left shirt front, including front edge folding, buttonholing, pocket attaching and hemming. A similar transfer street performed the shorter series of operations on the right front. The cut stack of shirt fronts was clamped in a tray and delivered to the machine. Pick up from the tray was by pressure-sensitive adhesive tape; it was then placed on a plate which moved the single front to the folder. After this, belts fed the fronts to subsequent operations. Pre-folded and pressed pockets were fed from magazines and transferred in a clamp device to the machine for attaching pockets. In all the automatic handling devices the work piece was oriented in direction and plane by controlling it from an aligned cut stack. Control over mating similarly derived from exact location in a cut stack. Control during sewing was through clamps. The machine as a whole never became commercially success-ful; it provided, in contrast to the Little report, a great deal of the technology that led for instance to automatic pocket setters, sequen-tial buttonholers and buttonsewers and to pick up and disposal devices. Again none of these operations attempted anything with a higher order of difficulty than 1 or 2 in the Little hierarchy.

Neither of these developments attempted more than relatively simple handling of standardised parts. Later developments have turned their attention to robotics and the concepts of 'flexible manufacturing', which are more in line with the needs of a fashion industry.

A robot is a reprogrammable, mechanical manipulator. A robot has to have a memory and must be capable of being programmed to repeat an operation precisely and continuously until reprogrammed. It must be capable of moving in three dimensions or two planes plus a rotary movement.

Research during the 1980s recognised five problems that must be solved before robots could ever undertake a significant proportion of the operations in clothing manufacture:

- The recognition of arbitrarily shaped objects.
- Ply-separation and pick up in a controlled manner of both large and small two-dimensional flexible garment parts.
- Alignment of flexible parts to each other and to the assembly machine in the same operation.
- Realignment of parts during the operation without loss of control.
- Sensing the need for, and taking appropriate corrective action during the operation.

In terms of robot capabilities, 258 operations on eight garment types were analysed and it was concluded that if there was a major invest-ment in research and development to solve these five problems, it would be possible to automate 37 per cent of the operations on these garments. However, these represented only two-dimensional opera-tions. The remaining three-dimensional operations would remain beyond the capabilities of robot technologies in the foreseeable future. Despite this widely held view, research proceeded on a number of fronts.

In the area of vision systems for the recognition of arbitrarily shaped objects, Taylor and Taylor (1992) describe several methods of using cameras to scan garment parts to identify their type and orientation, either at the beginning of an assembly sequence or at a later stage. Depending on the subsequent operation to be performed, the part may be moved to correct an erroneous orientation, perhaps by a robot, or sewing may take place correctly regardless of orientation.

A paper by Taylor and Koudis (1987) analysed the handling activities of typical sewing operations in a similar manner to that given in Fig. 4.16 and suggests that the difficulty of automating this handling may be assessed by imagining the results of trying to perform such operations manually but with eyes closed and perfectly numb fingers. An operator separating and picking up fabrics with the fingers generally uses three techniques – pinch, peel and rub singly or in combination, and it is these techniques that are reflected in the 'pick and place' devices that have been developed.

Taylor and Koudis (1987) describe five different methods that have been developed to separate fabric plies: vacuum, adhesives, pinching, pins and air jets. A very high degree of reliability is required in any devices that are developed since, if the separation process was required once for each time a three-second operation took place, a reliability of only 95 per cent would give on average one failure per minute. An operator would need to be available continuously to rectify these intermittent failures. Factors that affect the separation process are the cohesive forces between layers, such as could occur in a stack of knitted cotton which has been compressed at the cutting stage, and the degree to which the edges are bound together, either by the edges fusing during cutting or because of interlocking fibres.

A further review of the devices available to the industry in the USA in 1987 is provided by a report to the Apparel Research Committee published in that year. This gives a classification of limp fabric handling devices which can be used to define standard and specialised equipment. The classification indicates how they achieve the activities of ply separation, ply removal, transport and orientation and registration.

The pinching concept of ply separation is exemplified by the Clupicker, one of the most successful pick-and-place devices developed, which is manufactured by Cluett Peabody & Co. Ltd; it is designed to be adjustable to cope with a wide range of fabrics. It has a picking wheel with a rough surface which rotates and causes the top ply to slide against the second ply. This creates a fold of cloth which enters a shoe adjacent to the wheel and is gripped. Retaining fingers drop to hold the remainder of the stack and prevent the picker from taking two plies at a time. When the picker lifts, it takes the top ply with it. Placing is basically the reverse process. Picking speeds of 12 pieces per minute are feasible with this machine. Multiple pickers would be used on larger garment parts – for example, four would be used on a shirt front.

Brotherton and Tyler (1986) describe an investigation into Clupicker performance in which they found it to be generally very reliable, provided it was supplied with cut stacks with accurately aligned edges. One fabric gave significant problems only with different picking performance between different colours. Subsequent investigation of this fabric with the Kawabata KES-f surface tester showed a surprisingly large difference in surface roughness between the two colours of the same fabric. The general conclusion formed from this investigation was that much basic work on the fabric/machine interface still needed to be done.

Further work in the area of fabric handling is reported by Iype and Porat (1989), Govindaraj et al. (1992), Ono et al. (1992), and Leung et al. (1992).

Other developments in recent years have returned to the earlier idea of the transfer line but with new options for piece identification by means of vision systems and for movement by means of robotics. The Textile/Clothing Technology Corporation, known as [TC]², was set up in the USA in 1980 to investigate the automation of apparel manufacturing in an attempt to achieve substantial reductions in costs. By 1985 a laboratory prototype machine had been built at the Draper Laboratories, the contract research organisation to whom the initial work had been given. The Singer Company then took over to translate the technical success into a commercially viable system. The sections of the line consisted of:

♦ an automatic loader to insert parts to be loaded into the transfer line
♦ a viewing table that allows the automatic vision system to recognise the parts
♦ a robot that can fold and align the edges
♦ a transfer door that slides the parts to the sewing station
♦ a sewing unit with feed belts and a sewing machine under computer control

Lines were planned to assemble a complete jacket sleeve or trouser leg, and which would need three vision systems, two or three folding robots, and three sewing stations. This work is described in papers by Abernathy and Pippins (1986), Bray and Vento (1986), and Tyler (1989). Tyler identified the most difficult area of the system to be the folding robot, as the placing part of the pick and place operation has generally received less study and evaluation than the picking part. One machine that did get as far as production trials joined backs of jackets. This is illustrated in Fig. 4.18. This machine was used to align edges but not to fold and refold.

The Japanese TRAASS (Technology Research Association for Automatic Sewing Systems) project, some of which is described in the

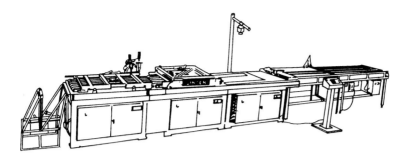

**Figure 4.18** The [TC]² coatback machine.

work by Ono *et al.* (1992), was active for ten years and produced some robotic systems for the sewing operations in making ladies' blazers. Marlowe (1992), in commenting on this, suggests that although technical solutions may, in many cases, be in sight, the equipment has so far been of such extreme complexity as to cast grave doubt on the economic viability of the systems envisioned. In his paper, which is mainly on the future of programmable sewing, he describes systems for monitoring thread tension and sewing faults such as mis-stitching while it is happening, for automatic switching of presser foot type when garment type changes, and for pre-programming such parameters as stitch length, presser foot pressure and top-feed ratio. He suggests that these more modest developments could reduce significantly sewing room changeover time between different batches of work and improve a factory's ability to respond quickly to changes in demand. Such incremental improvements appear to him to offer more realistic prospects of commercial benefit to the industry than the tantalising mirage of robotic systems, commercial exploitation of which seems likely to remain beyond our grasp, even well into the next millennium.

The 1980s saw research into automated, robotised systems in several countries proceeding with limited but important success, driven largely by an increasing need to react better to the economic pressures of cheap imports into those countries. Those same ten years saw extensive changes in large areas of the clothing industry caused by changes in the retailing scene, changes which require greater flexibility and improved speed of response.

Alongside this has been the marked globalisation of trade, with the US and Europe importing large volumes of clothing products from low-cost-labour countries. The conclusion can now be drawn that the 'equipment technology' route to competitiveness does not deliver a competitive advantage. The key problems have been engineering (the difficulties of controlling limp materials), the volatile market (the phasing out of mass production), and economic (the low value-added nature of clothing production).

Technological innovation will no doubt continue. However, the emphasis is likely to be on flexibility: integrating information, skilled operators, and sophisticated single-operation workstations to deliver more responsive manufacturing.

# Chapter Five
# Garment Accessories and Enhancements

The items and processes to be discussed in this chapter are those components, other than the main fabric of the garment, which are an essential part of the construction of the garment or which act as trimmings or fastenings of some kind.

As far as the separate items are concerned, no one term is in universal use to denote them. To many people, the word *component* includes the sections of main fabric that make up the garment as well as the additional items. The word *trim* tends to have decorative overtones, although many items are purely functional. Even that can change with fashion as the humble shoulder pad has shown, having swung with fashion from being a hidden support in tailored garments to being an ostentatious addition to a wide variety of garments. Many items are primarily fastenings but unless they are totally hidden they often provide decoration as well.

The total number of items available for use in garments in addition to the main fabric is extremely large and it is neither possible nor necessary to describe them all. Sewing threads are described elsewhere because their importance in terms of overall garment construction merits separate consideration. However, embroidery threads are discussed here, as their function is decorative rather than structural. In addition to traditional embroidery, several other decorative techniques are considered here: stencil embroidery, laser appliqué, motifs and badges, and sequins. Interlinings are divided into those sewn into the garment and those fused. The technology of fusing is sufficiently important that it is also given separate consideration. For the rest, it is proposed to discuss a selection of those that are most important and used most commonly.

The aspects of these items that are important are the functions they serve, the materials from which they are made, the methods by which they become part of the garment – i.e. are they attached to or applied to it? – and the performance properties that they must have. Their materials and performance properties are of importance only in the current context where they are relevant to garment construction, being otherwise more appropriate to a separate study of the properties of all clothing materials. However, a brief summary of the most important performance properties of these items will be given at the end of the chapter.

The accessories and enhancements that we will discuss are:

♦ labels
♦ decoration (embroidery, motifs and badges, sequins)
♦ fabrics for support and insulation (linings, interlinings, wadding, shoulder pads)
♦ narrow fabric trims (lace, braid, elastic, seam binding and tape)
♦ fastenings (hook and loop fastenings, eyelets and laces, zips, buttons, tack buttons, snap fasteners and rivets)

In most cases, the equipment used can be regarded as a modification of garment assembly machinery.

## Labels

No garment can be sold without some kind of label attached to it. Labelling listing fibre content is mandatory, size labelling is clearly necessary, and country of origin marking, though no longer required in every case, is likely to continue in extensive use. Care labelling is generally a voluntary rather than a legal requirement, but its use is on the increase as retailers try to ensure that garments do not fail the consumer as a result of incorrect action. Few manufactures or retailers would wish to sell a garment without including their brand name and, in addition, garments often carry information identifying the manufacturer who supplied the retailer and the date of manufacture.

Textile product labels have six main uses:

♦ informing consumers at the time of purchase, so that better decisions are made
♦ providing a service to customers regarding the care of the products
♦ a design feature, giving the product a brand identity (as part of a marketing strategy)
♦ stating that the product conforms to certain environmental standards
♦ identifying the flammability risk to help minimise injury
♦ incorporating a security tag to deter theft

Legislation sets out to promote standardisation in the marketplace and is concerned primarily with giving relevant information to consumers at the point of purchase. The rationale for knowing the fibre content is that this is difficult for consumers to determine for themselves, but is important to know to care for the product. A care labelling standard exists in Europe, EN 23758/94 (published by the European Committee for Standardization), which is identical to that published by the International Organization for Standardization, ISO 3758/91. A system of graphic symbols is used to provide information that is essential for the proper care of garments. US care labels are regulated by the Federal Trade Commission (http://www.ftc.gov) and use symbols approved by ASTM (American Society for Testing and Materials Standards).

Several countries have developed their own legislation on specific aspects of labelling, in some cases requiring flammability information. For example, in the UK, the Nightwear (Safety) Regulations 1985 are applicable to babies', children's and adults' nightwear. These regulations are made under the Consumer Safety Act 1978 and cover labelling, advertising and testing (BS 5722).

The voluntary aspects of labelling generally work well, as few manufacturers or retailers would wish to sell a garment without including their brand name, and few would want to supply a garment without some guidance on its care.

The majority of the items that are traditionally called labels are sewn into garments. The type of label and its cost are closely related to the type of garment and the level of the market in which it is selling.

The labels with the highest standard of appearance are *woven to a narrow width* with the necessary information woven into them as a jacquard design. They normally give the company's name and the garment size and fitting, and they are used in men's and women's outerwear and tailored garments, especially at the more expensive end of the market. In made-to-measure garments, the individual purchaser's name is sometimes embroidered on the label using a computer-controlled embroidery machine. These labels are usually sewn flat to a facing or lining, with the two raw edges turned in. Machines are available to sew the required rectangle of stitching automatically with a lockstich. Alternatively, a straight or zig-zag stitch may be used at both narrow ends.

The least expensive labels are *printed* on a large area of woven, thermoplastic fabric and *heat sealed to the narrow width* required. They can be delivered to the garment manufacturer as a roll of individual labels to be cut apart by hand, or already cut and sealed to length. As we mentioned before, these sealed edges are a frequent cause of discomfort when worn against the skin. These labels may be

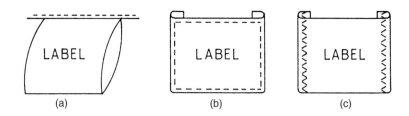

**Figure 5.1** Methods of sewing labels to garments. (a) Sewn flat; (b) rectangular sewing with automated machine; (c) sewn using zig-zag stitching.

sewn flat on to a facing, but are usually folded and inserted under the stitching of a superimposed seam or under the edge of a collar seam. They may be supplied ready folded. Examples of labels sewn to garments are shown in Fig. 5.1.

Garments often carry a label in more than one position. A lady's coat, for example, may have a woven label giving brand name and size sewn flat to the facing and a printed label inserted into the side seam of the lining giving the fibre content and care instructions. A common compromise to reduce the number of labels is to use jacquard weaving for constant information and overprinting for variable details.

Small, woven labels carrying a maker's name or logo are frequently inserted into a seam on the outside of a garment and are designed to show. They are commonly used on jeans and other casual wear.

## Decoration

### Embroidery

Embroidery is a decorative pattern superimposed on an existing fabric by machine stitching using polyester, cotton or rayon threads, or hand needlework using linen, cotton, wool, silk, gold, or silver thread. Open-width fabrics are embroidered using schiffli machines, whereas cut parts and garments are embroidered using multi-head machines.

A lustrous appearance is generally preferred for embroidery. Two types of embroidery thread dominate the machine embroidery market: polyester and rayon. Both are continuous filament threads with high lustre and can carry bright colours. As an alternative to rayon, mercerised cotton or spun polyester threads may be used. The embroidery designer has to consider end use and aesthetics when choosing threads.

According to Coats, a supplier of embroidery threads, the following factors should be considered at the thread selection stage: eco-

Embroidery thread comparison

| Thread type<br><br><br>Property | Continuous filament trilobal polyester | Spun polyester | Mercerised cotton | Mercerised cotton-covered corespun | Filament rayon |
|---|---|---|---|---|---|
| Sheen | excellent | poor | good | good | excellent |
| Sewability | excellent | excellent | excellent | excellent | excellent |
| Economics | good | excellent | excellent | excellent | fair |
| Abrasion resistance | excellent | good | poor | excellent | poor |
| Strength | excellent | good | fair | good | poor |
| Colourfastness to sunlight | excellent | excellent | good | good | good |
| Colourfastness to bleach | excellent | excellent | poor | poor | poor |

**Figure 5.2** Comparison of embroidery threads.

nomics, abrasion resistance, strength, colourfastness to sunlight, and colourfastness to bleach. Coats provide Fig. 5.2 as a comparison of popular thread types. Some of the fastness to bleach problems can be reduced by an appropriate choice of dyes.

As a working rule-of-thumb, about 6 m of embroidery thread is consumed for every 1000 embroidery stitches, and about 2 m of bobbin thread. The bobbin thread tension is set much tighter than the embroidery thread tension, so that only the latter appears on the surface of the fabric.

Many common embroidery problems are caused by an incorrect thread tension or a slightly bent or burred needle. However, garment technologists should give most attention to the way the embroidery design is translated into a sewing programme. There is usually some kind of trade off between cost and visual appearance, and in many cases, the embroidery looks poor because of inadequacies in the conversion of the design to the sewing program.

Regarding machinery, single-head, three-head, six-head and multi-head machines are produced to serve the needs of both small-lot manufacturing and mass production. Modern machinery operates at speeds of over 1000 stitches per minute. Variants include the size of the sewing area, the number of needles, features to assist changeover and reduce downtime, electronic control and the provision of programmability.

Embroidery may require the use of a backing fabric to ensure a uniform appearance of stitching. Backings are normally non-woven and may be 'tearaways' (removed afterwards by tearing loose material) or 'cutaways' (removed by trimming with scissors). Tearaway backings are preferred for economy of both materials and labour. Cutaway backings are used with higher quality embroidery designs.

Stencil embroidery uses the same computer-aided design (CAD) software to control both the embroidery machinery and a laser cutter. The cutter is used to produce stencils in a contrast fabric, and the embroidery machine sews the outline of the stencil on the garment. The stencil is then placed in the correct position as an appliqué and the embroidery machine is used to sew around the edges and complete the other parts of the design. This technique reduces the use of embroidery for covering large areas – a process that is costly and more susceptible to quality failure.

Miller (1995) has identified examples of poor embroidery that occur in three different areas: the quality of stitching, the quality of punching and the quality of design. The poor quality stitching can be traced to the embroidery machining operation, for example ends not trimmed properly, joining threads not trimmed properly, and uneven fabric stretching when loading. The poor quality punching relates to the digitising process, taking an image and representing it in electronic form. Punching needs to take account of the thread being used, the size of the design, and the fabric being embroidered. Failure to address these issues can lead to embroidery that does not adequately cover the background fabric, where details are too prominent visually and detract from the design, and where the fabric deforms because it is poorly matched with the design. Printed images are two-dimensional, whereas embroidery is a three-dimensional structure. Factors such as stitch direction, stitch colour, stitch length and stitch type must all be considered when preparing electronic instructions for a programmable embroidery machine. Poor designs tend to occur when embroidery is perceived as an 'add-on' feature, with the primary purpose of enhancing the value of a garment. The embroidery then tends to be abstracted from the whole garment, rather than integrated within an overall design. The resultant problems may relate to the size, the placement, the thread colours, the design theme and the ability of the wearer to relate the embroidery to the end use of the garment.

There is a challenging interface here between design, embroidery technology and garment production. Miller (1995) suggests that the apparent simplicity of computerised systems has encouraged novices to become responsible for punching embroidery designs, and that there is a great need for improved education and training in these areas.

Nergis and Özipek (1999) have investigated how laundering affects the dimensional stability of embroidered knitted fabrics. Area shrinkages were found to increase slightly with machine speeds, which were 350, 450 and 650 stitches per minute. The researchers suggested that the higher machine speeds introduced larger local distortions of the base fabrics, which were subsequently relieved by laundering. There was no discernible effect of thread tension, which varied between 20 and 80 g. Whilst the dominant dimensional changes were due to the fabrics selected for testing, the additional shrinkages associated with the embroidery were not insignificant, so this quality issue needs to be explored during product development.

## Motifs and badges

The term *motif* is often used to describe a decorative addition to a garment, but the use of motifs carrying a company's name, trade mark or logo is now widespread. Consequently, the subject of labels and the subject of motifs cannot be separated easily.

   Motifs are available in a wide variety of types, sizes and methods of attachment but the range will be limited here to small, decorative items that are attached flat to the outside of garments. The majority are either an all-over embroidery, a section of fabric with some embroidery on it, or a section of fabric neatened or sealed in some way at the edges and carrying a printed design. Many have special threads woven into the back to make them suitable for attachment by ultrasonic welding, the method for which is described in Chapter 6. This gives a secure attachment while at the same time maintaining the slightly three-dimensional structure that is an attractive feature of embroidered motifs. Printed motifs are often designed to be attached by a heat transfer process for which a special small heated press is used. Motifs may be attached by sewing but to do it freehand is likely to be slow and potentially inaccurate. For companies sewing large quantities of such items, lockstitch machines are available which can be programmed to sew the particular profile required.

   As programmable embroidery machines become more readily available, faster and more flexible, their use is tending to increase at the expense of attaching pre-made motifs. Direct embroidery on to the garment generally gives a more subtle and flexible motif with a higher quality appearance than sewing or welding on of a separate motif.

   This area of garment decoration has seen much innovation in recent years. For example, lasers can be used to 'engrave' the fabric surface without damaging it. The loose fibres are burned away and the engraved fabric has a different texture and colour from its surroundings.

## Sequins

Sequins come in a wide range of shapes and are usually made of plastic. They generally have a shiny, metallic finish, but some are nearly transparent and some are iridescent. Typical diameter ranges are 6–16mm. Sequins are used wherever colour, sparkle or glitter is desirable. Applications are found in partywear, dancewear, bridalwear, underwear, and costume and clothing with an ethnic design. Sequins are often attached to embroidery with, or as an alternative to, beads.

Traditionally, the method of assembly makes use of a special device called a tambour hook, often with an embroidery thread. They may be sewn in rows using large backstitches, applying one sequin with every stitch. Clothing manufacturers can use a purpose-built chainstitch machine to sew sequins one at a time, using a special foot to hold the sequins. Alternatively, pre-strung sequins or sequins attached to a backing fabric can be sewn using a lockstitch, chainstitch or zig-zag machine. The machine is fitted with a fine needle so that it penetrates the sequins without causing damage. The zig-zag machine should swing wider than the width of the sequins in order to secure them to the fabric. Fig. 5.3 shows a child's tee shirt decorated with sequins and embroidery.

**Figure 5.3** Child's tee shirt. The flower is made of sequins and beads. The stalk and the brand identity are embroidered.

# Fabrics for support and insulation

## Linings

Linings are generally a functional part of a garment, being used variously to maintain the shape of a garment, to improve the hang and comfort by allowing it to slide over other garments, to add insulation, and to cover the inside of a garment of complicated construction to make it neat. In many cases linings are selected to match the garment so as to be unobtrusive, but in others they are chosen to add to the design of the garment even perhaps as a subtle, identifying feature of the brand on an otherwise widely available style.

Linings are available as warp knits, but predominantly they are woven and are made from polyester, polyamide, acetate and viscose for use where a slippery material is required, and from cotton, polyester/cotton and wool or wool mixtures in plain or brushed versions where decoration or warm handle is required. Where non-slippery lining fabrics are used in garments, they are generally used only for the body, the sleeve being lined with a more slippery material to make putting on and taking off easier.

Lining material can be used for small garment sections such as pockets and for complete garments, either fully bagged out, i.e. sewn down all the way round, or sewn to the facing and open at the bottom.

For small sections such as patch pockets or pockets flaps it is necessary for the lining to remain hidden and it is in the construction of such parts as these that jigs with fulling bars as previously described would be used. For jackets, coats and raincoats the outer garment must not be constrained in any way by tightness in the lining and in these garments there is normally extra lining fabric in the body and the sleeve. In skirt and trouser linings, the stability of the outer garment in wear may be assisted by the lining being slightly smaller than the garment.

Linings made from polyester, polyamide or viscose can, in some constructions, be prone to the problem of seam slippage described earlier. Since these fabrics also tend to fray easily, a loss of seam allowance by fraying can contribute to seam slippage and it may be necessary to neaten seam edges during lining construction even though the garment and its lining will be totally bagged out and the lining edges will not be seen. Where a coat and its lining are open at the hem it is common to neaten the lining edges. In practice, if safety stitch machines are available, linings can be joined and neatened simultaneously at no extra cost except for the thread.

The actual method of attaching linings to outer garments depends on the garment type and on whether it is fully or partially bagged out. It also depends on whether the entire construction must be machine-sewn or whether some part of it will be finished by hand. Where the lining is left unattached at the hem on a garment such as a raincoat, it can be machine-sewn to the body and sleeve facings and turned through. If it is required to close the garment at the hem as well, a gap in the seam of the sleeve lining can be left through which the garment can be turned. This gap can then be topstitched closed on a lockstitch machine and it will not show on the outside. On men's jackets the body lining is normally attached to the jacket and, separately, the sleeve lining to the sleeve at the cuff. After attaching of jacket sleeves to jacket, each sleeve lining is attached to the body lining and turned through a gap in the forearm seam or vent, these gaps then being topstitched closed.

## Interlinings

Interlinings are used to support, reinforce and control areas of garments such as collars, cuffs, waistbands, hems, facings and the fronts of jackets and coats. They may be sewn into the garment or attached by means of fusing, the technology of which will be described in the next chapter. Although fusing is now very common as a method of garment construction, there are many fabrics that are not suitable for fusing, as well as small manufacturers who do not have the requisite equipment. The complexity of interlinings used varies greatly between tailored wear, especially menswear, and other types of garments.

In the non-tailored garments often referred to as 'light clothing', i.e. blouses, dresses, skirts, and lightweight jackets and coats, interlinings are sometimes laid into a garment section such as a collar or cuff and sewn around the edges when the part is constructed. They may also be joined to facings and waistbands when the edges are neatened and run into placket fronts via a folder. In all these cases they do not require to be stitched, other than in the seaming that will be part of the necessary garment construction. This is because, in general, they do not cover a very large area and consequently do not need attaching to the garment part they are to support other than at the edges. All that is necessary is to select an interlining which, by virtue of its weight, construction and fibre content, will perform satisfactorily in the wearing and washing or dry-cleaning of the garment.

In tailored garments, interlinings play a very important part in creating the shape of the garment and smoothing out the contours of the body. A man's jacket has an interlining all down the front which must be fastened invisibly into place, with others at hems, vents and sleeve heads, along with substantial canvases in the chest area.

Interlinings are available in a wide variety of weights and constructions to match the properties of the garment fabrics they will support. They can be woven or non-woven, both of which can be constructed to give a different softness or resilience in different directions.

Woven interlinings are, most commonly, plain weave construction. In the lighter weights they may have a cotton warp and weft, giving a soft handle in both directions, or a cotton warp and a viscose weft to aid crease recovery and retention of shape. More substantial constructions may include hair, wool and viscose blends. Finishing processes are used which may include a crease-resistant finish to give good crease shedding properties as well as stability to shrinkage.

Non-woven interlinings are made directly from textile fibres and are held together by mechanical, chemical, thermal or solvent means or by a combination of these. The fibres used can be viscose rayon to provide the harder handles, polyester to provide suppler handles, nylon to provide resilience and bulk, or some combination of these fibres to give specific physical and mechanical properties.

Non-woven interlinings have different properties according to the way in which the fibres are laid in making the material. The fibres may be laid at random for all-round stability, parallel to give stability in one direction with extensibility in the direction at right angles, cross to give extensibility in both directions (making them suitable for soft outer fabrics), and composite to give combinations of properties for general purpose interlinings. A variety of methods is available to bond the fibres together within the material and this also affects the interlining properties.

## Wadding

Wadding or batting are the names given to the fibre fillings used in garments where warmth is required without great weight. They aim to simulate the warmth and lightness of down, but with the advantage of washability and speed of drying as well as lower cost. The fibre used most commonly is polyester, although polypropylene is also used where a garment will not be subjected to the heat of dry-cleaning. For maximum insulation, as much air as possible must be trapped among or within the fibres, which must be as light and resilient as possible. The fibres themselves are of various diameters and may be solid or hollow with the possibility of one or more hollow channels within them. Different weights and thicknesses of batting are possible as a result of different densities of fibre material, different thicknesses of fibre, and different densities of fibre within the batt. At some stage in the construction of a garment, the batting must be quilted, i.e. sewn to an outer fabric. Present fashion demands that this quilting, where it shows on the outside of the garment, should be spaced as widely as possible. The more closely spaced traditional quilting does not require that the fibres in the batt are attached to each other in any way because they are held sufficiently in place by the quilting itself. The further apart the stitching is, the greater is the need for some kind of binding agent in the wadding, enabling the fibres to adhere together and not drop towards the garment hemline or the lower part of a stitched cube, box (the traditional diamond shape), or channel. The necessary bonding can be achieved in a variety of ways, mainly by the addition of a resin or the use of heat bonding. Heat-bonded battings are softer and are the result of the inclusion of a proportion of fibres of lower melting point or the making of each fibre in a bi-component form.

With such a variety of waddings available, care is needed in their selection and in the choice of garment construction methods if the designer's intentions and the performance requirements of a garment are to be realised. The main factors governing the choice of wadding are the amount of bulk appropriate to the style, the amount of insulation that must be provided, and the cost. Wadding is normally thinner around the limbs than the trunk. In terms of making up, the style may require the quilting to be visible on the outside or the inside or on both or on neither. Where the filling is sandwich-quilted, with garment fabric both sides as is the case in some reversible garments, and where it is quilted before garment construction commences, extensive use is made of binding to neaten edges and seams, sometimes adding contrast decoration in the process. Where an outer or lining fabric is wadded and quilted but will then be made up with a further loose layer of lining or outer fabric, or where the wadding is only attached to the fabric of the garment part around the edges, awaiting quilting when it has been bagged out with a further layer of fabric, the wadding may require a surface bonding or a light non-woven backing to assist cutting and sewing. Loose fibre battings could clog the moving parts of the sewing machine, especially the feed dog. If sewing must take place with one side of the wadding uncovered, a large, unjointed presser foot adjacent to the wadding is likely to cause the least problems.

It will be clear that quilting may take place at various stages in the construction of a garment and may even be one of the very last stages. Large garment sections such as jacket backs may be made with the wadding attached to the outer fabric just at the edges and then bagged out with the lining. The sections are normally then quilted in large squares or rectangles before the garment seams are joined.

Closely spaced quilting would be very costly if done at this stage as a multi-needle machine could not be used. The dimensions of the quilting will be determined by garment style and the requirement to support the wadding. Special feed mechanisms of the types described previously may be needed to overcome problems of creepage in sewing through such bulky materials. Compound feed is particularly useful for keeping the fabrics and wadding together without an excessive need for handling on the part of the operator.

When selecting fabrics to use with wadding it must be remembered that it has requirements similar to that of down in that, unless the correct kind of closely woven fabric is used over it, the fibre ends will work their way though the interstices of the weave and appear on the surface.

For showerproof garments, the problem of water penetration exists where an outer fabric is quilted. This may be overcome with thin wadding by the use of stitchless quilting by ultrasonic welding in the kind of box designs normally achieved by sewing.

## Shoulder pads

Shoulder pads have long been a standard item in tailored garments both for women and for men, but from time to time they become a fashion item and are seen in a much wider range of garments including knitwear and lightweight blouses.

The pads themselves are available in a variety of shapes and thicknesses to suit garment styles and to give the requisite amount of bulk, and in a variety of materials and constructions, depending largely on whether they are required to be washable or only dry-cleanable, and whether they are to be used in a lined or unlined garment.

The simplest are made from foam with a lightweight knitted polyamide covering; these are used in unlined garments such as blouses, dresses and knitwear. They are tacked to appropriate seam turnings using a buttonsew machine and are both washable and dry-cleanable. If a particularly neat appearance inside the garment is required, the pads might be covered with the actual garment fabric but it is essential to preserve the three-dimensional shape of the pad. Washable and dry-cleanable pads for lined garments often consist of an outer layer of non-woven material sandwiched over a foam or fibre inner. Large stitches through all the layers hold the pad together. They are attached by methods similar to those for the unlined garments.

For lined garments that will be dry-cleaned only, such as men's tailored jackets, the pads are normally built up of several layers of foam or various non-woven materials, and these layers may be needle-punched together. The pad is attached to the edge of the jacket at the armhole seam and also to the interlining, forming the chest piece, and accurate positioning is vital. Many companies now make use of pads on which there are small areas of adhesive resin of the type used in fusible interlinings. These pads can be attached to the jacket using an iron or, to be really sure that the jacket is in the correct shape that it will be when worn, using the type of shaped shoulder press that is common in menswear production. A flap can be folded back on the pad so that, after tacking into position by means of the adhesive, it can then be sewn to the garment without the sewing passing through all the thicknesses.

## Narrow fabric trims

### Lace, braid and elastic

The narrow trimmings generally referred to as lace and braid can be various natural and synthetic materials or mixtures. However, lace is predominantly made of polyester, polyamide, polyester/cotton or cotton; and braid is predominantly made of the same fibres plus wool and acrylic. They can also contain elastane fibres to give stretch and recovery. Their use is normally decorative although it may be functional as well. The term 'elastic' is being reserved here for those corded elastics and rubber strips used functionally in garments to draw in part of the garment in an elastic manner.

#### Lace

The term lace correctly refers to the type of open structure originally made by hand and now available in a variety of machine-made forms. Some are formed from twisted yarns, some are embroideries on net or more solid fabric, and others are knitted. For present purposes, the construction is important for the following reasons. Some types may be so open structured that stitch types such as 101 may not sew them satisfactorily. Some fray on one edge rather than being neat on both sides and these must be neatened during garment construction. This is common with the embroidered fabric known as broderie anglaise. Others have a scalloped edge and for maximum decorative effect must be sewn to the garment along the shape of the scallop.

#### Braid

Braids were originally braided fabrics, produced by interlacing yarns diagonally in a form of plaiting. They were either narrow flat fabrics or the type of narrow tube familiar as shoelaces. Flat braids of this type are still used and in wool and acrylic they make soft and flexible edgings for binding around medium and heavyweight garments. Since the edges do not fray, the simplest type of bound seam can be used. Corners on the garment would normally be rounded rather than square. The term braid is also used to describe other narrow fabrics that are woven or even knitted. In woven form they are similar to the many forms of ribbon available and in plain as well as jacquard constructions they are often used on children's garments, simply sewn flat with a twin-needle machine of an appropriate needle gauge (spacing).

Although lace and braid would traditionally have been regarded as totally separate in appearance and function, they are available as both stretch and non-stretch materials; in their stretch versions they have a number of similarities. Thus the elastication and decoration of the edges of garments such as ladies' briefs is accomplished simultaneously by using a narrow stretch material that has either the open appearance of a lace or the more solid appearance of a braid. Attachment requires metering of the elastic material as described previously, along with the bottom cover, top and bottom cover or zig-zag stitching in the versions also described earlier.

In the non-stretch version, lace is used frequently as a decorative edging on lingerie in a seam of class 7. If the lace is straight along the joining edge it can be attached with stitch type 406 or with 304, the former being necessary if the garment fabric is woven, and on the straight of the grain as it would fray along the edge. In many cases it is a shaped or scalloped edge of lace that is attached to the garment and for maximum effect the edge of the garment needs to be cut away to match it. This is slow and difficult to do by hand but machines are available which have a trimming knife operating below a plate adjacent to the needle. The operator joins the lace to the fabric with the lace above the plate and the fabric below and guides the machine to follow the shape of the lace, the knife trimming the fabric away just before they are sewn together. Stitch type 304, the lockstitch zig-zag, is normally used for flexibility of sewing shape. The shape of the seam is such that even on a woven fabric there is no significant fraying and no further neatening is necessary.

In virtually every case where braid, lace or elastic is applied to a garment it is applied at a stage in the construction such that it can be attached to a reasonably flat section of garment from an open edge to an open edge. This assists the use of edge guides in positioning the item and enables it to be fed from a long length on a reel via a rack guide rather than handled in short lengths.

*Elastic*

Where elasticated effects are required locally on garments but without added decoration, corded elastic of various widths and even flat rubber strips are used. Corded elastics contain rubber or elastane threads, which provide high stretch and recovery. Elastane is more common nowadays than natural rubber because of its greater durability. A typical use is on the waist of a loose-fitting dress or at the wrist of a sleeve that ends in a frill. A 3 or 4 mm elastic would be used and it would most commonly be sewn using a 304 lockstitch zig-zag. This stitches across the whole width of the elastic, which gives greater comfort than a straight lockstitch as it prevents the elastic rolling into a ridge. In addition, an alternating slightly pleated effect is produced on the outside of the garment, which adds to the decorative effect of the elastication.

Flat strips of rubber are used to provide control on the edges of garments such as swimwear and men's briefs. On swimwear they are normally attached to the fabric edge by overedging; the hem is then turned up and secured by sewing with stitch types 304 or 406, depending on the appearance required. On men's briefs, the elastic is inserted into the binding on the legs and waist as it is attached. This type of elastic can be supplied already joined into a ring of the required size for the hem, if the method of garment construction allows it to be used in that form, rather than open.

## Seam binding and tape

In some types of garment, neatening of seam edges by means of overedging is inadequate or inappropriate and the fabric edges are bound with bias cut strips of woven fabric, often a satin construction, passed through a folder. A typical garment requiring this type of finish is an unlined wool jacket or coat that is not constructed to be reversible but where a double cloth has been used, perhaps plain on the outside and check on the inside. The inside is intended to be seen and a binding gives a suitable finish. Another use is in the finish of trouser pockets. As with binding on the outer edges of reversible garments, sharp corners such as those occurring on facings are rounded.

Tape is often used along the joining stitching in a superimposed seam if there is a risk that the seam may stretch in wear and either distort the garment or cause the stitching to crack. Typical areas for use are shoulder seams on garments made from knitted fabrics and waist seams on dresses, especially where a flared or gathered skirt is joined on to the bodice. Machines with appropriate feeding systems can be set so that they do not stretch the materials while they are being sewn and in this case the tape can be run on flat from a roll as the seam is sewn. If stretch cannot be controlled during sewing it might be necessary to pre-cut tape pieces to length. The operator then ensures that the garment parts being sewn fit in to the length of tape. This is only possible on fairly short and straight seams; it would be impossible to handle the complete circle of a waist in this freehand manner. For economy, a narrow cotton tape in black or unbleached white is often sufficient although on more expensive garments colour matched ribbon is used. The possible problems of bulk and show-through must be considered and guides will be needed on machines to place the tape or ribbon in the correct position under the seam-joining stitching, e.g. under the 401 stitch in a (401.504) safety stitch.

For constructions such as sleeve-attachment in men's tailored jackets, where varying amounts of ease are needed at different stages in sewing the armhole seam, a programmable upper and lower feed machine can be used to set a tape or cord around the sleeve head with the correct amount of fabric eased on to it, and the sleeve can subsequently be attached to the body of the jacket as if the seam were being sewn flat.

## Fastenings

### Hook and loop fastenings

Hook and loop fastenings, e.g. Velcro, consist of two woven polyamide tapes, one covered with very fine hooks and the other with very fine loops. When pressed together they adhere securely to each other. They are very strong against the kind of shearing forces present in a simple lapped join yet they peel apart easily when required to be undone. Each side is joined to the garment part simply by sewing close to the edge with a lockstitch machine.

Hook and loop fastening is used in a limited number of garment applications, but where it is used its particular properties are extremely valuable. Since any part of one side will fasten to any part of the other it is used for adjustable fastenings such as closing cuffs and ankles on waterproof garments. Another advantage in this context is that it can be opened and closed easily, even when wearing gloves or mittens, and it is useful to provide a secondary, reasonably waterproof closure over zips on such garments. This ease of handling is also useful for disabled people who find buttons or other fastenings difficult to handle or who need additional openings in garments so that they can dress themselves without assistance.

Unfortunately, the ability of the hook side to close anywhere on a section of loop side means that it will also close on any other reasonably fibrous surface. Thus garments fastened with it can, depending on their material, fasten almost anywhere as well as in the right place, and when undone the fabric begins to be damaged by the tearing action of the hook side. Repetition of the attachment of the hook side to items other than its correct opposite number will cause the hook side gradually to acquire a build-up of fluff which limits its effectiveness. The same effect will occur if garments are washed or cleaned without the fastening being closed on itself. Because of these difficulties, it is important to select carefully which side of the fastening to use on which side of a closure and how much of each to use. In adjustable fastenings, a small section of hook side normally moves over a larger section of loop side. Another reason why the fastening has limited use as a substitute for zips or buttons is the poor appearance arising from its relative inflexibility, especially on lightweight garments. At the other extreme, however, it is substantial enough to be used a great deal as a fastening for casual shoes.

## Eyelets and laces

Garments frequently require small holes in them in the form of eyelets for a variety of purposes such as for the prongs of buckles on belts, for ventilation on waterproof garments, for the emergence of drawstrings at waist or around hoods, and for use with lacing as a fastening.

Machines are available of the chainstitch buttonhole type which will stitch a small round hole and these are often used on belts, especially on more expensive raincoats. Since the prong of the buckle is normally of polished metal, the sewn eyelet does not suffer great wear. A more common and more hard-wearing alternative to a sewn eyelet is a metal eyelet and reinforcing washer in brass or steel with a plated or coloured, lacquered surface. Eyelets that are likely to become wet must be rustproof. These eyelets are appropriate to all the uses described above but a special machine is required to attach the two sections that make up the eyelet. The centre of the visible circle of the eyelet has a short tubular projection on the back. The attaching machine presses the two eyelet sections together through the fabric, with the projection through the centre of the reinforcing washer, and spreads out the end of the tubular section over the edge of the washer so that they become held together permanently.

Different sizes of eyelet are available as appropriate to the end use and garment type and it is essential that the material to which they are attached is sufficiently substantial. Underarm ventilation holes do not take any stress and are strong enough applied through a single thickness of any material that is likely to be used, but any application that is to have a drawstring or lacing of any kind through it must be reinforced with another layer of fabric or interlining.

A drawstring or the lacing of a fastening can be one of many materials, from the plaited braid shoelace type described earlier, possibly with filling yarns to make it round, to narrow strips of leather or suede, or to fabric run through a narrow folder producing a spaghetti or topstitched effect. In most cases, these are finished in some way at the cut end, possibly in a sufficiently bulky manner that the end cannot be drawn accidentally through the eyelets. The plastic sealed end common to shoelaces can be used, even on the sewn fabric ties, and the sewn ones might also be tied decoratively in an overhand knot. Where synthetic materials are used, the ends can be cut and sealed simultaneously and, if necessary, knotted afterwards. Another functional and decorative end is provided by the shaped metal or plastic item often referred to as an acorn. Where an end finishing is not used, a drawstring may be sewn to the garment with a short lockstitch tack, for example at the centre back for a waist drawstring tied at the front.

It should be remembered that, in the interests of safety, the *Children's Clothing (Hood Cords) Regulations 1976* prohibit the use of drawstrings in the hoods of all outer garments (e.g. raincoats and anoraks), that measure not more than 44 cm across the chest when laid out flat. An enclosed elastic is normally used.

## Zip fasteners

These are the principal items used in clothing that are partly textile in nature and partly non-textile, hard material. They provide a neat, strong fastening in garments, and can be functional or decorative or both. They provide two edges that will mesh together and resist pulling apart when stressed, on a tape support that can be sewn into the garment. They can vary in the materials of the tape, the form and materials of the meshing sections, and in the overall construction and function of the zip. The latter affects predominantly their methods of attachment to garments.

The major types of zip are:

♦ individual metal teeth
♦ spiral coil
♦ plastic moulded teeth
♦ invisible zips

The tapes are most commonly woven and can be of cotton, polyester, polyamide or mixtures. The meshing sections can be individual teeth of metal, typically brass although aluminium can be used to reduce the cost. For aesthetic reasons, a variety of finishes have been developed: antique brass, black oxidized, nickel, antique nickel, and copper. Alternatively, they can consist of plastic teeth. These are either attached to tape by injection moulding or they are made from a continuous spiral of plastic (polyamide or polyester). Whichever form the teeth take, they must be fastened securely to the tape, and when closed remain securely meshed together against all reasonable lateral forces. When fully opened, an end stop holds the zip together; this must be strong enough to withstand considerable forces when the garment is being put on or taken off. The slider must move smoothly up and down when required, but keep the zip closed against a lateral pull by means of a small stop that rests between the teeth. For ease of sewing to the garment, a construction that gives a flat back to the zip but a well defined ridge of teeth or coil on the face side enables the machinist to sew accurately with the presser foot as a guide.

The slider should be considered the most important part of the zip. It has four parts: the body, the spring, the bridge (or cover) and the pull tab. When selecting the appropriate slider, consideration should be given to convenience of use, functional performance, laundering, and aesthetic appearance. For example, ball and chain sliders or sliders with large pull tabs or rings are usual on skiwear and other outdoor garments because they can be grasped by gloved hands.

Zips are available in a variety of forms, principally:

- made to length with stop and slider
- invisible, made to length with stop and slider
- continuous with added stop and slider
- made to length, open ended with slider
- made to length, open ended with two sliders

The first, which is made to a particular length, is the simplest; these zips are common in ladies' and children's wear. In heavier versions, these zips have teeth of metal or plastic, but in lighter versions a plastic spiral is the norm. An opening of appropriate length is left in a seam as it is joined and the zip is inserted into the opening. When the zip is fully open, some strain should be taken on the backtack at the end of the seam as well as on the stop on the zip. The zip may be concealed by setting it centrally in the seam or to one side, as shown in the seam diagram in Fig. 5.4(i); a zip guard may be included, especially on skirts and trousers.

Special narrow toed or single sided presser feet for sewing zips were described in Chapter 4. These enable the stitching to run closer to the teeth or spiral than the width of a normal presser foot. Skilled operators are required for this work in order to achieve straight stitch-

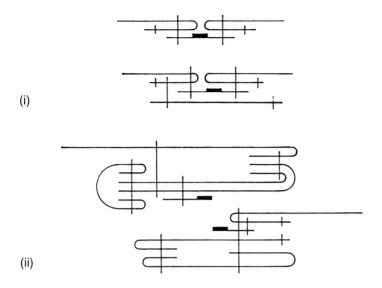

(i)

(ii)

**Figure 5.4** Zip insertion. (i) Concealed skirt zip insertion. (ii) Men's trouser zip fly construction.

ing with even edge-to-edge or overlapped fabric and an avoidance of any stretch in the fabric as it is sewn. Even the common differential feeding effect when a soft fabric is sewn on top of a more rigid one can cause the fabric to be stretched on to the zip, and the garment will then not lie flat in wear. Careless sewing can also insert a twist into the garment if differential feeding occurs as the operator sews down one side of the zip and up the other, leaving the top edges stepped.

Two types of zip that require less skill are the invisible and the continuous zips. Invisible zips have the teeth turned on to the inside of the garment; they are used mainly in ladies' skirts to give a smooth line over the hip with a barely detectable gap in the seam and no visible stitching. Their attachment, using a special presser foot, was described in Chapter 4. Apart from a neat appearance in wear, they offer advantages in terms of operator skill during assembly because the zip is sewn to a single thickness of fabric rather than to a folded edge, with the seam allowance clearly visible; accuracy is easy to obtain. When considering using invisible zips, the design of the garment is important as they cannot be used across a seam such as a yoke or Basque seam on a skirt. The stitching that attaches the zip to the garment is so close to the zip teeth that the extra bulk of a cross seam would cause it to jam. It is also important to ensure these zips are 'fit for purpose', as there have been many cases of side seam failure with invisible zips.

Continuous zips are of the polyamide spiral type and can be purchased either as a reel of closed zip or with the two sides separate.
In the closed form, they can be inserted into a variety of seams, for
example in the back of a child's or lady's dress; a twin-needle machine
can be used. The end stop and the slider are added later by means
of special machines. No top stops are needed, provided there is a
seam across the top as part of the garment's construction. One of
the most important advantages of continuous zip tape, however, is
found when it is used unjoined as it often is in the construction of
men's trousers. It is a common construction sequence with men's
trousers that each leg is assembled completely, with a partly or even
completely finished waistband, and the garment then completed by
joining the crutch seam and the zip. Attaching a length of tape and
spiral to each side of the trouser, flat and in the correct position, is a
simple job compared with attaching a complete zip to the fly section.
The crotch seam can then be joined, the waistband completed
if necessary, and the stop and slider added to the zip. An example
of a typical construction of the fly area of a man's trouser is shown
in Fig. 5.4(ii).

Zips that can be opened at the lower end are required in garments
such as cardigans and jackets which have to be undone completely
rather than stepped into. They are also used when a garment section
might be removed for some situations of wear, e.g. anoraks and ski
jackets with zip-out sleeves or with an inner body-warmer that attaches
by means of a zip. The two sections of the garment can only be joined
or separated when the slider is fully to the bottom of the zip. This
type of zip may have chunky, plastic teeth and slider and be decorative as well as functional.

Insertion of an open-ended zip into a garment can be much easier
than the closed type since the two sides can be separated. This is a
help in the more complicated types of constructions needed for
jackets and anoraks such as where a lining must also be sewn to the
zip. Away from clothing, open-ended zips are seen where the reasons
for their use appear to be entirely connected with construction rather
than function. An example is a tapered sleeping bag, of a type not
designed to attach to another one, where the zip finishes with an open
end immediately above the shaped foot section. There is no functional
need for the zip to separate at the bottom; indeed, if accidentally
separated it is difficult to rejoin because there is so little free movement of the two sides. It appears to be used solely to assist construction in that it enables each side to be sewn on separately.

Zips with two sliders are used on longer length jackets and waistcoats where there would be a strain on the bottom of the zip when
the wearer is seated. Both sliders must be fully to the bottom for the

zip to be joined or separated, but in wear the lower slider can be pulled up and the lower end of the zip opened when required.

Zips supplied to the British market must meet the BS 3084 : 1992 standard. However, most retailers have higher standards, because of past problems from zip failure.

There are legislative restrictions on the amount of nickel allowable in zips linked to BS EN 1811 : 1999 and the EU Nickel Directive 94/27/EC. This has led to the development of chemical finishes that have a nickel appearance. Other regulative constraints concern the toxicity of paint (BS EN 71–1) and the zip fastener test (BS 3084).

## Buttons

Buttons are hardware items used in conjunction with buttonholes for the fastening of garments. They can add decoration as well as providing a closure; buttons can be used alone as decoration.

The variety of materials from which buttons can be made is considerable, including natural wood, bone, horn and mother-of-pearl, and man-made metal, polyester, polyamide, acrylic, urea formaldehyde and casein. In addition, plastic and metal can be combined such as when a metal ring encircles a button, and plastic can be covered with the fabric of the garment. As is normal with such materials, the natural materials provide buttons with some variability in colour and pattern and possibly in size and shape, at a higher price, while the man-made materials are more uniform as well as less expensive. Which is chosen depends largely on the garment type and its market but the prime requirement from the point of view of garment construction is that for situations of moderate-to-high volume production it must be possible to sew on the buttons by machine. This requires that the buttons can be held in a clamp in the machine while sewing takes place; for very high volume production such as that of shirts it requires that they can be fed to this clamp automatically from a hopper system.

Buttons are sewn to garments by means of the type of cam-controlled, automatic-cycle machine described earlier. They make use of single-thread chainstitch, lockstitch or simulated handstitching, the latter being used only on tailored outerwear. Single-thread chainstitch, as explained earlier, offers insecure button attachment, but the machines are in wide use and their replacement with lockstitch machines would be costly.

Buttons that are sewn directly through the face have either two or four holes and it is important that where they are functional rather than decorative they are sewn with a sufficient thread shank that the button is not so tight against the garment that it distorts the buttonhole. On a four-hole button, the direction of sewing does not matter, but on a two-hole button, the stitching should be parallel to the buttonhole to minimise distortion and the need for a long thread shank.

The other type of button available has no holes showing on the face, but has its own shank on the back. This type must be clamped in the machine on its side so that the stitching passes alternately through the hole in the shank and to one side of it. Fabric-covered buttons are also of this shape. A selection of buttons was described when discussing buttonsew machines.

## Tack buttons, snap fasteners and rivets

The use of metal components on garments has increased in recent years, especially with the wide acceptance of denim in jeans, skirts and jackets for casual wear. A sewn button on the waistband of a pair of jeans tends to suffer such abuse that the sewing is quickly over-stressed or abraded and the button becomes detached. The fabric is capable of withstanding considerable stress and there is a need for the strength that can be provided by metal tack buttons or other metal snaps or studs as fastenings and by rivets as reinforcement. Similarly, rivets on pocket corners provide greater strength as well as providing a more interesting decoration than a sewn bar tack.

### Tack buttons

Tack buttons consist of two sections. The outer button fastens with the buttonhole and has a similar appearance to the previously described shank button, except that it is not attached by sewing. The inner tack penetrates the fabric from the inside of the garment and is secured into the shank of the button by means of a special machine. There is not thread to come undone or be abraded and the broad base of the tack spreads the load which is placed on the button when it is in use. The two parts can be brass or steel and the button can be made with a decorative design or logo, but it must be rust proofed. Once attached to the garment, they cannot be moved and it is thus more important that positioning is accurate than it is with sewn buttons. The garment fabric must be sufficiently strong, with the addition of an interlining if necessary, to take the stress to which such a button will be subject.

### Snap fasteners

Snap, press or stud fasteners come in a variety of types. They all consist of four elements: a cap and socket that fit together and form the outer, female part of the fastening, and a stud and post that form the inner, male part of the fastening, not normally seen when the garment is fastened (Fig. 5.5). The cap and post may also consist of prong rings where the fastening is being used in lightweight, non-decorative applications. Prong fasteners are the only type suitable for use on knitted fabrics. This type is suitable for use on infants' playsuits and pyjamas and it is designed to avoid puncturing the fabric with large holes. It also lies completely flat. Failures usually arise from the method of application rather than defects in the fasteners. Typical failures are the result of the material being too thick for the fastener, excessive force used during attachment, and uneven materials. Fasteners should never be attached through a single thickness of material, but a backing fabric should be used, especially with knitted fabrics. The size used must be appropriate to the number of thicknesses and weight of fabric. The rim of the ring must not cross varying thicknesses of fabric and fastening through binding is preferably avoided. A common-sense test is to insert the fingernail between fabric and rim; if this can be done, failure is probable. The sections of a type of snap fastener (in this case the type with a spring in the socket), and the assembly of them, are shown in Fig. 5.6.

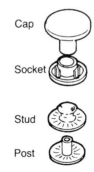

Figure 5.5 Four elements of a snap fastener.

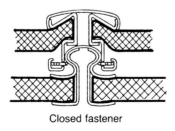

Closed fastener

Figure 5.6 Spring snap fastener.

Snap fasteners can be made from plastic, steel or brass with a design on the cap if required. The metal can be enamelled and thus colour-matched to the garment if required. They can also have plastic caps on an otherwise metal assembly, which gives further design and colour possibilities. They have wide uses, both decorative and functional, and in appropriate sizes and materials are used from heavy denim jackets to infants' stretch suits. They are quick to attach using appropriate machinery which automatically feeds the separate sections into position.

### Rivets

Rivets are used for decoration and reinforcement on garments, mainly jeans, and may consist of one or two sections but in both cases a special machine is required to attach them. When the rivet is used alone, the tubular section on the back of the rivet that is passed through the material is spread out by the machine on the inside of the garment. In the two-part system the rivet is attached to a cap or a washer on the other side, and depending on the appearance required, either side may be used on the outside of the garment. A variation known as a rivet and burr can be used in twos or fours to attach the ends of the metal logo plates used decoratively on jeans.

## Performance properties of components and trims

The performance requirements of the items that are incorporated into garments in addition to the main fabric are largely the same as those of the main fabric but with the additional complication that they comprise a wide variety of materials, many of them non-textile. Garments must be capable of being constructed, worn, and washed and/or dry-cleaned in particular ways and to a particular standard which is appropriate to the end use of the garment and the market it will be sold in. Assuming that an acceptable standard has been set for the main fabric, all other items must be compatible with it.

Where items are textile in nature, the requirements are similar to those for the main fabric. Shrinkage during manufacture and cleaning must be controlled so that the garment retains its size and is not distorted. Other textile performance properties such as strength, pilling, snagging, creasing and abrasion resistance may also be important. Resistance to heat may be important if a garment made wholly or predominantly from natural fibres is trimmed with a synthetic ribbon or lace or a PVC binding as the ironing temperature required to give a good appearance to the main part of the garment may be high enough to cause damage to the trim.

For non-textile items, the main requirement is often strength. This is not difficult to achieve where metal is used but metal is not suitable for every application. Bikini fastenings, for example, must be strong but they are also exposed to the sun and if made from metal they can absorb enough heat to cause burns when they touch the skin. In this situation, a plastic, usually in the form of polyamide, would be used. Where a metallic appearance is required, it can be achieved by plating the polyamide.

Where items are made from metal, the main consideration is the problem of rusting if they are made from steel. For most trims, buttons, clasps etc., the base material is steel or brass, the former being cheaper but also subject to rusting, even when electroplated. For inexpensive garments, those that will not be washed or exposed to rain or sea water, or for removable items such as dungaree clips, brass or nickel-plated steel may be satisfactory, the plating offering protection from rusting unless scratched. For more expensive garments and those requiring higher performance, brass should be used.

If there will be frequent exposure to salt water, as on some sports clothing, plastic is more suitable. If there is doubt as to the base material of an item with a plated finish, steel items can be identified by their magnetic properties.

One of the most important properties of all items that go together to make garments is their colour, both initially and after wear and cleaning. It applies to all the items discussed in the present chapter and also to the sewing threads described elsewhere. Thus it is normally necessary for all the components of a garment to match the main fabric or to provide a specific colour contrast, in whatever circumstances they are viewed, for the match to remain throughout the lifetime of the garment, and for contrasting colours not to run or bleed into one another.

Where items are chosen to match the main fabric, the degree of match required will vary according to the visibility of the item. Zip fasteners and lining fabrics are normally concealed partly or wholly by the garment and an adequate match can be obtained from the range of stock shades carried by the manufacturers. Buttons, depending on their raw material, may be surface dyed to match but this is not a difficult process. The highest standards of colour matching are required of sewing threads and despite the commonly used threads being available in several hundred shades from stock, and a further thousand or so shades at short notice, special dyeing is occasionally required.

Traditionally, an inspector using a light cabinet and swatches of fabric dyed to the specified colour has carried out colour matching.

More recently, numerical specifications of colour are used, together with colour difference equations that specify the tolerances that are acceptable. The colour co-ordinates are measured using a colorimeter. Further details of these practices, and the complexities of assessing colour continuity are found in Chapter 10.

Colours must not only conform to the specified standard; they must also be fast. Exposure to light, washing and ironing may cause unacceptable changes. These are also the subjects of routine testing. Further comments are to be found in Chapter 10.

Other less common and rather specialised situations exist which present special hazards to components from the point of view of colour and other problems. Examples are the extreme laundering and dry-cleaning conditions used with contract rental workwear, and medical and food applications where threads might be required to be non-toxic and fast to autoclaving. Component manufacturers can normally advise on the most suitable thread and sewing conditions and, if necessary, special finishes can be developed.

# Chapter Six
# Alternative Methods of Joining Materials

We have stated several times that the dominant process in the assembly of garments is sewing. Many attempts have been made to develop other processes but achieving the speed and flexibility of manufacture required, along with the seam appearance and performance, is often elusive. The processes that have been developed as alternatives to sewing are very important in specific contexts. They have a significant commercial impact and they change the way garments are designed, constructed and assembled. However, their use must be supported by pre-production development and process control during manufacture. Those to be considered are:

- fusing
- welding and adhesives
- moulding

Of these, fusing is an established routine process for attaching interlinings; welding used to be a very specialised technology for niche products but is currently experiencing an explosion of interest in sportswear and lingerie; applications of true adhesives has always been a niche technology, but 'adhesive' is often employed today for some welding applications (thermoplastic materials that are melted to bind two fabrics together); and the major use of moulding continues to be bras, headwear and shaped supports for use in structured garments.

## Fusing

The purpose and nature of interlinings were described in the last chapter but the discussion was confined to interlinings sewn into garments. When interlinings are sewn in, it can be difficult on parts such as collars to avoid a wrinkling of the interlining inside the collar and pucker around the edge. On large parts such as jacket fronts, the attachment of interlinings by sewing is expensive and requires skill if a high standard is to be achieved. The alternative process that has been developed is that of fusing, whereby the interlining is bonded to the outer fabric by means of a thermoplastic resin.

The fusible interlining consists of a base cloth, which may be similar to that used for a sew-in interlining, and which carries on its surface a thermoplastic adhesive resin, usually in the form of small dots, which will melt when heated to a specific temperature. If it is laid flat with the resin side on to the garment part, and heat and pressure applied, the resin will flow into the fabric of the garment and it and the inter-lining will become permanently attached. For the remaining assembly of the garment, this laminate will be handled as one piece of material. This simple explanation hides a great deal of technology but it serves to introduce one of the most significant developments in garment construction methods to have taken place in recent years. Not all garment fabrics can be fused, and there will always be some situations where sew-in interlinings continue to be used, but in the vast majority of garment making today, fusing is the more common process. The reasons are both economic and technical.

## Advantages of using fusible interlinings

In most cases the use of fusible interlinings shortens manufacturing time with a consequent *reduction in direct labour cost*. In large area applications such as jacket fronts, the fusing operation replaces complex basting operations. In some small area applications such as reinforcing tapes it replaces sewing, but in others it can actually add a stage to the manufacturing process. If the parts of a collar are to be sewn together in a jig, a sew-in interlining can be laid into the jig at the same time as the collar parts at only a small extra cost in labour. If the collar is to be fused it must be done separately from the assem-bly of the collar.

There is a *reduction in the skill* required in many operations involv-ing fusing compared with the sewing in of interlinings and this leads to a reduction in training time.

It is easier to achieve *consistent quality* in the lamination process than it is with many of the operations of sewing in of interlinings, especially on modern lightweight fabrics. Traditionalists sometimes claim that in individual cases a craftsman using traditional canvas interlinings can produce garments with a subtlety of contour, and a softness and a crease recovery that fusing cannot; however the overall cost of manufacturing by this method is high enough to be uncompeti-

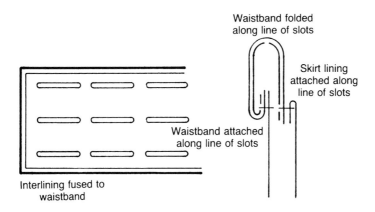

Waistband folded
along line of slots

Skirt lining
attached along
line of slots

Waistband attached
along line of slots

Interlining fused to
waistband

**Figure 6.1** Skirt waistband with slotted interlining.

tive for all but a few people, and this softer appearance, when rarely seen, has become less fashionable.

Fusible interlinings provide opportunities for *alternative methods of garment construction*; in some of which the interlining might be said to be operating as a 'work aid' in the sense that the term was used earlier, with all the advantages of speed and quality that work aids can confer. Most notable of these methods are those involving slotted interlinings. In this case the interlining will have been purchased cut to a specific narrow width, perhaps that of the pattern piece for a waistband, with lines of long narrow slots, about 20 mm by 2 mm, cut out of it along the intended folds of the waistband. When fused to the waistband and sewn to a skirt or trouser along one line of slots, the band will fold more easily in the correct positions to give the correct width. This type of application is shown in Fig. 6.1. It can be used in many other applications, as well, such as forming the edges of pleats and hems.

## Requirements of fusing

The process of fusing interlinings to garments must fulfil certain requirements and avoid certain problems if the garment is to have a satisfactory appearance and performance throughout its life.

The laminate produced by fusing should show the *aesthetic qualities* required by the designer in the finished garment. This relates in particular to the stiffness or draping qualities of the garment. These increase beyond those of the two components, singly or together, in a way that is not predictable. Achieving the required stiffness, handle or draping qualities is a matter of trial and error before manufacturing begins. The factors over which the garment manufacturer can exercise choice are the drape of the fusible's base cloth, and the type and quantity of the fusible resin forming the bond. In the search for a softer handle, the choice may be a compromise between the strength of the bond, as measured, and those qualities referred to as stiffness, handle and drape, based on a subjective judgment. Other fabric properties that could be affected adversely by the fusing on of interlinings are crease recovery and air permeability. A laminate will normally show crease recovery properties somewhere between the better and worse components and it may vary with the grain direction of the fabric. Fusing normally reduces air permeability and if it is both low to begin with in the outer fabric, and an important requirement in the finished garment, consideration must be given to it when interlinings are chosen.

The *strength of bond* of the laminate must be sufficient to withstand handling during subsequent operations in the garment manufacturing process as well as the flexing that takes place in wear. The bond must resist either the temperature and degree of agitation of a washing and drying cycle, with perhaps subsequent ironing, or the solvents, temperature and agitation of a dry-cleaning process, and in some cases both. The garment should carry a care label appropriate to the requirements of the fused interlinings as well as to the rest of the garment materials. If there is not a complete and even bond over the whole surface of the laminate when first fused, or if delamination takes place at some stage in the garment's life, it will appear as a 'bubbling' in the outer fabric of the garment. Parts that appear to be satisfactorily fused initially could have a bond that is below the required strength and may subsequently fail. Certain fabrics are particularly difficult to fuse to, notably showerproof rainwear fabrics. Both the showerproof finish on the fabric and its typically smooth, hard surface make a good bond difficult to achieve.

Fusing must take place without either *strike-through* or *strike-back* occurring. When the softened adhesive resin is pressed into the garment fabric, it is important that it does not go right through to the face side of that fabric, and that it does not go back to the outside of the interlining base cloth. These problems are known as 'strike-through' and 'strike-back' respectively. If strike-through occurs it may show on the right side of the garment as a pattern of dots of resin; if it occurs on a garment subject to high temperature ironing such as a shirt collar, it may be picked up on the iron and lead to marking of the garment. If strike-back occurs, it can contaminate parts of the equipment used in the fusing process, and may also adhere to the garment lining during pressing.

The fusing process must not cause *thermal shrinkage* in the outer fabric. Fusing commonly takes place at around 150°C and at this temperature many fabrics may be subject to thermal shrinkage. If this occurs, it can cause garments to fit together badly during manufacture and be incorrect in size after manufacture. To minimise shrinkage, some fusing presses have a pre-heat zone, set at a lower temperature.

A further possible effect of the heat of the fusing process is that of *dye sublimation*. Fabrics may change colour to a level that is unacceptable, causing a mismatch between the fused and unfused parts of the garment. This phenomenon can sometimes be pronounced. In one company, a polyester fabric was so affected by the fusing process that it was decided to send all the garment pieces through the press, whether or not they required the attachment of a fusible interlining. Only in this way could they avoid shading in the garments.

Since the fusing process involves pressure, there is a risk that pile fabrics may be subject to *crushing* during fusing. Fused and unfused parts of the garment, when sewn together, may have a different appearance.

Where showerproof fabrics are fused, there is a possibility that the presence of a fused interlining in the garment may *wick water* through the fabric in the fused areas while the unfused areas remain satisfactorily showerproofed. Water-resistant interlinings have been developed for these situations.

The achievement of these requirements, and the avoidance of the problems described, require that care is taken in the selection of an interlining for a particular outer fabric at the design stage, having in mind the intended appearance, handle and end use of the garment and the equipment available for fusing. It also requires careful control of the fusing process in the factory. Fusing operations pose problems of a different order from those of cutting, sewing and pressing for the simple reason that a satisfactory outcome of the operation cannot be judged visually. While some of the problems described show immediately, in most cases they will appear only after wearing or cleaning, by which time many faulty garments may have been made. In most other clothing manufacturing operations, the eye provides the information required to make a judgment about acceptability. In fusing, it will be seen that the temperature at which it takes place, the pressure that is applied, and the time during which the heating and pressing operate, are critical for satisfactory fusing, but their effectiveness can be measured only by specific, destructive tests performed on samples of fused fabric and interlining. Setting up and maintaining fusing operations requires a closer and more continuous co-operation among materials suppliers, production managers and the manufacturers of the equipment than is required in other operations.

## The fusing process

The means of fusing are temperature and pressure, applied over a period of time, usually in some kind of specialised fusing press. The rise in temperature at the 'glue line', the interface of resin and outer fabric where the resin is active, is caused by the electric heating elements of the press. This changes the state of the resin from a dry solid to a viscous fluid. Only with appropriate pressure will this flow among the fibres of both the outer fabric and the fusible base cloth. On cooling, the resin re-solidifies and forms a bond between the two components of the laminate. The heat has to pass through fabric to activate the resin, and this requires a time, measured in seconds, that varies according to the nature of the fabric and the type of resin.

Every fusible resin has an optimum temperature at which it flows satisfactorily. If this temperature is not reached, a longer time or higher pressure will not compensate and the bond will be weak. If the temperature is too high, the resin becomes too fluid, giving rise to strike-back and strike-through. Most specifications of optimum temperatures for fusing include a tolerance to cope with small variations in operating conditions.

In addition to the outer fabric of the garment, three factors determine the properties of the fused laminate:

♦ base fabric of the interlining
♦ type of fusible resin
♦ pattern of application of the resin to the base cloth

### Base fabric of the interlining

Base fabrics are available in the woven and non-woven constructions described for sew-in interlinings and also as warp knits. The warp knits are either a lock-knit or weft insert construction.

Lock-knit, using more yarns and with more interlinking of loops, gives a satisfactory stability where simple warp knit would not be stable enough. The most usual fibre is nylon, which gives very soft handle and draping. In some applications, the smooth surface may fulfil part of the role of a body lining. Weft insert fabrics consist of vertical chains of loops with yarns laid in horizontally and interlaced with the vertical chains. This construction should, in theory, give the vertical suppleness and horizontal resilience of a woven interlining, but in practice the properties are rather unpredictable. Finishing involves heat setting and, depending on the nature of the inserted yarn, may include chemical treatment.

*Type of fusible resin*

Just as there is a range of stitch and seam types to achieve a range of assembly objectives and finishes, so there is a range of resin types to cover a range of laminating requirements. The choice of resin is restricted by limits imposed by the outer fabric, the fusing equipment to be used, the end use requirements, and the precise behaviour of the resins in response to heat. The particular requirements of resins are as follows:

♦ The fusing temperature needed must not be so high that it will damage the outer fabric or its colour. The usual maximum is 175°C, with 150°C most common.
♦ The fusing temperature needed must not be so low that the bond is inadequate to withstand garment making. The lower limit is generally 110°C, although leather may require even lower temperatures.
♦ The resin must provide a bond that is suitably resistant to washing and/or dry-cleaning.
♦ The thermoplastic nature of the resin must be such that adjustment of temperature is sufficient to permit it to penetrate the outer fabric to give a bond, without flowing excessively to give strike-through or strike-back.
♦ The resin must contribute to the achievement of the desired handle of the laminate.
♦ In the majority of end uses, the resin must be white or transparent. It must also have low dye retention properties.
♦ The resin must be harmless in processing and in end use.

An ideal resin would have a high degree of cross-linking ability, i.e. it would be a thermosetting resin with no danger of being affected by subsequent higher temperatures. Such resins are still under development.

The resins used are mostly chemicals whose names will be familiar from other uses. All are capable of modification during manufacture to give a wide range of properties, both as fusible resins and for these other uses. In the present context, a detailed understanding of the properties of the resins is not necessary, but it is important to appreciate the range that is available.

*Polyethylene coatings* are available in different densities and with different values of a property known as the melt flow index. The value of this index determines the extent to which the resin flows during the fusing operation and the higher its value, i.e. the more easily it flows, the lower will be the subsequent resistance of the laminate to dry-cleaning solvents. The effect of varying the density of the resin is to give a greater resistance to dry-cleaning solvents, and a higher softening point, with increasing density. All the polyethylene resins used in fusible coatings are washable and, in the higher densities, they are both washable and dry-cleanable. They require high bonding pressures on the fusing press. Their main use is in interlinings for shirt collars.

*Polypropylene resin* is similar in properties to high density polyethylene but reaches its softening point at a higher temperature. This makes it especially suitable for fusing applications where rapid, high-temperature drying is part of the garment laundering process. The resin will withstand temperatures at the glue line of 150 °C before delaminating.

*Polyamides* can have a wide range of fusing properties, according to the proportions of the basic ingredients of different nylons employed as well as the amount of plasticiser added. The objectives are to vary the melting range and lower the softening temperature. Polyamides are used widely in dry-cleanable garments. Polyamides in the higher temperature melting range are generally washable up to 60 °C but in the lower melting ranges they are dry-cleanable only.

*Polyesters* have a similarly wide range of fusing properties as a result of varying the constituents. These resins are used in garments that are dry-cleanable and washable, because polyesters are less water-absorbent than polyamides and therefore resist washing better.

*Polyvinyl chloride (PVC)* is generally printed on to base fabrics as a plasticised paste; the fusing temperature is determined by the amount and type of plasticiser used in its formation. It is both dry-cleanable and washable. It is used commonly in large area applications on coat fronts.

*Plasticised polyvinyl acetate (PVA)* is normally in the form of a continuous coating for fusing to leather and fur at low pressures and temperatures. It is not dry-cleanable and has limited washability.

A small number of other chemicals have been tried but they are not in widespread use.

## Methods of applying resins to base cloths

There is further scope for varying the properties of an interlining and its effect on the outer fabric of a garment by varying the application of the resin to the base cloth. The most popular methods used are:

- ♦ scatter coating
- ♦ dry dot printing
- ♦ paste coating

All the methods involve the use of carefully selected particle sizes of the various resins. Scatter coating uses the largest particles, from 150 to 400 microns; dry dot printing uses particles from 80 to 200 microns; and paste coating uses the smallest at 0 to 80 microns (1000 microns equals 1 mm).

In *scatter coating*, specifically designed scattering heads are used to provide an even scatter under automatic control. The resin is then softened in an oven, pressed on to the base cloth and cooled. This is the cheapest method of making a fusible but the product is neither as uniform nor as flexible as printed coatings.

With *dry dot printed coating*, the powdered resin fills engraved holes on a roller. The base cloth passes over a heated roller and then against the engraved roller. The powdered resin adheres to the cloth in the form of dots. Oven heating follows the printing operation to ensure permanent adhesion. The temperature and pressure on the two rollers is varied for different resin types. Patterns of dots can vary from 3 to 12 dots per centimetre according to the garment manufacturer's requirements. Generally, lighter weight garment fabrics require interlinings with smaller dots in higher concentration, while heavier weight fabrics require larger dots in lower concentration to allow good penetration into the fabric surface and give a satisfactory bond.

With *paste coating*, fine resin powders are blended with water and other agents to form a smooth paste and are printed on to the base cloth. Heat removes the water and the dots coalesce into solid resin. This type of coating gives precisely shaped dots and is used to produce the finer dots used in shirt collar fusibles.

Others methods of applying resins to base cloths include preformed systems, where a preformed net is laminated to a base cloth to form precise dot patterns such as are used on top collar fusibles; extrusion laminating, producing a continuous film of polyethylene, also used in shirt collar applications but resulting in a very stiff product; and emulsion coating, for instance by dipping the base cloth into a bath of emulsion, squeezing out excess resin by rolling, and drying in an oven to produce double-sided coatings.

Choice of resin type and method of coating relates to cost, fusing characteristics, suitability for use with particular fusing equipment, durability when washing and dry-cleaning, and particular garment end use. It will be clear from the variety of base fabrics, resin types and resin applications that are available that the total range of possibilities when these are used in combination is very wide. Within one company, which makes a limited range of garment types and has only one method of fusing, a small selection only will be needed. Making the correct choice requires careful investigation at the design stage, often with the help of the interlining companies and their laboratory facilities. Cost will often be a consideration but it should be remembered that the cost of the interlining is often small in relation to the total cost of the materials in the garment, whereas the cost of failure of unsatisfactory garments, returned after wearing and cleaning, could be extremely high.

## Means of fusing

Fusing equipment must control three factors:

- ♦ temperature
- ♦ pressure
- ♦ time

### Temperature

This must be high enough to achieve the necessary temperature at the glue line which will change the dry thermoplastic resin into a partially molten state in order that it will flow. For each resin there is a limited range within which the correct level of flow is achieved. Too low a temperature gives poor flow and poor subsequent adhesion. Too high a temperature gives too much flow, resulting in strike-back and strike-through and a reduction of performance in most respects.

### Pressure

The equipment must provide enough consistent pressure to ensure intimate contact between interlining and outer cloth over the whole surface of the interlining. This ensures correct transfer of heat to the glue line and correct penetration of resin among the fibres of the outer fabric. Too low a pressure reduces penetration with consequent low adhesion. Too high a pressure provides excessive penetration of resin resulting in strike-back and strike-through.

### Time

The equipment must give enough time to allow the temperature and pressure to induce melting of the resin and penetration of the outer fabric in order to produce a satisfactory bond; too much time may result in strike-back and strike-through. It will be appreciated that if a thick fabric and an interlining are put into a heated press in a cool state, it may be several seconds before the resin reaches the required temperature.

These three factors are interrelated. A change in one may necessitate a change in the others, though there is a limit to the extent to which one factor will compensate for another. If the temperature in the press is not high enough, no amount of extra time will enable the resin to soften and flow.

## Fusing equipment

The equipment used for fusing can be divided into:

- ♦ specialised fusing presses
- ♦ hand irons
- ♦ steam presses

### Specialised fusing presses

A number of different types of fusing press have been developed over the years, providing control of the heat and pressure applied to the garment part and providing for fusing to take place on flat sections of garments that have not yet been sewn. In many companies, such fusing presses are sited in the cutting room and the fusing operation takes place before transferring the garments to the sewing room. On some garments, notably men's jackets, it is necessary to add further sections of fusible interlining to the already three-dimensional garment during construction; different equipment must be used for this.

Fusing presses vary in the way they operate and these differences affect both the quality of the fusing and the productivity of the operation.

*Flat bed fusing press* A diagram of the principle of operation of this type of fusing press is shown in Fig. 6.2. It consists of two horizontal metal platens between which the fabric and interlining laminate are

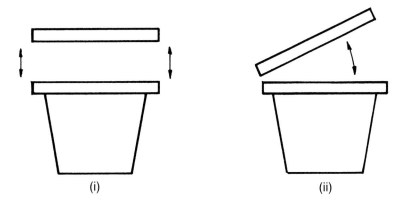

**Figure 6.2** Flat bed fusing presses. (i) Vertical action. (ii) Scissor action.

sandwiched. The top platen is unpadded but the bottom platen has a resilient cover, typically silicone rubber, though it may be a felt pad. Both platens have an outer cover of PTFE, which can be cleaned easily to prevent straining and build-up of resin that would cause garment parts to adhere to the platen. Heat is provided by electric elements, usually in the top platen only, but sometimes in the bottom as well. The elements provide a uniform temperature over the whole surface.

The press manufacturer aims for a standard of control allowing a variation of 5 °C either way from the required temperature over the whole surface area. Pressure is applied by closing the platens together mechanically, hydraulically or pneumatically. The pressure system must be robust, provide accurate closing over a large area, and be free from distortion through heat, wear or mechanical faults. The resilient bottom cover should be changed regularly to avoid pressure problems. Vertical action closure, as shown in Fig. 6.2(i) and in Fig 6.3, gives more accurate pressure than the scissors action shown in Fig. 6.2(ii). Fusing time is normally controlled by an automatic timer, whose cycle can be varied to suit different requirements. It is typically of the order of 8–12 seconds.

In the simplest mode of operation, the operator places the garment part face down on the lower platen, places the interlining resin side down on top of it in the correct position, and closes the press. This is slow and time-consuming as the operator can do little that is productive for the duration of the fusing cycle. These presses do not cover

**Figure 6.3** Vertical action flat bed fusing press under manual control. (Reproduced by permission of Macpi Group.)

a very large area, often no more than one metre by half a metre, and the number of garment parts that can be fused at one time will depend on their size. If a small end section of a larger garment part has to be fused it may be possible to insert only the end of the part into the press. A change in the type or style of garment to one needing large areas of fusing could present difficulties for a company having only a small area fusing press. Where small parts are being fused, output may be increased by laying them on a sheet of card which is then placed in the press. By this method, the placing of garment and interlining parts can take place while the previous parts are being fused. Accuracy of positioning of the interlining on the garment part is important, not just for the garment, but for the cleanliness of the press. Where the whole area of a garment part is being fused, the interlining pattern is normally slightly smaller than the garment pattern so that there is no possibility of the interlining extending over the edge of the garment part. If this happens, resin is transferred to the cover on the lower platen and subsequently to the face side of another garment part. This is a potential problem whatever the method of fusing used.

Variations in the design of these presses can improve productivity, in particular by having a twin-tray system that slides in and out from under the top platen, or a three-station carousel which has two operators at separate loading and unloading stations. In both of these, loading and unloading takes place during the fusing cycle, but the principle of operation of the press remains the same as the simple version described above, in that the garment parts are held firmly between the platens for the duration of the fusing cycle.

One of the advantages of this type of fusing press is that in the simplest version, their small size and relatively low cost allow their use by the smaller clothing manufacturer. They also tend to reduce fabric shrinkage since the fabric is held under pressure throughout the fusing cycle. A disadvantage is the tendency to crush pile fabrics such as velvet because of the length of time that they are held under pressure.

*Continuous fusing systems* These systems operate by passing the garment part, with its interlining placed on it, past a heat source, and either simultaneously or subsequently applying pressure. Heat is provided in one of three ways:

♦ With direct heating, the conveyor belt carries the components to be fused into direct contact with a heated surface, either a drum or curved plates.
♦ With indirect heating, the components to be fused are carried through a heated chamber (see Fig. 6.4).

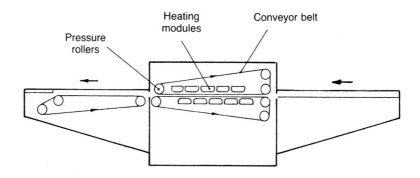

**Figure 6.4** Mode of operation of a continuous fusing press.

♦ With low temperature, gradient heating, the components are carried through a pre-heating zone. Heating is either direct or indirect. With this approach the temperature reached at the glue line is only just above that required to make the resin a viscous fluid and in some cases fusing takes place satisfactorily with a glue line temperature of only 120 °C. This reduces the possibility of heat shrinkage in the outer fabric and is a feature of some of the most recent fusing presses.

The maintenance of the required temperature is less of a problem inside a fully enclosed, continuously operating press than with a flat bed press, especially with modern electronic temperature controls. On drum presses, the tension of the conveyor belt presses the components continuously against the heated drum during the complete fusing process. Where conveyor belts carry the components past heating plates (direct) or through a heating chamber (indirect), nip rollers apply pressure to the assembly after heating. The pressure time is very small compared to that in flat bed presses and has to be controlled more precisely. The loading on the rollers is applied by springs or pneumatically at their ends. Rollers must be maintained parallel, unbowed and free of wear to give even pressure. The rubber covering of the rollers is available in a range of hardnesses. Usually shirt top collar fusing requires the hardest rollers and outerwear fabrics require softer rollers. Fusing times depend on the speed of the conveyor belt, which can be adjusted to give various dwell times in the heated zone.

Companies engaged in high-volume garment production generally use continuous fusing systems, both for the quality of the fusing they give and for the productivity gains. Presses are now available of such a size that as many as six operators can be loading simultaneously from specially designed workplaces. Unloading may be by operator at the far end, or by automatic catcher, or the press may divert the fused parts back to the loading station. It should be mentioned here that care is needed in handling newly fused parts while they are still hot as distortion or marking can occur.

Small width presses will have a join in the belt, and this is where failure generally occurs. Larger widths are within the range of circular weaving machines and woven fabric can be used to produce seamless belts with a significantly longer belt life.

These fusing presses can require a total floor area as high as 30 square metres. By contrast, special narrow continuous fusing presses are available for use where companies require large quantities of narrow parts fused. They are particularly used for waistbands and belts; in a company making only trousers, this might be the only fusing press they would need. High productivity is obtained by cutting the interlining in continuous strips directly from the roll (by cutting through the roll at the required width), and setting this to run continuously through the press. Waistbands are cut slightly longer than will be needed and are fed into the press, on to the interlining, one after the other by the operator. A small overlap should be made in the waistbands so that there are no gaps where adhesive from the interlining would be transferred to the press. The operator can stop the press when necessary. The fused waistbands can be rolled up automatically at the far end of the press and in many cases can be presented in this form to the sewing operator. If waistbands are being attached to trousers or skirts through a folder, time is saved if they are in a continuous strip. The joins in the waistbands will become waste between garments. A continuous fusing press is shown in Fig. 6.5.

**Figure 6.5** Continuous fusing press. (Reproduced by permission of Macpi Group.)

Continuous fusing presses generally reduce any problems associated with fusing pile fabrics such as velvet because the duration of pressure on the fabric is short. For the same reason, though, fabrics prone to heat shrinkage are likely to shrink more when fused in a continuous press than when held firmly in a flat bed press.

*High frequency fusing* In the fusing presses described so far, heat has been provided by electric heating elements. This limits the number of thicknesses of fabric that can be fused at once because of the time taken for the heat to transfer through the fabric to the resin. The heat may also produce shrinkage and colour changes. If multiple layers of fabric and interlining can be stacked up and fused simultaneously, productivity might be increased. Over a number of years, attempts have been made to do this by generating the heat by means of high frequency (HF) energy, in the same way as in a microwave cooker. This method offers the possibility of eliminating shrinkage and colour changes.

The alternating waves from a high frequency generator are absorbed by certain types of polymer, thereby generating heat. The platens of the press are the plates generating the high frequency field and the heating effect is distributed uniformly in length and width and is the full height between the platens. This effect is known as dielectric heating. The heating effect is different for different polymers, and many fibres are not affected at all. The fusible adhesive material heats up much faster than either the interlining base fabric or the garment fabric. This results in bonding at the glue line without excessive heat being generated in the fabric. Multiple plies of garment and interlining can be stacked up to 70 mm high, and since the heating effect is not dependent on its distance from a heat source, the adhesive at each joint should be raised to the same temperature. Less pressure is needed than with conventional fusing presses. The time required to generate the heat depends on the capacity of the high frequency unit and the weight of the load to be fused. For a typical 30 kW unit, operating times of 1–3 minutes may be achieved for loads of 5–20 kg.

The difficulty that arises with this method of fusing is that the press must be set to allow for the particular natural or man-made materials being used, the weight and thickness of those materials, and their moisture content. This has not been found easy, especially in the case of the moisture content. If incorrect estimates are made, the press may overfuse and bond the whole stack together, or underfuse and produce a poor bond on each garment part.

### Hand iron

Only those interlinings that can be fused at relatively low temperatures, low pressures and in relatively short times are suitable for fusing by hand iron. There are a number of difficulties. The operator cannot know the temperature at the glue line and cannot apply pressure uniformly. The operator estimates the time subjectively. Only small parts can be fused with any degree of success, and then only by pressing the iron for a fixed time on to the fusible, covering the area step by step and using steam to help the heat transfer. In this situation, garment parts may appear to be satisfactorily fused initially but deficiencies will show up as delamination during wearing or cleaning of the garment.

When the iron is used merely to position an interlining part or tape temporarily, to be followed by pressing on a steam press, fusing conditions are more satisfactory. This is common in menswear where additional, reinforcing, fusible tapes are often added during the construction of a jacket, in positions such as pockets, vents and hems. The garment is placed on a shaped press (described in the next chapter), the interlining sections are positioned using the hand iron, and the press is closed to effect complete fusing. On jacket hems, a slotted interlining tape is often used; once this is fused on, the iron can be further used to press up the hem along the line of slots before further sewing.

*Steam press*

In this case fusing takes place on presses of the type used for intermediate and final pressing of made up garments. Temperature at the glue line is achieved by steam from the head of the press. The temperature reached depends on the steam pressure at the press head, the efficiency of the press and its cladding. Pressure is provided mechanically or pneumatically by closing the press head on the buck. Vacuum in the lower part of the press, or buck, assists rapid cooling. The head is less likely to meet the buck with even pressure if it works with a scissors action. Best results are obtained if the pressing cycle is controlled automatically. The resins that fuse most successfully on a steam press are polyvinyl acetate and the lower melting range of polyamides, but fusing is not as effective as when using a dedicated press.

A specialised use of a steam press for fusing is in the positioning and initial attaching of fusible shoulder pads in men's jackets, as described in Chapter 5. A shoulder press would be used.

## Methods of fusing

All the descriptions of the fusing process that have been included so far have represented it as a single piece of interlining, laid resin side down, on a single piece of garment fabric, laid right side down. This is referred to as single fusing, and is the safest in the sense that it is easiest to set the press conditions to achieve the correct temperature at the glue line. Several other configurations are possible, both in terms of the presentation of the parts to the fusing press, and in the parts that are included in the garment. Some of the variations will now be described; illustrating them will demonstrate some of the methods of garment construction that involve fusible interlinings. The main variations are:

♦ reverse fusing
♦ sandwich fusing
♦ double fusing
♦ block fusing (HF fusing, described earlier)

### Reverse fusing

In this method the outer fabric lies on top of the fusible. It is some-times used in fusing shirt and blouse collars. On flat bed presses with elements only in the top platen, it is necessary to adjust temperature settings. Since the interlining part is normally slightly smaller than the garment part, accurate positioning may be difficult.

### Sandwich fusing

This is effectively carried out only on a horizontal continuous press where heat is applied both from above and below. Two pairs of com-ponents, forming two laminates, are fused together, with the two outer fabrics on the outside of the sandwich (of four layers) and the two interlinings on the inside. With correct temperature settings, the glue line temperature may be achieved in both laminates, but the potential for strike-back occurring and causing all the layers to adhere together is considerable. A small amount of fusing time will be saved but preparation will take longer and the quality of the results may be unsatisfactory.

### Double fusing

This is the fusing of two sorts of interlining to the outer fabric in one operation. It is most commonly used in shirt collars and men's jacket fronts.

*Shirt collar fusing* The majority of shirts manufactured today are made with one-piece collars rather than the more expensive, traditional two-piece collars. In the creation of a satisfactory one-piece collar with a

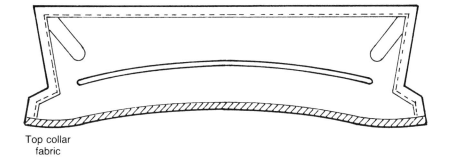

Top collar
fabric

**Figure 6.6** One-piece collar construction with interlining in the seam.

definite break line, fusible interlinings play a very important part. Two different constructions are in common use, both requiring two thicknesses of interlining to be fused to the top collar section in what is referred to as a skin and patch construction.

The *one-piece collar with turning* is shown in Fig. 6.6. One layer of fusible interlining skin is fused to the edge of the fabric, except on the neck edge, and a second layer of fusible interlining patch, cut to fit within the sewing line and with a 3 mm slot along the break line, is fused on top of it. This double fusing process requires the achievement of two correct glue line temperatures in the two layers of resin. The collars are normally fused with the patch lining towards the hot press surface, if only one platen is heated, and it is necessary to ensure that the glue line temperature furthest away, i.e. the one between the face fabric and the interlining skin, reaches the required level. This may require the glue line temperature nearest to the press surface, i.e. between skin and patch, to be slightly above that required. However, because of the generally thin face fabrics and interlinings and the tolerance built into the interlinings, the two glue line temperatures can be balanced to give good performance without excessive flow of resin.

In this construction, precision is all important in the cutting and locating of the interlinings. They are usually die cut and the two sections are spot welded together before being placed on the collar piece. A locating notch ensures correct positioning on the collar. This type of collar can be sewn in an automatic jig or profile stitcher and the interlining skin gives support to the fabric during stitching. It does, however, produce a thicker collar edge than the alternative method. All the component parts are cut and fused warp to warp to ensure minimum shrinkage during fusing and after-care.

The *one-piece collar with nett interlining construction* looks similar at first glance to the one described above, but both the skin and the patch interlinings are cut to the same size and fit within the stitch line on the collar piece. This is shown in Fig. 6.7.

The interlining edges are used as a profile for stitching directly on to the fabric collar plies, usually with a small wheel beside the presser foot acting as an edge guide. Automatic profile stitching machinery cannot be used. There is no excess interlining in the seam and this gives a thin edge that does not require topstitching.

*Fusing of tailored jacket fronts*   A wide variety of different constructions are used for the foreparts of men's jackets; a small selection only will be described here. The main requirement is a different level of support in different sections of the jacket between the shoulder and the hem and an additional support in the chest area which does not go into the lapel. To retain a good appearance in the jacket, despite the movement of the body, the interlining should provide a recovery from bending in the horizontal direction, coupled with a softness and flexibility in the vertical direction.

In the *floating chest piece*, shown in Fig. 6.8, the body interlining is fused over the whole of the front and a chest piece is made by

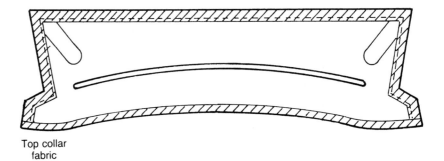

Top collar
 fabric

**Figure 6.7** One-piece collar construction without interlining in the seam.

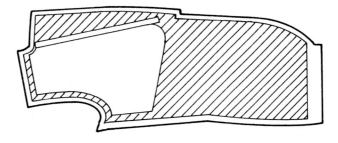

**Figure 6.8** Jacket front with floating chest piece.

fusing two interlinings together and attaching them to the front by means of a fusible bridle tape.

The *fully fused forepart* has a body interlining fused right across and a chest piece and shoulder piece fused on top of it. This is shown in Fig. 6.9.

A *multizonal fusible interlining with extra fusible felt shoulder* is shown in Fig. 6.10. Interlinings are available that are graduated in weight, usually in three stages, across the width of the cloth. If the interlining parts for the garment are cut across the piece it is possible to create a garment with heavier interlining at the top and lighter interlining at the hem. With some garment end uses, such as washable school blazers, this might be adequate on its own. For a higher quality garment, additional lapel and shoulder pieces are fused on to it. If the lapel becomes too bulky by this method, a separate piece of interlining may be used in that area.

Not all types of fusing press are suitable for the methods of fusing described here; in every case, very careful setting of the press conditions is necessary.

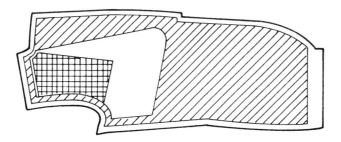

**Figure 6.9** Jacket front with fully fused forepart.

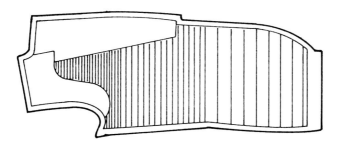

**Figure 6.10** Jacket front with multizonal fusible interlining.

## Quality control in fusing

It is clear from a number of statements made so far that careful control of the fusing process, after careful selection of interlinings, is essential. Assuming that a company has purchased a press appropriate to its needs, and sited it where extraneous factors such as draughts will not affect it, checks must still be made on a routine basis that the press and the garments being produced on it are satisfactory. Separate checks can be made on the factors of temperature, pressure and time, and on the quality of the bond being achieved in the laminate.

### Temperature control

It is necessary to calibrate fusing presses before operating them, in order to relate actual glue line temperatures to thermostat settings in all the conditions and over all the time cycles likely to be met during normal manufacturing conditions. The glue line temperatures required for fusing will always be lower than the thermostat temperatures displayed owing to the insulating effect of press cladding, interlining and outer fabric. A further factor is the heat required to remove the regain, the natural moisture contained within materials, which is a variable factor. If the machine is not fitted with a sensor, two methods of checking temperature are available:

A portable *pyrometer* is a device consisting of a long wire probe that can be inserted into a press, between plies of interlining and fabric; the pyrometer shows on a dial the temperature achieved after a certain time of closing of the press. It can be used only on a flat bed press and should be calibrated itself using heat sources with known temperatures, e.g. boiling water.

A *thermopaper* consists of a narrow strip with a series of heat-sensitive areas. Each section along the thermopaper is marked with a temperature and it changes from white to black if that temperature is reached while it is in the press.

Whether the press is being calibrated initially, or is in use for fusing, it must be allowed sufficient time to reach its working temperature after switching on.

### Pressure control

Adequate and even pressure over the whole area of a fusing press is essential, and although there will probably be a dial showing the pressure in the compressed air line supplying the press, this does not provide a very good indication of the actual pressure on the platens.

In practice, only the evenness of the pressure can be measured. The method uses strips of paper in different ways according to the type of press. For example, with *continuous presses*, provided access can be gained to the rollers in the press, strips of paper can be passed through the press which is stopped when they are partially through the rollers. Pulling out the strips by hand will show if there is any bowing in the rollers.

The most important check, however, is whether the desired bond strength is achieved, and this laboratory test should be carried out as a matter of routine (*see* Garment quality control, below).

### Time control

In the calibration of a press, the representation of time on the press controls must be related to the actual time of fusing, i.e. the time of press closure for a flat bed press or the time of heating in a continuous press. It should not be assumed that the time in seconds given on a dial is what is actually happening. Both types of press can be checked with a stop watch.

In the course of checking the temperature on each type of press, the time cycle required for the desired temperature to be reached will be discovered. This will change for different fabrics and interlinings, as with thicker fabrics more time will be needed for the heat to penetrate to the glue line. When a garment is designed, and the interlining is selected, checks should be made to establish the fusing conditions, which must be specified for production.

### Garment quality control

To ensure that the quality of the fusing of the garments is satisfactory, the *strength of the bond* between the outer fabric and the interlining must be tested by measuring the force required to peel them apart. Of interest is the initial bond strength after fusing and cooling, as well as the bond strength after the washing or cleaning procedures which will be specified for the garment. Tests for bond strength should take place at the design stage when interlinings are being selected and as a routine quality control procedure during production. Standard tests are available, for example BS 4973: 1973 (Part 2).

Tests for bond strength are made by fusing a large enough section of fabric and interlining so that it covers the full width of the press. Strips 5 cm by 15 cm are cut from this laminate in the lengthwise direction. A small amount is peeled apart by hand so that clips can be attached separately to the interlining and the face fabric and the force required to continue peeling apart the two sections is then measured. The most accurate method of measurement uses a laboratory tensile testing machine which records on a chart the variations in the peel bond strength along the length of the strip. If this facility is available it may be used at the design stage but it is unlikely to be available for routine testing during production. More appropriate is a spring balance which, with practice, will give reasonably good and reproducible results. The sample is suspended from a fixed point by the clip attached to it, the spring balance is attached to the clip on the interlining, and the force required to peel them apart is noted. Alternatively, a series of different weights can be used, and the strength of the bond accepted as adequate if the lightest weight that will peel the bond apart is above a certain level.

It is not easy to specify the figures that should be obtained for peel bond strength for a particular combination of interlining and outer fabric. Figures must be obtained which can be related to actual satisfactory performance of garments in wearing and washing or dry cleaning and with time a company can build up a library of useful information. For each new style of garment, a figure must be established as the required standard. Tests for peel bond strength should be carried out at least twice each day during the production run of the style, the figures recorded, and action taken to investigate the cause if inadequate strengths are discovered. By measuring the bond strength at intervals across the press, a check is made on the uniformity of temperature and pressure across the press since they determine the quality of the bond.

In establishing the correct level of peel bond strength at the design stage, sample pieces should be subjected to the appropriate washing and/or dry-cleaning tests and the peel bond strength checked after drying. This will show whether there is an unacceptable loss in strength during these processes. The samples can also be examined visually for delamination. During the production run, weekly wash or dry-clean tests should be made on garment parts or, preferably, on complete garments. This should be part of an overall programme of checks on the performance of the materials and construction of the garments being manufactured and should include wearer trials.

As part of the investigations made at the design stage to decide on a satisfactory interlining and fusing conditions, the outer fabric should be checked for *heat shrinkage* and *colour change* during fusing. Shrinkage must also be checked for during washing and dry-cleaning since this is a common cause of delamination.

A final point to make concerning the control of quality standards in production relates to *cleanliness* of the press and surrounding area.

Fusing presses tend to acquire a build-up of resin on their various parts which is made worse by the addition of frayed threads and lint from fabrics. This can be severe enough to affect the evenness of pressure in a press and it can also lead to the transfer of adhesive resin onto the face side of garment parts and to threads and lint being trapped between the garment fabric and the interlining during fusing.

## Welding and adhesives

The process of fusing described applies to the attachment of interlinings to garment parts over an area that may be large in the case of a jacket front or small in the case of a reinforcing tape. Whatever the situation, the fused part is not subjected, in the course of normal wear and tear, to any forces that would tend to pull it apart. Over the years, many attempts have been made to join normal garment seams by methods other than sewing, usually using some means of welding or sticking the seam. It will be remembered that a large proportion of the seams used in garment construction are superimposed seams, and when sewn with the correct selection of stitch type and sewing thread these can be made adequately strong for a particular fabric and garment end use. Unfortunately, when this type of seam is joined with any kind of adhesive or some method of melting a thermoplastic fibre fabric and bonding the material together, the seam may pull apart easily, unless it is substantial and possibly ugly. The effect is similar to the undoing of the hook and loop fastening described earlier or to the peeling of adhesive tape from a roll.

The situation in which a welded or stuck seam works well is in the lapped seam but in the majority of materials this presents problems of raw edges. Experience of a hook and loop fastening on a garment or on footwear shows how strong it is against a shearing force and the same applies to a long seam which is bonded together. Unfortunately the more complicated lapped seams that lend themselves well to sewing by means of folders cannot be constructed easily for any other method of joining.

Further properties of sealed or adhesive seams also cause problems. The seams tend to be less flexible, and have less stretch and recovery than sewn seams; both these problems can cause the seam to break down. If a seam is joined incorrectly, it may be impossible to alter it. While stitching is, in most cases, simple to undo and re-sew, seams joined by other methods are likely to become damaged if separation is attempted.

All these difficulties, however, do not mean that there is no scope for using such methods of construction. The main areas of use of the methods outlined here are:

- welding decorative motifs to garments
- sealing of the edges of sewn garment parts and other garment components to prevent fraying and avoid the need for additional sewing
- formation of vents, button holes and eyelets
- production of close-fitting performance garments (sportswear and underwear)
- waterproofing previously sewn seams in garments made from waterproof materials
- attaching garment parts by means of adhesives where subsequent stitching, such as topstitching, will prevent the parts peeling apart

## Welding

Welding as a process in garment manufacture involves the joining of two fabrics using a thermoplastic material. However, the heat is not applied externally as is normally the case with the fusing of interlinings. The heat must be focused on the thermoplastic material. There are four ways of achieving this:

- Radio frequency welding (also known as RF or dielectric welding). An alternating electric field is applied to two shaped electrodes between which are the materials to be seamed.
- Hot air welding. Hot air is directed to the join-line between the fabric plies, and a roller applies pressure to facilitate flow of the melt.
- Ultrasonic welding. The seam assembly is placed under a metal head which is vibrated at ultrasonic frequencies. This creates a melt and the pressure of the head ensures flow.
- Hot wedge welding. Two shaped heated jaws are brought together, between which are the materials to be seamed.

In all cases, welding melts a thermoplastic material, allows the melt to flow into the fabrics to be joined, and then cooling secures the bond. If the fabrics are themselves thermoplastic, there is a decision to be made as to whether the welding melts these fabrics, or whether another material, of lower melting temperature, is introduced. This other material may be a separate film or it may be a coating on the back of one or both of the fabrics being joined.

*Radio frequency welding*

Some polymeric materials are known as 'polar', which means that they are responsive to the presence of an alternating electric field. Each polymer has a north and south pole and can behave like a tiny magnet. In the presence of a suitable field, the polymers experience stresses and internal energy dissipation leads to heating until the polymer melts. Suitable polar materials are polyvinylchloride (PVC) and poly-urethane, both of which can be either used as a coating or inserted as a film between plies. The electrodes for creating the electric field are preformed to the contour of the seam. They are also used to apply pressure on the assembly, so that the melt flows correctly. In the UK, the permitted frequency is 27.12 MHz. As there are health and safety issues, these machines must be regularly monitored and located so as to minimise hazards.

Since the electrodes are preformed to follow the seam line, there are significant setup issues for this joining technology. It is not easy to combine HF welding with a requirement for flexibility in manufac-turing. The assembly to be joined is two-dimensional, with welding times of a few seconds.

*Hot air welding*

Hot air welding is important as a method of joining or sealing the seams on garments made from materials rendered waterproof by means of a coating of PVC on one side of a textile material. When joining, a tape is fed into the seam and melted by the hot air. The seam then passes between a roller that ensures the melt flows before cooling and then creates the bond.

A sewn seam in materials with an impermeable coating allows ingress of water between the layers of the material or through the needle holes, depending on the configuration of the seam. When sealing such a seam, the subassembly is fed through the hot air welding machine and a tape applied to the line of stitching.

In either situation, whether sewn first or not, the seams may become bulky and inflexible compared with the rest of the material of the garment. Garment design is important; both because of this bulk and because of the cost of assembling the seams. Garments of this type normally have a minimum of seams of carefully planned shape. Since they are usually looser-fitting outer garments, the loss of shaping pos-sibilities may not be too much of a constraint. However material costs can be high when, for instance, jackets are cut in one main body piece with no shoulder, armhole, yoke or centre back seams. To introduce more flexibility to this area and to enhance the design potential, one supplier offers a tape of 13 mm (instead of 22 mm).

## Ultrasonic welding

If two hard materials are pressed together and one is vibrated against the other, energy is generated at the point of contact. If plies of thermoplastic materials are placed between the points of vibration, heat energy will be generated internally in the materials where they touch; if the dissipation of energy is sufficient, the materials will melt and can be pressed together so that a bond is formed. A device that changes an input of electric current into mechanical vibrations is known as a transducer, and it is this which is used to generate the heat. If the speed of vibration is below about 18 000 cycles per second, audible sound will be produced. This could be painful and even dangerous to work with. Consequently, and for technical reasons to do with the welding of clothing materials rather than other types of materials, frequencies in the ultrasonic region of around 20 000 cycles per second are used. In *ultrasonic welding* of clothing materials, the vibrations developed in the transducer are transferred to a 'horn' and the heat is generated between this vibrating horn and a stationary anvil. Fabric plies are placed between the horn and the anvil, and the horn, in addition to vibrating, maintains the pressure necessary to form a weld once the surfaces to be joined have been melted. Horns can vary in size up to a maximum of about 25 cm by 4 cm if rectangular, or about 9 cm in diameter if round. The actual shape of the horn relates to the particular welding operation to be achieved.

The amount of heat generated depends on the amplitude of the vibrations, the frequency, the pressure between the two surfaces, and the length of time they are allowed to continue vibrating in contact. The amplitude is pre-set for a particular application, depending on the materials to be welded and the type of operation, i.e. joining, edge finishing etc. Pressure is adjusted by experiment and the time is usually around 2 seconds. The horn and anvil remain cold to the touch at all times.

The materials to be welded must be at least 65 per cent thermoplastic, although there is scope for welding materials made of natural fibres if a plastic film is inserted between the plies being sealed together.

Typical uses are the application of motifs to garments, the cutting and sealing to length of ribbons and straps, and the shaping of small garment parts that would otherwise be costly and time-consuming to sew. Motifs must be designed to be attached by the welding process and have suitable threads woven into the back of them. Ribbons and sewn straps made of suitable materials can be simultaneously cut to length and heat sealed at the ends to prevent fraying. It is particularly useful where narrow straps or ties for a garment have been made by sewing through a folder since the ends are, in this case, very awkward to neaten. A neat, non-bulky end is achieved very rapidly by means of welding.

Another item that can be cut to exactly the right dimensions and sealed at the same time is the hook and eye tape used as a fastening on bras. This is supplied as a continuous strip, and cutting it into sections with scissors is inaccurate and leads to a costly neatening operation afterwards. In instances such as this, where the garment part to be welded will be worn against the skin, care must be taken that the edge remains sufficiently soft that it will not cause discomfort.

In addition to the stamping and plunge type operations described above, the welding principle can be used in rotary machines. In this case a rotating wheel replaces the anvil and, if the wheel has a dot pattern on it, an effect similar in appearance to stitching can be created. The garment parts must be conveyed accurately through the machine to obtain the correct seam line. The appearance of the machine is similar to that of a flat bed sewing machine but without the thread control systems. In deciding whether to weld or sew garments, the constraints described previously must be remembered.

More substantial operations have been welded. One example concerns waistband ends on sports shorts. The waistband can be bound to the garment in the manner described previously and a specially shaped horn made to cut and seal the waistband end into a pointed shape and, at the same time, weld in the buttonhole. Another use on the same type of garment could be to create a small vent at the lower end of the side seam. Both these operations are costly to do in the conventional way. Welding saves time and guarantees accuracy of shape in the finished part. This type of construction is acceptable on a garment for the less expensive market but would not be appropriate on expensive styles.

### Hot wedge welding

Two jaws are shaped to follow the seam line and mounted so that they can be brought together. The jaws are heated and the materials to be seamed are sandwiched between them. The heat melts the thermoplastic material and, because the assembly is held under pressure, the melt flows and forms the join.

### Contemporary trends

The past decade has seen many developments in machinery and applications of welding technologies. A review of seamless knitting and stitch-free technologies for performance apparel is by Thorp

(2006), documenting the way many performance brands are now offering stitch-free products. Apart from waterproofing, the main advantages are described as increased durability with lighter weight, reduced bulk of seams reducing abrasion, good stretch and recovery performance. These properties are identified as relevant to sports-wear and underwear, and both these markets are now being supplied with products having a greater proportion of stitch-free seams, as illustrated in Fig 6.11. Ultrasonic seaming is emerging as the most popular welding technology, but machinery suppliers are equipped to develop whatever technologies are appropriate for the seaming operation. As an example of innovation, Pfaff and ProLas have been developing laser sewing in combination with ultrasonics. This has industrial textile joining in mind, but there are also applications in technical apparel, where the laser sewing facility can be used to join electro-conductive yarns.

Research in these technologies is still very limited. The machinery suppliers do not have a tradition of publishing, and most develop-ments are confidential to the customer. Shi and Little (2000) con-sidered ultrasonic welding and identified significant parameters as amplitude, pressure and weld time. This is significant because machin-ery settings have not allowed these parameters to be pre-set, so an experienced technician is needed to prepare the machine for seaming, and this has to be done via a process of experimentation. Hayes and McLoughlin (2007) have compared the mechanical behaviour of welded and sewn seams, providing documented evidence for welded seams having enhanced compliance and reduced resistance

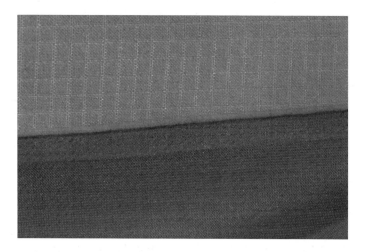

**Figure 6.11** Welded seam in a football shirt. All the seams in this shirt are welded (except for label insertion).

to bending, but also for reduced durability when compared with sewn seams. There is clearly scope for much more work to be done to allow anecdotal evidence to be critically appraised.

For technologists entering this domain, it is important to carry out a programme of tests with the materials, the equipment and with the garments. Usually this is done in conjunction with the machinery supplier. It is important to know what adjustments can be made to machinery settings and how much experimentation is needed to optimise these settings. Suppliers of machinery and materials for use in stitch-free seaming should provide manuals to support the use of their products, and these should be used to guide all applications of these technologies.

## Adhesives

The term 'adhesive' is used here to mean a substance that is initially a 'sticky' fluid that can flow over a substrate, and then it hardens/solidifies to form a bond. The main way of achieving this hardening process is polymerisation, whereby time, heat, pressure or light leads to chemical changes in the adhesive. Heat-activated adhesives are made of copolymers that melt, flow and polymerise at higher temperatures.

There are potential ambiguities about the terminology used to describe thermoplastic tapes or films for joining fabrics. If they are melted by the input of heat energy, caused to flow and then cooled, that is welding. If, however, there is a chemical change within the material used as the tape or film, that is adhesive bonding.

Welding and adhesives have some similarities in the problems that arise in the construction of seams using them, but there are also a number of differences.

The number of garment construction methods that make use of adhesives for seams is limited. The main growth area is in tapes or films, where there is a substantial overlap with welding technologies.

Three other applications are worth describing. One is the use of an adhesive thread that can be sewn into the edge neatening of a hem as one of the looper threads. When the hem is pressed up to the correct position, the thread melts and holds it in place without sewing. The obvious restriction here is the problem of alteration of the garment length. Another use of adhesives is in seams that will take no strain or will subsequently be topstitched. Patch pockets can be attached to garments by means of a strip of adhesive around the edge, the top corners being reinforced subsequently with a sewn bar tack. Yoke seams can be similarly attached using an adhesive and topstitched afterwards. Adhesive seams such as these are not in common use at present and it is not proposed to describe in detail the methods of achieving them.

The third use of adhesives does not relate to the construction of seams but is a means of waterproofing them, in this case when the materials are waterproof by virtue of a coating on the inside rather than the outside. Many waterproof materials nowadays are made from a strong woven nylon with an inside coating of neoprene, PTFE or other synthetic material, often of a type that gives breathability as well as waterproofing. Aesthetically these materials are often superior to the PVC-coated materials described earlier and with good flexibility and handling properties they can be sewn easily with strong seams, either superimposed or lap felled. These are then rendered waterproof by the application of a sealing tape along the seam on the inside. A special machine heats the tape to make it stick and then rolls it under pressure firmly into place along the seam. Although these materials can be sewn more easily than the PVC-coated materials, the process of seam sealing adds greatly to the manufacturing cost of the garment, and as with the garments described previously, careful garment design is required to reduce the number of seams and control their shape.

## Moulding

The inclusion of moulding under a heading of alternative methods of joining garments is not entirely accurate since the process of moulding actually eliminates seams as opposed to creating them. It results in a three-dimensional shape without introducing seams. However, because it has some importance as an alternative method of manufacture, it is included here.

The development of moulded garments brings together a number of technologies, without which moulded garments would be impossible. These include automatic knitting machinery, thermoplastic yarns, texturising processes to give fabrics made from these yarns an acceptable handle, stretch fabrics, and heat setting. Moulding causes the fabric of the garment to be permanently stretched or shrunk or both, by heating it until it just begins to soften, deforming it into the required shape, and then cooling it so that the new shape becomes permanent. Knitted fabric is essential since it must be capable of being both stretched and compressed; the synthetic content must be at least 65 per cent.

A particular development some years ago applied the technique to ladies' trousers, which it proved possible to make with no sewing other than a seat seam. The appropriate size of knitting machine was used to knit tubes for the legs and a hem was knitted in at each end. Each tube was heated and moulded over a suitably shaped form to provide a hip, knee and ankle shape, and a section of each was cut out so that they could be joined together at the seat seam to make a pair of trousers. Other garment types, or parts of them, have been moulded by similar methods but for this type of garment the process has not been widely used.

Moulding precludes an important element in the creation of aesthetic appeal in garments – the placement of seams – and styles made by this process are inevitably rather simple. Moulding is used in the manufacture of hats and in standardised garment components where shape can be created in a cost-effective way.

The main exception to this lack of success is the moulding of bra cups, where the combination of a garment which changes little in shape and a fashion for a softer, lighter, less supporting construction has enabled the technology to be applied widely. A high-stretch material of polyamide and elastane is normally used and the sections to form the cups must be cut larger than the actual cup size. This is a disadvantage because it wastes fabric, but it is necessary so that the edge of the cup can be clamped in the moulding machine. Moulding takes place over a hemispherical metal surface and the central area of the cut cup becomes moulded to that shape. No attempt is made to make the moulded cup exactly the shape of the section of the body it will cover since some stretch remains in the material and the garment is designed to be worn in a slightly stretched state. Following the moulding stage, the spare fabric is trimmed from the edges of each cup, and construction of the bra continues in the same way as for a bra with cup sections that are sewn together to create the shape. The saving in seaming costs for the cup is, to some extent, offset by the additional fabric that must be used. Moulded bras represent a significant proportion of the total number of bras now manufactured but this could change if fashion reverts to a firmer, more structured look.

# Chapter Seven
# Pressing and Related Garment Finishing Techniques

Pressing makes a large contribution to the finished appearance of garments and thus their attractiveness at the point of sale. Steam and pressure are frequently applied during garment assembly to ensure the quality of the final product.

The largest use of pressing is in the mass production of tailored garments, particularly menswear. These products receive their shape by a combination of pattern, the attachment of canvasses and/or fusible interlinings, and pressing. The presses have specially designed surfaces that impart shape to selected parts of the garment. By contrast, traditional methods of tailoring (the classic Savile Row suit in the UK) employ specially constructed canvasses that are made to suit a particular customer and give a permanent three-dimensional shape to the garment. These products need be pressed only with a hand iron; there is no requirement for shaping using large presses.

It should be noted that garments that are presented well may not retain their shape in wear and laundering. For example, when a mass-produced suit is dry-cleaned, it will be re-pressed, but not with shape-imparting presses. The result is that the garment becomes flattened. Specialist dry-cleaners will hand iron after cleaning, which will preserve the shape for longer. Savile Row suits, by contrast, will keep their shape during cleaning.

Although the word 'pressing' is often used as a generic term for a variety of different operations involving the use of steam, this chapter will distinguish between pressing, creasing, steaming and pleating.

## The purpose of pressing

### Presenting the fabric for retail

Final pressing is undertaken to smooth away unwanted creases and crush marks. In garment manufacture, creases and crushing occur as a result of operator handling; this is particularly bad when garments are handled between operations in bundles, whether tied up tightly or piled on trolleys or in boxes. However, the increasing use of materials with a high standard of crease recovery, along with the reduction in work in progress that results from the installation of hanging transport systems or the working of team systems, has reduced the problem for many types of garment.

Final pressing also refreshes the fabric appearance after manufacture. Especially during underpressing, the surface of the fabric may be altered. A common symptom is gloss or glazing, induced by extreme pressure of press or iron in order to achieve a firm edge or seam. A related but lesser symptom is a generalised flattening of the nap of the fabric, which no longer shows the richness intended by its designer. With the long-fibred naps, as in corduroy or velvet, this becomes much more important.

## Making creases

Creases are obvious design features in trousers, skirts (where a series of creases is often referred to as pleating), and some collar styles. Creases are less obvious but still require pressing when they are hems and cuff edges, front edges, top edges of waistbands, pocket flaps and patch pocket edges as well as pressed open seams, which from a pressing point of view are two creases sewn together.

## Moulding the garment to the contour of the body

This does not refer to the specialised technique of garment moulding described in Chapter 6, but to the enhancement of shape already largely determined by seams and darts. It is mainly effected in wool or wool-rich fabrics in tailored garments. This sort of moulding involves two kinds of deformation (together or separate): shrinking and stretching. After moulding it is not possible to unpick the seams and return garment parts to their former flat state. The chief areas where this moulding takes place are around the ends of darts, collars, shoulders, armholes and sleeveheads, and sometimes trouser legs. Thus the chest and waist of a tailored jacket created by the pattern's seams and darts can be accentuated by pressing on shaped presses. Generally, where the body has a prominence, extra length is created, and where the body has a hollow the fabric is shrunk.

## Preparing garments for further sewing

The term 'underpressing' is reserved for pressing operations on partly constructed garments, while top-, off- or final pressing is used for completed garments, the actual term varying according to the sector of the industry. The stages at which a garment is underpressed will depend on many factors. It normally takes place when several sewing stages have been completed but the garment parts are still accessible by the press equipment. An obvious example is a jacket and its lining before assembly, after which pressing of the separate sections is no longer possible. Underpressing also makes further sewing easier to do, or easier to do to a high quality standard. It may be possible to topstitch a collar that has not been pressed, but it is likely to be more quickly and accurately sewn if it has. In the case of topstitching collars, it has been possible to incorporate pressing as an integral part of an automated workstation.

Underpressing operations must be scrutinised carefully during product development. Dimensional mismatches, for example, may be the cause of unnecessary underpressing. This may be particularly important if underpressing has been used to make up design samples but has not yet been written into the product costing.

## Categories of pressing

Pressing serves to highlight the variety and extremes that exist within the clothing industry across the different garment types, the levels of style change and the volumes of a style that are produced. Specialised pressing equipment is costly and often relates to a specific garment type, and even a particular shape. Style change may render it redundant. As with sewing machinery, the more flexible the equipment, the more skill is required of the operator. It is useful to divide garments into categories according to the amount and type of pressing they require.

*Garments that require no pressing* may include bras and other foundation garments, stretch swimwear and dancewear, and briefs and other items of underwear. Manufacture achieves a satisfactory finished appearance through topstitching of seams and the use of fabrics, sometimes synthetic and usually knitted, that do not require shaping, refinishing or creasing. In factories making garments solely from these fabrics, there may be no pressing equipment whatsoever.

*Garments requiring minimal pressing or finishing* include simple, single-ply garments such as slips and nightgowns, often in knitted synthetics, tee shirts and other knitted leisurewear, quilted or wadded items such as anoraks, and some laundered and garment-dyed products. The term 'finishing' is used here because this category includes garments that require no more than a light steaming since pressing in the sense of applying pressure is not necessary.

Some production systems reduce the need for pressing by eliminating bundle handling. Both unit production system and teamworking systems can bring garments into this category.

For the opening of seams, creasing of edges, and pressing garments with gathers and fullness, and in situations where style change is frequent, *pressing with an iron* is common because it is simple and flexible.

*Garments requiring extensive underpressing and final pressing* include those that require the pressing open of seams and the setting of edges during manufacture. They are often of more mouldable fabrics, which use large areas of interlining and are usually wholly or partly lined. The category includes men's jackets, trousers and waistcoats, many skirts, women's tailored jackets and trousers, topcoats, trench coats and other lined rainwear. Style change in many of these garments is infrequent and a range of specialised, shaped press equipment has been developed.

*Pleating or 'permanent press' finishing* will be described later.

## The means of pressing

Cotton creases during wear and washing. In terms of its fibre chemistry, this is due to the breaking and reforming of hydrogen bonds between cellulose chains, which occurs easily when the fibres are deformed or heated or exposed to water. The process is reversible, so if the fabric is placed in a particular (uncreased) position and exposed to heat and moisture, the hydrogen bonds will reform and the fabric will take up the new shape. This is what pressing seeks to achieve. Other fibre types have hydrogen bonds, but their tendency to crease is not so pronounced.

The means of pressing are heat, moisture (usually as steam) and pressure, singly or in combination. These means deform or reform fibres, yarns and fabrics in order to achieve the effect intended by the designer.

Equally important, after the application of heat and moisture, is the application of vacuum, which sucks ambient air through the garment as it lies on the buck (the lower part of a press) or pressing table. This dries out residual moisture from the garment (and the buck cladding) rapidly and ensures that the set imparted by pressing is retained. The suction is created by an exhauster operated by an electric motor. In the simpler finishing processes, it will be seen that hot air or infrared heating may serve the same purpose.

Research in the past into the pressing of wool and polyester/wool mixture fabrics has shown the importance of temperature in obtaining a satisfactory standard of pressing but also the difficulty of achieving the required temperatures. Although the pressure of the steam in the supply line to the press will be above atmospheric pressure, and the steam temperature consequently above 100 °C, the steam released from the supply line and through a press and its cladding will cool as it expands. Steaming of garments on a press without the head of the press locked closed produces garment temperatures just short of 100 °C and it is only by locking the press head closed for at least ten seconds and adding further steam that the required temperatures of around 130 °C can be achieved. For polyester/wool trousers, where a durable crease can be set into the material, a period of head lock of 30 seconds should be used to achieve the necessary temperature and at the same time allow the molecules of polyester in the fabric to rearrange themselves in the position of the crease. An application of vacuum for five seconds or more is needed to cool the fabric and prevent the development of unwanted creases during handling by the operator immediately after removal from the press. Precise positioning of the trouser on the press is essential since these creases, once set, are virtually impossible to remove.

It is important to realise that pressing during garment manufacture is often only one set of applications of heat, moisture and pressure during the life of the fabric. The fabric is set during finishing, by a variety of processes depending on the type of fabric and its fibre content, and will be re-pressed for the consumer after dry-cleaning or by the consumer after domestic washing.

A concern of the garment manufacturer, especially one using woollen fabrics, is the possibility of excessive shrinkage during pressing, resulting from relaxation of tensions from inadequate setting during fabric finishing. The problem with tailored garments is that a certain amount of consistent shrinkage is required in order to mould the garments during pressing, but not so much dimensional instability as to result in sporadically undersized garments. Some manufacturers carry out their own shrinkage operation before spreading and cutting, usually by a form of steam blowing or decatising, but occasionally by immersion in cold water with a wetting agent followed by air drying at room temperature (the so-called London shrinking). Knitwear is normally finished flat to the correct dimensions by inserting a wire frame into the garment before the application of steam and vacuum. This is crucial for acrylics, and the stabilisation process may additionally be carried out before cutting.

## Pressing equipment and methods

In categorising garments into the various types that require pressing, reference was made to some of the equipment that is used and it might seem that different companies adhere rigidly to different types of equipment. In practice, many companies combine the use of several types of pressing equipment to achieve satisfactory and economical pressing.

## Irons

The most common type of iron in general use is the steam electric. The iron is heated by an electric element, controlled by a thermostat, and supplied with steam, either from the factory's main steam supply, or from a small boiler adjacent to the pressing unit. The steam function of the iron is activated by the touch of a button, when a powerful jet of dry steam is produced. At extremes, the weights of irons vary from about 2–15 kilos. Several shapes are available including a roughly triangular one similar to a domestic iron, the 'tailor's shape' which has a pointed nose and parallel sides, and a narrow one used for operations such as seam opening on sleeves and trouser legs.

There is a range of workplaces available for ironing. In a situation where a variety of parts and shapes of garments has to be pressed, a simple pressing table, similar in shape to a domestic ironing board, is used. Modern tables have a supply of vacuum to hold the garment in position and dry and set it after ironing. This vacuum facility can also be used as a work aid in the sense that the term was used earlier. A section of a flat garment part can be held in place while the operator moves the remainder of the part to create a fold or pleat, which they then press. The position of the fold can be marked on the press cover for accuracy. The flat table can be fitted with swivel arms, which present bucks of varied shapes to allow the laying of sleeves, shoulders and collars without distortion or the danger of creasing. Each of these has the vacuum facility. Alternatively, the basic table may consist of a very large flat area, or a smaller curved surface, each with additional sections to be swung into position if required. The principle is one of flexibility, with some units able to accept a change of pressing surface so that the most suitable shape is always available for the production of a particular batch of garments. A blowing function is also available on some of these pressing surfaces which gives a billowing surface on which to press. This enables some difficult materials, such as thin, hard rainwear fabrics, to be pressed with less risk of seam impressions showing.

Self-contained units, incorporating a steam boiler and electrically driven vacuum and air blowing facilities, are used increasingly both in the underpressing of tailored garments and the pressing of unstructured garments, because they can be moved from place to place at much less cost than conventional steam presses or the older irons,

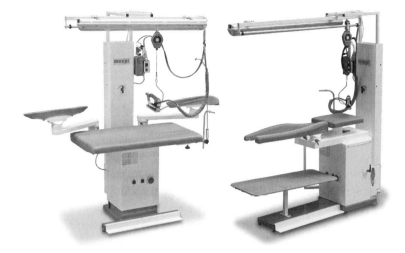

**Figure 7.1** Ironing units showing a variety of surface shapes. (Reproduced by permission of Macpi Group.)

both of which are linked to the factory steam supply. This means that they can be sited within a production line of sewing operations to enable underpressing to be undertaken at minimum cost. Examples of some of the types of ironing unit that are available are shown in Fig. 7.1. The iron is rested at the right-hand end of the flat surface; alternatively the weight of the iron can be taken on the spring fitment on the upper gantry. This reduces operator fatigue in continually picking up and putting down the iron.

The use of an iron and pressing table may require considerable skill on the part of the operator, especially when finally pressing complex dresses or blouses, because of the handling involved around a surface shape which is never exactly that of the garment. Additionally, the amount of steam and vacuum used is left to the operator, and the quality of the pressing may suffer if the operator is tempted to hurry in the interests of high output.

## Steam presses

A steam press consists of a static buck and a head of complementary shape which closes onto it, thus sandwiching the garment to be pressed. A general-purpose, manually operated press is shown in Fig. 7.2. It consists of a frame carrying the buck, which is generally rounded in shape for pressing a variety of garments, linkages to close the head by a scissors action, a pipe system distributing steam to head and buck, a vacuum system to provide suction through the buck, a table

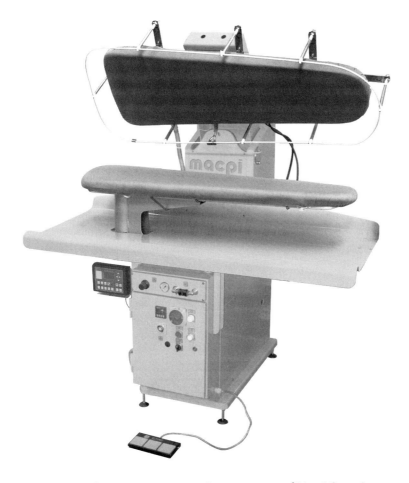

**Figure 7.2** General-purpose steam press. (Image courtesy of Macpi Group.)

around the buck to aid handling of the garment, and foot controls for head closure and vacuum, with hand and/or foot controls for steam. These is also a means of varying head pressure.

When pressing a garment such as a skirt, a typical pressing cycle might be: apply steam from the buck, lock the head to press the garment, further steam from the head or the buck, release the head, and apply vacuum to cool and dry the garment before it is moved around the buck for the next part of it to be pressed. When pressing is completed, the garment is hung on a hanger. Adequate time of application of vacuum is essential if the garment is not to remain damp and to distort at this stage. In the case of a manually operated press, the duration of steam, pressure and vacuum are left to the skill and judgment of the operator, as is the manipulation of the garment around the buck, often rather different in shape from the actual garment.

Where large quantities of a garment shape are being manufactured, there is scope for using bucks, and, of course, matching heads, which are close to the shape of the garment. In particular, in men's jacket production, the total pressing of all the parts of the garment is broken down into many stages, both of underpressing and final pressing, and at each stage a specially shaped press is used. An example of a machine for pressing collars and shoulders is shown in Fig. 7.3. Stocking alternative bucks is a capital intensive practice, and the lead times for supply of new bucks are several weeks long. Consequently, it is increasingly unrealistic to develop garments that require different bucks during pressing.

In some cases, an iron is available beside the press for the operator to touch up local areas of the garment before pressing with the head of the press. This facility can also be used to add sections of fusible interlining to partly constructed garments, especially tailored jackets. The example quoted previously was of a slotted tape interlining being added to the hem of a jacket. It would be attached in position by means of the iron, fused properly by closing the press, the hem could be folded up along the slots, again by means of the iron, before pressing the hem up finally with the press.

Manually operated scissor-action presses have been improved considerably by the use of electronically controlled pneumatic power. The compressed air takes the heavy, fatiguing work of closing the press from the operator, and allows the introduction of automatic timing of the pressing cycle. A decision can be made at the beginning of a production run as to the correct cycle for the fabric and garment style, and the press can be set to reproduce it.

Another improvement is in the mechanical principle in the operation of steam presses. This employs a vertical head movement in addition to or instead of a scissors action, giving the benefits of much finer control and a more even distribution of pressure over the whole surface of the buck, especially where contoured shapes have to be aligned. At the same time additional functions can be incorporated such as head vacuum and air blowing from the buck. The combination of these three factors enables easier pressing of fabrics such as gabardines, where impressions of seams and pockets can cause a problem. The air blower is used in conjunction with head vacuum at the end of the pressing cycle to reduce impressions. The correct pressing cycle can be designed and maintained through the use of microprocessor controls.

A development in press operation is the carousel press. Here a pair of bucks rotates between the operator and either a single or a double head, depending on whether the bucks are identical or an opposite pair for pressing the left and right of a garment part. The operator

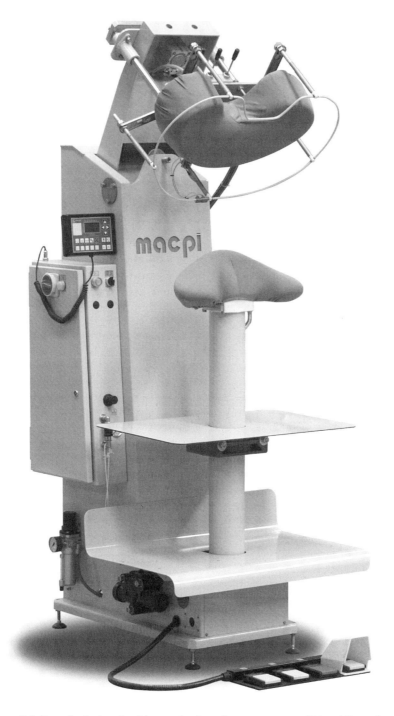

**Figure 7.3** Press for jacket shoulders and collars. (Image courtesy of Macpi Group.)

loads the garment on to one buck which is then moved away to be aligned under the head, often behind a screen that keeps steam away from the operator. Both scissor-action and vertically acting heads can be used but the latter are increasingly common. While the machine carries out the controlled pressing cycle, the operator loads the other buck. This enables the operator to achieve a much higher output because the handling time of the operation takes place during the pressing cycle, leading to higher machine utilisation. An example of a four-station carousel press designed to finish trousers without pleats is shown in Fig. 7.4.

Trouser pressing is conventionally carried out in two operations, in addition to the underpressing of the seam: legging on a flat press, which sets and creases the legs, and topping in a series of lays around the top of the trouser on a contoured press. If the trouser features a pleat at the waistband, the leg crease must be run into it accurately. The problem is to provide firmly set creases at the same time as an even finish to the fabric overall, without impressions of pockets, fly and seams showing. Traditionally, these impressions were removed in

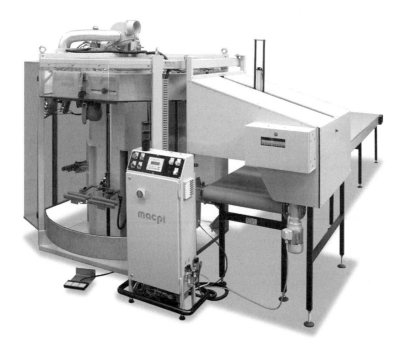

**Figure 7.4** Carousel press with four stations for finishing trousers without pleats. (Image courtesy of Macpi Group.)

a subsequent 'touching up' operation with an iron, on those fabrics such as gabardines where the steam press leaves an unacceptable finish, but on most fabrics this should not be necessary. Trouser legging also moulds the legs by pressing away fullness in the underside below the seat area, and by shaping the calves in closer fitting trousers. In addition, the presser must set the crease in the correct position in order that the crease might hang centrally over the shoe of the wearer. Usually the pattern cutter designs the pattern in such a way that the presser achieves the desired effect by aligning inside leg seam on outside leg seam up to the knee and the inside leg seam then runs back a few centimetres at the crutch.

A number of machines combine the topping and legging in one operation by suspending the trousers, from the waistband, vertically over an upright 'buck' and pressing from each side. Certain difficulties arise with this method, in particular achieving consistency throughout the size range and flexibility of mechanical pressure on critical areas such as waistbands, pockets and fly. The term 'trouser' covers a wide range of garments, including jeans, women's trousers of perhaps simpler construction and requiring a less sharp crease, men's trousers including four pockets, and suit trousers. Whether combined topping and legging is acceptable at the moment will depend on the construction of the trousers, the sharpness of the crease and the required quality standards at the point of sale. Thus separate topping is still frequently used.

The machinery available for pressing legs also includes double leggers, which press two legs simultaneously, with the top hanging down between two separate bucks, onto which one complete head closes. This is shown in Fig. 7.5. Vertically acting heads, carousels and microprocessor controls are also available. In an attempt to avoid impressions and gloss at the side seam, a split head action (with a vertically acting head) applies steam to the whole leg but no pressure to the seam area. Automatic unloading after pressing, which keeps the legs flat, is also available, the first serious approach to mechanising the handling elements in a pressing operation. Other than this example, handling between press and hanger is still a significant part of pressing operations.

### Press cladding

Bucks of steam presses and the tables used with irons (vacuum boards) are commonly covered with a heat-resistant silicone foam. This is protected on the outside by a top cover of woven polyester (or stretch nylon with the more highly contoured bucks). Although it is generally

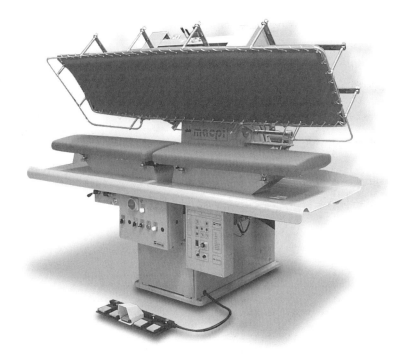

**Figure 7.5** Trouser press: double legger. (Image courtesy of Macpi Group.)

heat-resistant it is normal to protect the underside of the silicone foam from the continuous heat of the buck by a layer of synthetic felt. The silicone foam has a life of several months without compacting. It remains resilient enough over a long period to absorb the thicknesses of seams and inhibit impressions in the finished garments. Both the stretch nylon and the woven polyester top covers should be smooth enough to allow easy manipulation of the garment from one pressing lay to the next.

The heads of steam presses may be covered with a sandwich of materials which contains, from the metal head outwards, a layer of metal gauze, (sometimes copper or more often aluminium) which makes for even distribution of steam, a layer of synthetic felt to protect the next layer, the main layer of knitted cotton padding, and a final layer of outer cover as on the buck. An alternative for certain fabrics and applications is an aluminium grid plate, with perforations for the emission of steam, and contoured to fit the head of the press. While these general approaches to covering head and buck are typical, there are many variations according to the needs of the operation. For instance, a need for firmer pressing will reduce the thickness of padding in a few underpressing operations to merely an outer covering.

*Control of the pressing process*

Despite considerable developments in steam presses in recent years, especially in programmable controls designed to ensure that all of the garments in a batch receive the same, satisfactory cycle of steam, pressure and vacuum, there is considerable variation in the success of the pressing of individual garments. The easiest aspect of the pressing process to measure is the time cycle but with many presses connected to the same steam supply and to the same vacuum line, an individual press may not always receive the supply that it should. Thus the required temperatures may not always be achieved, nor may satisfactory cooling. In addition, there may be unevenness between a head and a buck which affects the pressure achieved on a garment.

Recent developments in sensor technology have made it possible to quantify the conditions inside the press by measuring the temperature profile during the pressing cycle, the pressure on the garment and the strength of the cooling vacuum. Evenness of each parameter across the area of the press can also be measured, as can thickness and compressibility of cladding. This equipment has greatly increased the possibility of setting presses correctly to achieve an acceptable standard of pressing. Test methods for factors such as sharpness of crease have also been developed.

*Creasing machines*

A special type of small press performs an extremely useful function in what is, in effect, an underpressing situation. Creasing machines fold over and press the edges of clothing components such as pockets or cuffs to prepare them for easier sewing. In particular, a patch pocket that has already had the top hem sewn, is pressed ready for the operator to sew it to the garment with no handling of the seam turnings. The operator positions the component over an appropriately shaped die and blades manipulate the fabric to form the creases around it and exert pressure during the pressing cycle. The means of pressing may be heat alone, coming from elements in the machine, or heat and steam for some fabrics.

## Steam air finisher

This equipment is often referred to as a steam air bag, a form press or a 'dolly' press. It consists of a frame carrying a steam distribution system, compressed air distribution system and a pressing form which is a canvas bag in the approximate shape of the garment to be pressed, i.e. a body shape but with no sleeves. There are controls for steam and air release, and timers controlling the steam and air cycles. The equipment aims to reduce the positioning and re-positioning in pressing operations by pressing the whole garment at the same time, though finishing is a better term in this situation since very little pressure is applied to the garment. The operator pulls the garment on to the form from above, and the form is then expanded to its full size and shape as steam is blown through it from the inside. A cycle of, perhaps, eight seconds' steaming is followed by a further period of hot air drying, also by blowing from the inside.

This equipment can remove accidental creases and refinish the fabric, but will not form creases or mould the garment, and will not help much with cellulosic fabrics. It is extremely useful for garments such as nightdresses, tee shirts and blouses, and is sometimes worth using for simple dresses, even though the hem might have to be pressed flat separately with an iron or a steam press. Distortion along buttoned openings is prevented by a sprung, padded, clamp which holds the section of garment in place and an additional attachment is a spring-loaded sleeve former. Care must be taken when finishing garments in knitted fabrics which may stretch, as the size and shape may be distorted to that of the bag covering the unit. If this is a problem, a slipover may be made from a rigid, woven, press-covering fabric, to the pattern shape of each size of garment, and put on the covering bag as a restrainer before pressing each size of the garment style. An example of a steam-air finisher for shirts, jackets and coats is shown in Fig. 7.6.

A variation on the shape described here can be used for jeans and other casual trousers which do not require a crease. The trouser is clamped in a ring at the waist and clamped again at the ankles. Steam followed by hot air is blown through it, while maintaining slight downward tension on the legs.

## Steam tunnel

Another garment finishing process where pressure is not applied to the garments but where handling during the process is reduced is in steam tunnel finishing. It can be used for a variety of simple garments in man-made fibres and blends. In addition to manufacturers, these systems are used extensively by mail-order companies to re-present garments. Some garments on hangers are fed under automatic control through a cabinet on a motorised rail, passed through sections with superheated steam, and dried by air blowing. Alternatively, tee shirts and similar knitwear are loaded on to frames and passed through the tunnel on a conveyor. The tunnel reduces the need for any other pressing process before or after its operation and sometimes elimi-

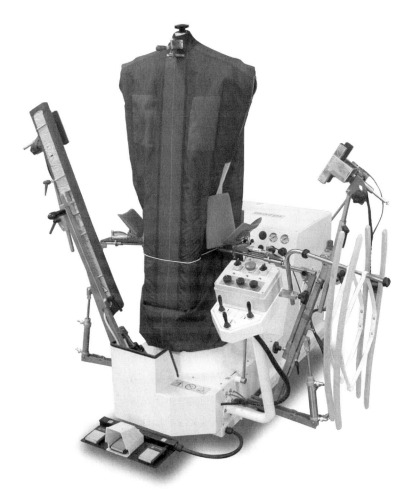

**Figure 7.6** Steam air finisher for shirts, jackets and coats. (Image courtesy of Macpi Group.)

nates it. The aim of the steam is to relax natural fibres, that of the heat to relax man-made fibres. With the garments on hangers or frames, gravity or tension pulls out the wrinkles, and the turbulence of air blowing provides additional energy to relax wrinkles in woven fabrics. Such turbulence should be restricted with fabrics such as acrylics, since excessive agitation makes the fabric pliable and subject to deformation. This fabric responds well to infrared drying, a feature of some tunnels. The setting of steaming and drying conditions in the tunnel can be varied for different fabrics. The operators have only to load and unload the hangers or frames. An example is shown in Fig. 7.7.

**Figure 7.7** Steam tunnel for garment pressing and finishing. (Reproduced by permission of Macpi Group.)

## Pleating

Pleating is a special type of pressing, the aim of which is to produce an array of creases of some durability according to a geometrical pattern. This may be an overall pattern of small pleats, formed as a result of machine pleating a complete roll of cloth, or larger pleats formed by hand pleating of garment sections that have been previously cut to shape and, in the case of skirt sections, hemmed. Examples of machine pleating are fluting and crystal pleating; hand pleating includes box pleats and the fan-shaped pleats that taper to nothing at the waist known as sunray pleats. Like other forms of pressing, the means of pleating are heat, moisture and pressure.

Machine pleating is of two types. The first is a rotary machine in which the rollers are fitted with complementary dies similar to gears. Extensive areas of tiny pleats such as crystal pleating or accordion pleating can be produced on this machine. Different geometrical patterns can be achieved only by changing the complementary dies.

Second is a blade machine in which pleats are formed by the thrust action of a blade or blades. The pleats are set by heat and pressure as they pass between a pair of mangle-type rollers. Some machines have steaming boxes that steam the fabric before pleating. The pleating takes place between two layers of paper and the pleated fabric is re-rolled for delivery along with the paper. This process is normally carried out by specialist firms, rather than by clothing manufacturers. The subsequent cutting of garment sections from the pleated fabric is not easy and sizing can be very variable.

In hand pleating, the fabric is folded between two complementary card patterns, which are scored in such a way as to fold at the lines where pleats are required. The fabric is placed on the first card, the second card is laid over the top, and the cards with their enclosed fabric are then folded tightly into the pleat pattern that is scored on the card. With flimsy fabrics it is possible to insert two plies.

In traditional hand pleating, the folded cards with their enclosed fabric are rolled up inside a further layer of unpleated card, tied round to hold them in place, and put into a steam box or autoclave. This enables pressure to be built up and steam temperatures of around 130 °C to be achieved. This sets the pleats, whose durability is related to the temperature and duration of the steaming, as well as the nature of the fabric being pleated. The time in the autoclave could be as long as half an hour. The autoclave is large enough to take several dozen garment parts at once. Only a small number of clothing manufacturers have their own autoclaves, mainly those who expect always to include pleating in their garment styles and/or those who are geographically remote from the main centres of clothing manufacture. In these centres, specialist firms provide a pleating service. Cut garment parts are hemmed if necessary, then sent out for pleating, and making up continues when they are returned. This delay in between sewing operations is disruptive of production flow and is one of the problems of including pleating as a feature in garment styles. Another problem is the cost, much of which is the result of the large numbers of pleating cards that are needed.

A way of reducing both these problems for certain types of pleat is provided by a specialist pleating press, which enables a garment manufacturer to do pleating within the factory more simply than can be done with an autoclave. The press consists of large, upper and lower flat platens, both of which are heated, and a supply of steam to the lower platen. The garment part is sandwiched between card formers which are steam permeable and the pleats folded into place. Only pleats that will lie flat can be done by this method; it will not create sunray pleats. Several garment panels can be put in the press side by side and a typical pressing time is one to two minutes. Heat, humidity, pressure and time can all be varied to obtain sharp pleats. A separate cardboard-folding machine enables the clothing manufacturer to make his own pleating cards. If necessary, in box pleat and similar designs, the two cards of a pair are folded to slightly different dimensions to allow for fabric thickness.

Before any pleating process is planned for a fabric, checks should be made to ensure that it will not suffer from shrinkage or a change in colour during the process. If there is a likelihood of colour change, other sections of the garment should be put in the autoclave with the parts to be pleated.

## Non-iron garments

In the 1950s, cotton fabrics were given a 'permanent press' treatment to help them compete with the easy-care properties of polyester and nylon. The basis of the treatment was a resin finish imparted to cotton fabrics during finishing, which was subsequently heat-treated (curing) to form permanent chemical bonds within the cellulose (much stronger than the hydrogen bonds) and thereby impart a resistance to subsequent creasing. While the finishing treatment achieved this goal, it adversely affected other fabric properties such as tear strength, abrasion resistance and some shrinkage. Furthermore, nylon and polyester fabrics always dried faster than permanent-press cotton.

In subsequent decades, the emphasis shifted towards easy care garments. Research with cotton fabrics was directed at achieving easy care properties, requiring little or no ironing. Initially, polyester/cotton blends were investigated. The polyester fibres were heat-set using a hot press and then the cotton fibres were cured in an oven. There are now five commercially available non-iron processes:

- ♦ *Pre-cure*. The fabric is cured during finishing and no further operations are needed by the clothing manufacturer.
- ♦ *Post-cure*. The fabric is resin-treated during finishing, and then dried. After making up the garment, with any pleats or creases pressed into place, the whole garment is passed through a curing oven.
- ♦ *Dipping*. Untreated fabrics are made up into garments, which are then treated with resin. After drying, the garments are pressed to shape and then cured in much the same way as in the post-cure route.
- ♦ *Metered spraying*. Resin is applied to a finished garment by tumbling in a drum with the resin being introduced in precise quantities in a fine mist. The garments are then

dried, pressed and cured as for the post-cure and dipped
processes.
 ♦ *Vapour phase.* Finished garments are placed in an enclosed
vessel and treated with gaseous formaldehyde, acid catalyst
and steam. There is no subsequent curing stage.

Each of these processes has advantages and disadvantages, of which
only a selection can be considered here. Pre-cure is low cost, but it is
unsuitable for garments that need pleats or formal creases, and it
creates problems in sewing (particularly seam pucker). All the other
processes require the clothing manufacturer to invest in machinery
or to sub-contract to specialists. The post-cure, dipping and metered
spraying processes require careful choice of fabrics, threads, trims,
components and interlinings to ensure compatibility. Fabric softeners
are generally applied to improve the handle. The vapour phase process
produces a softer handle than the other non-iron processes, but it
places even more demands on the clothing manufacturer in the choice
of materials and the control of the process (which is potentially haz-
ardous). The most common non-iron processes used in the UK are
post-cure and dipping.
   There are numerous product development issues that have to be
addressed in order to achieve the desired product performance.
Fabrics will shrink to some extent and there may be a problem of
puckering. There will be some degradation of fabric performance, and
this must be taken into account as decisions are being made about
the product specification (for example appearance, crease retention,
abrasion resistance, shade and handle). All auxiliary materials must be
scrutinised for potential loss of performance as a result of the non-iron
processing.

## The state of pressing

Not nearly as much attention has been paid to the technology of
pressing as to the technology of sewing and cutting. What has been
achieved is the means to press all fabrics and garments, refinishing
the fabric and producing a temporary or durable set in the three-
dimensional shapes required.
   A number of interesting points may be noted:

 ♦ The percentage of total manufacturing work content
involved in pressing is generally not known across
the industry. Individual cases noted show a range of
5–15 per cent.

♦ Actual pressing time as a percentage of the total time in pressing operations has not yet been analysed as it has for typical sewing operations. The capital requirements for pressing are large in comparison with other aspects of clothing production. Constraints on expenditure have limited the developments taking place. These are mainly in the area of electronic control (digital rather than analogue) and reprogrammable cycles.

♦ The possibilities of automation have been explored for some steam presses, but most pressing operations are batch processes that require the continual intervention of humans.

♦ Great advances in the general area of non-iron garments and easy care are by no means complete, although this concept involves textile structures and finishing as well as sewing and fusing technology.

♦ Loss of shape in wear and laundering is still poorly understood.

# Chapter Eight
# Technology and Management of Colour

There has always been a general problem throughout the clothing supply chain of understanding and managing colour. This ranges from the selection of a colour palette by designers, the production of standards, dissemination of those standards to relevant stages in the supply chain, and correctly using those standards.

Colour communication may be based on visual assessment. In such cases, words are needed to describe the perceived problems and the responses that are needed. Traditionally, subjective phraseology has been used (such as: 'more sunshine is needed in that yellow') but, whilst this can be meaningful between colleagues who are used to working together, it does not work when the people communicate only by email or telephone, and it does not work across cultures.

Colour communication may be based on numerical data. This is where instrumental assessment of colour is made and spectral data are recorded. Although this brings objectivity to the definition of colour, there are still major problems interpreting those data against the standard and deciding on appropriate responses.

Often, colour matching of materials is required, for example, the matching of thread or other components to fabric. This can be a difficult process requiring equipment, experience and skill. There are several problems present in any matching situation, relating to the person doing the matching, the materials being matched, and the surroundings. Leaving aside the problem of actual colour blindness, which would bar a person from working with colour in any way, individuals vary in their ability to distinguish shades. Thus two people may see a shade match differently, one regarding it as a good match and the other a poor match.

In this chapter, we start by looking at the physics of colour, go on to identify the problems of gamut mapping, and then address the issue of colour specification. Finally, we consider the different colour management approaches that can be adopted.

## Physics of colour

There are many sources giving an introduction to colour. A good starting point is the ASBCI (2005) handbook is for industrial users (designers, buyers, technicians and sales personnel) who want to know how the science of colour can be applied to the world of textiles and fashion.

People see colour in two ways:

♦ from light emitters (such as the sun and computer colour monitors)
♦ from light absorbers (such as fabric, skin, hair, printed materials)

The sun gives us a complete spectrum of visible light, as is apparent when we use an artificial glass prism or look at a rainbow, which is a natural means of refracting light. Other emitters are more restricted in the colours they offer: tungsten filament lights have more yellow and red than sunlight and low-pressure sodium street lights are almost monochromatic with an orange light (wavelength 589 nm) that leaves everything looking washed out. Computer aided design (CAD) screens have been cleverly designed to allow users to perceive millions of colours by combining the three primary colours: red, green and blue (RGB). The human vision system combines these colours to give oranges, yellows, white, etc. Our eyes have three receptor cells that are sensitive to these three colours and our brains combine the signals and allow the perception of all the colours of the rainbow. CAD screens work by adding red, green and blue together to create the perception of a continuum of colour. This is referred to as 'additive' colour.

Light absorbers work rather differently. Pigments in a material absorb certain frequencies and allow others to be reflected. Human vision senses the reflected frequencies and registers the colour of the material. The colour that is seen is the result of selective absorption of incident light and is referred to as 'subtractive' colour. Human vision is able to combine the colours Cyan, Magenta and Yellow (CMY) so as to reconstruct the primary colours. Therefore, in principle, CMY colours can be used in printing to reproduce the colours available via a CAD screen. In practice, the colour gamut is more restricted and colour printers often have to use other colours to achieve desired colour effects. Furthermore, to get a good black, printers use a black ink (K) rather than a combination of CMY. Hence, the standard office colour printer has four colourways: CMYK.

Commission Internationale d'Eclairage (CIE) colour space was developed in 1931. The colour standards resulting from it are intended to

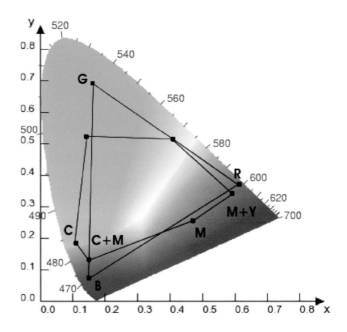

Figure 8.1 CIE colour space.

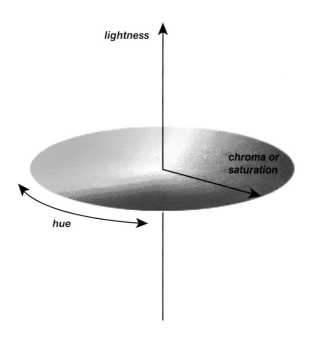

Figure 8.2 CIE colour wheel plot, with changes in intensity in the vertical axis.

**Figure 8.3** The Kaledo Color Match for colour management and communication, with calibrated VDU, portable spectrophotometer and light cabinet for swatches. (© Lectra Systems and used with permission.)

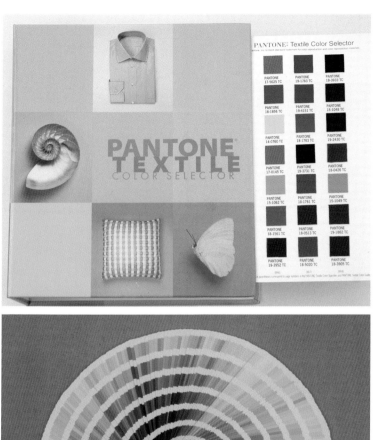

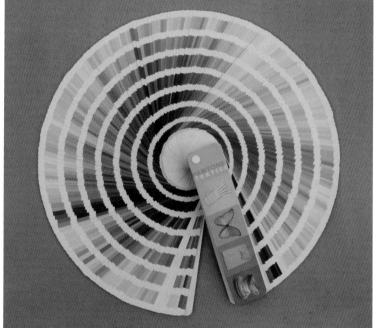

**Figure 8.4** Pantone products for colour specification.

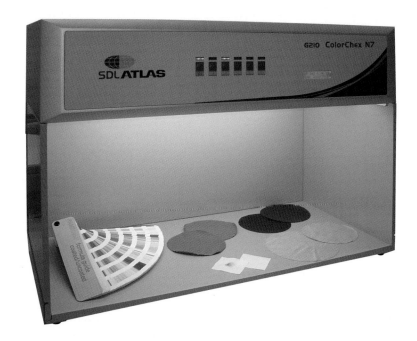

**Figure 8.5** Light cabinet. (Reproduced by permission of ASL Atlas Inc.)

**Figure 8.6** The Farnsworth-Munsell 100 Hue Test Kit. (Reproduced by permission of farbstandards.de.)

model the vision sensitivity of a human observer. The main advantage is that the colour produced by one set of inks can be matched to the colour produced by another set of inks by adjusting them to produce the same CIE coordinates.

CIE space is represented by an x–y plot with green, blue and red primaries occupying different limits of the colour space. The graph is also referred to as the CIE chromaticity diagram. Moving around the boundary allows a change of *hue*: moving anticlockwise goes through the spectrum: red, orange, yellow, green, blue, indigo, violet. In Fig. 8.1 (Plate 1) numbered locations along the curve are the wavelengths (in nanometres) of the colours. The filled area represents the space of colours that can be perceived by the human eye.

As one moves from the outside margin to the centre, there is a reduction of the colour: the hue becomes less saturated. There is a white spot in the middle (x = 0.3138, y = 0.3310) which represents daylight. Illuminant D65 is associated with this spot, where the letter D refers to daylight, and the number 65 refers to the colour temperature of 6500 K.

Also marked on Fig. 8.1 (Plate 1) are the colour gamuts for a CAD screen (RGB colour) and for a four-colour printer (CMYK). These are considered below.

In 1976, the CIE colour space was reworked and presented as the CIELAB system. This was intended to provide something equivalent to the way humans see colour. It has been very successful, and Lab coordinates are now widely used. The plot becomes a three-dimensional one, with the vertical axis (L) defining the lightness or darkness of the colour (Fig. 8.2; Plate 1). The other two dimensions are represented as a plane cutting through the vertical axis: there is a green–red axis (referred to as the a axis) and a blue–yellow axis (referred to as the b axis).

By specifying hue, chroma and lightness, the total range of theoretical colours can be defined. A summary of this terminology is as follows:

*Hue* gives the colour of the spectrum (red, yellow, green, blue).

*Chroma* is a measure of depth of colour, e.g. vivid, pure colours versus pastel colours (red is highly saturated; pink is relatively unsaturated).

*Lightness* is the perceived intensity. Lightness is the word used for light-reflecting objects, whereas the word brightness is used for light-emitting objects (light bulb, sun, computer screen).

Since Lab coordinates represent the colour perception of the human eye, it is necessary to link each set of coordinates with three parameters:

- ◆ coloured object (utilising spectral data)
- ◆ light source (most commonly D65)
- ◆ observer (most commonly 10° standard observer)

(In some sectors of the paper printing industry, Hunter Lab coordinates are used, which are defined differently from the CIE Lab coordinates. To avoid confusion, there has been a practice of writing CIE coordinates as L*a*b*. However, this convention is not used here, as Hunter Lab coordinates are not found in the clothing and textiles sector.)

Printers, CAD screens and other tools for communicating colour are not able to reproduce all the theoretical colours. For each, a colour gamut must be defined. Fig. 8.1 (Plate 1) shows the restricted colour gamuts of a computer monitor and a four-colour printer. These colour gamuts, if known, will inform the user about the colours that are within the capability of the office printer, CAD screen, scanner or textile printer.

Different manufacturers produce monitors with slightly different gamuts. Furthermore, as monitors age, the phosphors emitting RGB colours deteriorate and the gamut changes. Clearly, any attempt to standardise the colours seen on CAD screens will require calibrating the monitors. A similar situation applies to printers because inks exhibit signs of ageing.

## Gamut mapping

A good example of a colour management issue is that experienced by users of desk top printers. The task is to reproduce a specified image using the printer and inks available. The problem is that a four-colour printer cannot reproduce all the colours seen by the human eye. It has a reduced colour gamut. Consequently, compromises have to be made. The techniques used are known as gamut mapping, two of these being colorimetric correction and photometric correction.

Colorimetric correction matches exactly all the colours within the gamut of the print system being used, and adopts the closest match for all the others. This may deliver acceptable results, but it has the reputation of being unsuitable for photographs with significant out-of-gamut colours. Perceptual (or photometric) correction applies a common correction to all the colours, so that all can be located within the gamut of the print system. This means that the printed image will have less saturated colours than the original, but there will be an internal consistency in the way colours are represented. CAD systems associated with printing software will normally offer the user several options.

An alternative strategy is to enhance the technology by increasing the number of inks (by using a 6, 7 or 8 colour printer) or by improving the quality of the inks being used with the 4 colour printer.

## Colour specification and standardisation procedures

Often the starting point for colour selection by designers is not standardised. Some may work from a CAD screen (RGB colour), some will use swatches of fabric from suppliers or a Pantone standard (spot colour), and some will start with a printed or scanned image (CMYK colour). In practice, a variety of materials have been used as alternatives to fabric swatches: a length of yarn, a magazine cutting, a sample of plastic. These different starting points have to be addressed by any colour management system subsequent to the design work.

The tools used to process colour at the design stage are CAD systems, scanners, digital camera images and office printers (which have RGB and CMYK gamuts). Thus, in many cases, spot colours are converted to a digital format in order to process them digitally. This is not a problem if the spot colour lies within the gamut of the particular tools being used, but it is a problem if it cannot be accurately reproduced by RGB or CMYK gamuts. Fig. 8.3 (Plate 2) illustrates one system, the Kaledo Color Match system, for colour management and communication.

The finished product, if dyed or screen printed, has a spot colour and if digitally printed, it has a CMYK colour gamut. If the designer starts by specifying a colour outside the range of dyes or pigments being used, or outside the gamut of CMYK printing, then there will be problems reproducing that particular shade and producing true-colour printed images of the product.

## Standardisation using standard swatches

It has long been a practice of textile manufacturers to provide samples of their materials dyed up to different shades that satisfy the forecasted colour trends and that show their products off to the best advantage. These samples then become standards within organisations and their suppliers: defining the shades that are being used. The system has the merit of ensuring that the standard colours can be achieved using commercial dyeing procedures. Problems can arise when the designer or buyer selects the fabric, but requires it to be dyed to a particular shade. This is where samples have to be produced and approved before sample swatches can be circulated within the supply chain.

The system has served the clothing industry for many years, but there are numerous limitations. Swatches can show signs of wear and they can get dirty. There are opportunities for confusion about which sample was approved. However, the main problem is that the process of approving samples and circulating standards is slow. This does not sit comfortably with the general trend of reducing lead times and delays in the supply chain.

## Standardisation using Pantone colour standards

Pantone Inc. has made a business based on providing standard swatches, linked to CAD data that can be incorporated into colour palates (Fig. 8.4; Plate 3). Designers choose colours and develop palates using the Pantone colour book. The principle is that the starting point is standardised, and that the supply chain can acquire the same standard swatches and incorporate them within their quality systems. Experience suggests some beneficial effects and some limitations.

The major positive impact is that colours are selected and specified by a unique number. The Pantone range of colours can be acquired by all who need them, and there is no requirement to circulate standard swatches to define the colour. There is still a need to prepare and approve samples that are intended to match the selected Pantone standards, but time savings are already gained and the procedures for approval are simplified.

However, it should be noted that Pantone colours are not without some variability. Differences between Pantone books have been reported by users, and there may be changes within an individual book with time and with humidity. The Textile Colour Guide carries a caution, alerting the user to colour changes because of 'uncontrollable fading of printed, coated or dyed materials'. Furthermore, although a colour may exist as a Pantone swatch, there is no guarantee that a printer (or a dyer) can match the shade. This is a major issue with digitally printed technologies, but is also relevant to conventional dyeing and printing processes.

Until recently, Pantone Inc. did not define its colours numerically (in terms of spectral reflectance data) and the supply chain had the task of matching shades that are defined only by a swatch. RGB information has been provided, but without specifying which RGB system has been used. So these data provide only ballpark colours for CAD users and so do not serve as standards for the supply chain. For these reasons, alternative colour management systems have been sought. However, in March 2007, Pantone announced an initiative with Clariant International Inc. with the title *Pantone for Fashion and Home*. This provides colour books, swatches, spectral colours and dye recipes for the 1925 colours in the range. The impact of this initiative will become apparent in coming years. The thinking behind it is sound, and is discussed in the following section.

## Standardisation using colour standards linked to spectral data

Colour control is possible by specifying spectral reflectance data. Ultimately, this is the most meaningful approach for textile dyers and printers. The main difficulty is that the rest of the supply chain lacks familiarity with colour technology and procedures for the quantification of colour standards. In particular, designers and buyers are not used to working with spectral values. The language of colour for these people is typically drawn from aesthetic, poetic or emotional sources. The culture gap within the supply chain can be immense.

It should be noted that this situation is not static, and designers are perfectly capable of using computer tools when these are perceived as enhancing the design function. Developers of colour standards based on spectral reflectance values have sought to provide tools that 'capture' spectral data in the earliest stages of design work, in a way that is unobtrusive and that does not inhibit creativity.

Contemporary CAD software systems are capable of managing colour to link sample, monitor display, paper printing and textile colouration. This is done by extensive calibration of components and software routines that ensure the whole system is coordinated. Calibration is necessary for the screen display (RGB colour) and the paper printer (CMYK). Tools and software routines for doing this are becoming widespread.

Small, desktop spectrophotometers are available for the use of design personnel. The device can capture the spectral reflectance data of a swatch, magazine image or photograph, and provide an RGB representation of the data on the designer's CAD screen. The designer does not need to know anything about the meaning of these data, only that a 'fingerprint' of the colour has been stored for reference by others downstream in the supply chain. The principle is essentially very simple. Once the fingerprint of the colour has been defined, an integrated system of colour management through the supply chain is viable.

Several colour management systems have been developed that incorporate libraries of physical swatches, covering the range of colours accessible to the designer. These systems can be linked to spectral data and dye recipes, and can be transported easily throughout the world.

There is, therefore, convergence between the colour management systems appropriate for dying solid colours and those appropriate for digital printing. If the output required is a dyed fabric, the designer needs to start with colours within the colour gamut of the approved dyes. If the output is a printed textile, the designer needs to start with colours that are obtainable by the screen printing system or the digital

printing system (as appropriate). The principles of colour science outlined above are relevant here, and the tools offered by CAD software
should be capable of handling issues of gamut limitations in a way
that is understandable to users.

## Clothing technologists and colour

Clothing technologists have been involved in two ways in the management of colour. First, technologists have been asked to contribute to
the *installation* of a colour management system for their company.
This has necessitated familiarity with all the issues discussed above.
Second, technologists have been involved in *maintaining* colour management systems, checking that all users know what they are doing,
and ensuring that informed colour assessment decisions are made
regarding each test sample. This is the topic reviewed below.

There are essentially two formal ways to assess whether a swatch
matches a colour standard.

- ♦ a visual assessment may be made under controlled illumina-
  tion conditions
- ♦ a spectrophotometer may be used to obtain spectral data,
  which is then compared with the standard

Both routes are covered by widely used standards. These include:

BS 950-1:1967 – Specification for artificial daylight for the
   assessment of colour. Illuminant for colour matching and
   colour appraisal
BS 8475: 2006 – Instrumental colour measurement of
   textiles – Method
BS 6923:1988 – Method for calculation of small colour
   differences
AATCC Evaluation Procedure 9 – Visual assessment of colour
   difference of textiles
AATCC Evaluation Procedure 6 – Instrumental colour
   measurement
AATCC Evaluation Procedure 7 – Instrumental assessment of the
   change in colour of a test specimen

Visual assessment makes use of a special light cabinet containing
one of each of the types of illuminant under which a match might
need to be made. The box is painted a standard grey on the inside,
the samples are viewed at a standard angle to the light, and the lighting in the room surrounding the box is also specified. If a light box is
not available, matching should be done in good natural north daylight

or in a room lit by BS Artificial Daylight. The fabric samples used should be at least 10 cm square, held at an angle of 45° to the light source and maintained stationary with the thread whilst a decision is made. They should be viewed against as plain a background as possible. Whether a light box is used or not, if sewing threads are being matched, the thread should be sewn into the fabric since a single strand will generally appear paler than the thread on the package. If a clothing manufacturer does not have satisfactory conditions for thread matching to the high standards that are required, the service can normally be provided by the thread suppliers on receipt of a fabric swatch. It is important that the equipment is maintained in good condition and that it is used in a predetermined manner. The equipment is illustrated in Fig. 8.5 (Plate 4).

Spectrophotometers require only a small area of material to be analysed and the output is a set of spectral data. The equipment needs to be calibrated and maintained, and housed in an atmosphere with humidity control. The output can be understood as a fingerprint of the colour of the sample and it can be linked to dye recipes. Computerised systems exist to take this data and to calculate dye recipes necessary to achieve the shade. The colour of dyed samples can also be measured and compared with the original sample across the whole spectrum of recorded data. Various colour difference equations exist to describe the variance and these also allow pass–fail limits to be established. How large a colour difference is acceptable will depend on a particular garment manufacturer's standards for the market, but to many visual observers it would be undetectable.

Inevitably, there are some complexities in the process of colour matching. Phenomena in the materials themselves can affect the ease of achieving a good match. *Metamerism* describes the situation where a colour may match perfectly under one illuminant but may be a mismatch under a second. Some dyes will produce a shade which matches a standard in, say, artificial daylight but not in the tungsten light used domestically. Some retail stores use special tubes that use less energy but can give a different colour effect from domestic lighting. These retailers will need to ensure that the match is good in the display situation in the store as well as domestically.

The dyer, therefore, should choose dye combinations carefully so that as well as matching under the specified illuminant, the match is reasonable under other illuminants. This has been a relatively easy task since the advent of computer dye recipe predictions. The computer can examine all possible combinations of these dyes and inform the dyer beforehand as to the level of metamerism that can be expected in the final product (expressed as a metameric index). Metamerism should be checked when: there is an unknown combination of dyes in the source; when alternative combinations of dyes are used to get the same end colour but with reduced cost; and when matching across systems (i.e. pigments and dyes).

A related problem is known as *geometric metamerism*, an apparent change of colour as the direction of viewing is changed. It tends to occur more with fabric panels than with threads and trims but it can affect the judgment of their colour.

Another difficulty with dyestuffs is that they may *fluoresce*, i.e. absorb light in the ultraviolet part of the spectrum and re-emit it in the visible part. This phenomenon is actually made use of in white materials to make them look brighter, but if it is present in dyestuffs producing other colours it may cause shades to match in strong sunlight but differ in poor daylight or tungsten lighting. This issue is growing in importance because of the use of lighting with a high UV content in night clubs and discos. Clothing with dyes that fluoresce look good in this lighting, but care is needed to establish the criteria for effective colour management. For example, the spectrophotometers used must have the capability of working with UV light.

These complexities suggest that colour management needs to be the task of trained personnel. They need to understand and maintain the equipment, to interpret the data, and to supplement instrumental data with their own skilled judgment. To do this, the observers must have good colour vision.

Tests are available to check people's ability to see colour accurately and these tests should be administered to anyone involved in choosing or checking a colour match. For example, the Farnsworth-Munsell 100 Hue Test Kit (Fig. 8.6; Plate 4) is a set of coloured tiles which individuals must place in shade order to assess their colour perception. The Ishihara Colour Blindness Test Chart Kit provides coloured images with embedded patterns that are only visible to people with normal vision. These charts offer a useful screening test for colour vision deficiencies prior to using the 100 Hue Test Kit.

In matching fabric and other items, the surface characteristics of the items being matched can have a significant effect upon the final visual shade. It is not possible to produce a coloured continuous filament thread, with its high lustre, so that it will appear exactly the same as a coloured spun or corespun thread which has a fibrous, matt surface. In addition, the surface character or twist of the thread may be changed as it goes through a sewing machine and this may affect its shade. The local density of a fabric in a seam may also cause difference in the shade of the seam compared to a single ply of fabric elsewhere in the garment and this may affect apparent thread match. Buttons, ribbons and other items may also have a glossy surface compared with the main fabric which will make matching difficult.

Having chosen a suitable shade to match the material to be sewn or to contrast with it for decoration, it is important that the selected shade remains colourfast throughout the life of the finished article. The *colourfastness* of any material is the resistance of its colour to the different agencies to which it may be exposed during manufacture and use. This usually means wash fastness and light fastness but other factors may be involved such as fastness to rubbing, pressing, cold water, sublimation, chlorination, dry-cleaning, bleaching and perspiration. Colourfastness is assessed in terms of change of shade in the item itself and staining of material adjacent to it. The tests used for colourfastness in sewing threads and other components follow the same lines and use the same Grey Scale methods of assessment as are used in investigations of other textile materials. The need for colourfastness to some of these factors is largely self-explanatory but others may be less clear. Colourfastness to rubbing is necessary so that items used for contrast do not stain any adjacent fabric against which they may be rubbed constantly during use. Hot, wet pressing represents one of the severest tests of fastness; to test it, a wet sample of thread or other trim is placed between one piece of wet cloth and one dry piece and pressed with a hot iron for 15 seconds. In practice, wet and dry parts of a garment may be pressed together during ironing. The cold water test covers the situation where a garment containing a strongly coloured trim is left lying wet. This condition could be more severe than washing since no relative movement occurs and permanent staining could result. This particular problem can vary with the fibre content of the material being stained and bulked synthetic fabrics present a particular difficulty. They are sometimes referred to as 'scavengers' as they tend to attract any spare dyestuff to themselves.

Where thread is concerned, a wide range of colourfast shades are available in cotton threads for use on cotton fabrics, and in polyester and polyamide threads for use on cotton, polyester and polyamide fabrics. The problem of *sublimation* may arise when garments are subjected to permanent press curing processes. Temperatures as high as 175 °C can be required and at this temperature some dyestuffs can sublimate, i.e. the dye vaporises and changes the colour of the substrate. Moreover, it may be deposited on a cooler fabric surface, causing staining. This problem may affect polyester garments, for example, where some of the garment pieces are fused and others are not.

Permanent press treatment of garments to give them easy care properties generally involves chemicals and high temperatures which may adversely affect sewing threads in several ways. The main factors are shrinkage, strength loss and sublimation. Cotton threads are generally unsuitable because of loss of strength and shrinkage, although they are normally free from sublimation. Spun polyester and polyester core-spun are suitable with respect to strength and shrinkage and dyes are generally used on them that are fast to sublimation, but it is advisable to mention the particular end use when ordering the thread. *Chlorination* is a hazard when articles are exposed to certain bleaching agents, swimming pool water and many anti-felting treatments for wool, the latter being particularly severe. Cotton threads are unsuitable as they can become bleached but polyester is normally satisfactory.

Where any items are being put together in a garment in a situation of contrast, the colourfastness requirements are higher than when they match; it is always advisable to notify the suppliers of a contrast item that it will be used in that situation, as well as notifying them of any special processes to which the garment will be subject, so that special care can be taken with dyeing or different materials can be used.

A special problem of colour, though not of colourfastness, is the *yellowing* of white materials and threads. Aside from any problem of white garments becoming soiled in manufacturing, problems occasionally arise when apparently perfectly clean garments are found to have yellow stains in places on them when they are unpacked before sale. Considerable investigation has been applied to this problem and an important factor appears to be exposure of the garment to oxides of nitrogen or hydrogen sulphide in polluted atmospheres. The pollution could arise from such things as vehicle exhausts or boiler or cooker emissions and tends to be worse during the winter months. Numerous other factors are also implicated such as fluorescent brightening agents, which may be prone to yellowing and which may migrate and concentrate in certain areas of the garment such as hems and seams, chemicals present in (or contamination of) cardboard and polythene used for packaging, and the particular tendency of some white polyamide fibres to yellow if exposed to certain pollutants. Close scrutiny of packaging materials, fabric finishes, sewing threads and associated trimmings will reduce the possibility of yellowing and work continues to find satisfactory chemical inhibitors which could be applied to these items.

## Implementation of colour management procedures

From what has been written above, any management scheme must incorporate:

- ♦ properly maintained visual assessment systems
- ♦ properly maintained and calibrated instrumental colour management systems
- ♦ an appropriate testing environment

- trained personnel who understand the systems
- brand owner involvement to create specifications and establish tolerances

Of these elements, the second is highly desirable but not essential. It should be noted that many dyehouses throughout the world do not yet have a spectrophotometer as a resource, and are not equipped to participate in colour management using instrumental data collection. However, all the other elements are crucial to the success of colour management.

Thus, designers and buyers are part of the process, and they need to communicate in ways that are meaningful to the supply chain. Failure to do this means that there will be no benefits in the timescales or costs associated with the approval of samples, whatever investments in equipment have been made by suppliers. The appropriate response to this is to accredit personnel in the brand owner/retail organisation who are trained and competent to manage colour communication.

Within the supply chain, there is a similar need for trained and accredited personnel who will participate in communication, use the equipment and interpret data.

In it anticipated that in each of these organisations, clothing technologists will play a significant part in training, implementing and participating in the colour management process.

# Chapter Nine
# Clothing Technology and Product Development

This chapter is concerned with the application of clothing technology know-how. What is the role of clothing technologists in the process of garment manufacture? Are clothing technologists trouble-shooters in manufacturing? Do they work with designers helping to make products commercial? Do they have a role in retail organisations? The answer to these questions is 'yes' – but the way the technology is introduced is not always the best or most cost effective.

## Late-stage technology inputs

Traditionally, much clothing technology input has been at the pre-production stage in manufacturing plants. This is indicated in the simplified process map in Fig. 9.1.

In the past, the writer was responsible for setting up the manufacturing system that would make a child's top. The first sight of the garment was an approved sample that was forwarded from the design office about two weeks before the production line was scheduled to commence work on the garments. Management and supervisor looked through the operations sequence given on the cost sheet and planned the processes and the allocation of operators to each operation. However, one operation was a problem: the pockets were topstitched with two curved lockstitch seams separated by a few millimetres. The people who had made the approved sample were approached: how was this operation done? The answer was that a sample hand had marked the lines of sewing and had followed these lines very carefully using a lockstitch machine. This was not a commercial way of carrying out the operation: it was too slow and there were too many quality hazards. A specially designed jig had to be made, using a twin-needle machine. This jig took some time to make, resulting in delays to the start of the style. There was a further problem because even with

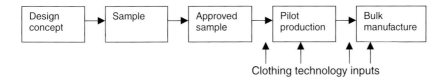

Figure 9.1 Technology inputs in a traditional product development route.

overtime, the jig operation was a capacity constraint on production, so that 'catching up' with the schedule was not possible. There were thus several significant excess costs associated with this style. These costs were assigned to manufacturing excesses, but the reality was that they were late-stage product development costs.

This scenario is by no means unusual. Similar things could be reported from all sectors of the industry and also from non-clothing sectors. Design and design development costs are relatively low and these are normally regarded as budgeted product development costs. The process planning stage is often the first time technologists get to work on the product, and it is not unusual for changes to be made at this stage. These changes are often costly, because many (if not most) aspects of the product are part of a contract with the customer and the options for modification are much reduced. If there are subsequent changes during bulk manufacture, the costs can be very high. The cost build-up is illustrated in Fig. 9.2.

## The problem of communication

Companies have been organised traditionally along functional lines. Consider a manufacturing company with an in-house design capability. Traditionally, Design, Production, Sales and Finance are distinct parts of the company, often with their own director and management structure. This creates problems of communication between functions and may adversely affect communications outside the organisation.

Designers operate in a design office, often close to their customers, and they talk the language of aesthetics, creativity and fashion trends. Their primary communications are with customer buyers, but the buyers have their own agenda. Their brief is to achieve commercial benefits from selling garments, and their language relates to market demand, margins and volumes. There is common ground regarding fashion trends affecting demand, but not all buyers can operate well in a design culture.

Technologists and manufacturing people are typically based on distant sites and have a different language still. Technologists are

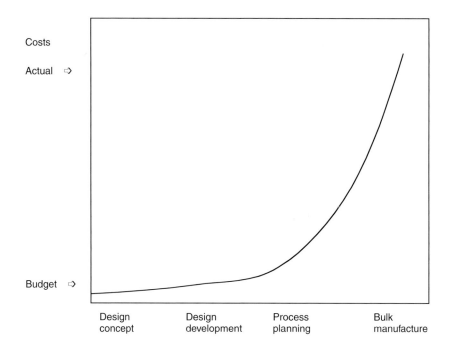

**Figure 9.2** Staged contributions to product development costs.

people who work with specifications and who are used to measuring things. The manufacturer culture is concerned with materials management, people management, the allocation of resources and unit costs. The diversity of these individuals is portrayed in Fig. 9.3. Effective communication between them may be elusive.

There is, of course, an element of caricature in the above analysis, and work experience does broaden people's ability to communicate and to have worthwhile judgments outside their specialist areas of expertise. The point that is really being made here is that traditional organisational structures do not provide the kind of communication that is necessary to manage the product development process.

There is a case for change, but people will only change when they perceive benefits and where there are cost drivers. To elaborate on this, we shall look at an example of a late-stage product change that resulted from inadequate product development and the use of technologists as fire-fighters.

## Late-stage product development: quantifying costs

The case study documented in this section concerns a major quality problem that disrupted the manufacture of a 500 dozen blouse

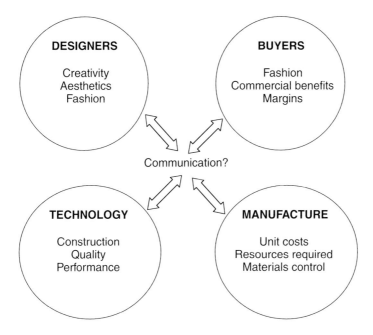

**Figure 9.3** Contrasting cultures within traditional organisations and the communication problem.

contract. Factors affecting costs have been investigated. The production line was organised as a product layout, with a manual overhead rail transporter system. Bundles of varying size, but typically of two dozen garments, were carried on diabolos. The line had 16 operators, three of which were recent trainees.

The blouse was almost identical to another that had previously been made up by the line. This previous style had been free of quality problems, and none were anticipated with the new style. The difference in making-up was just one additional row of stitching around the neck. The previous style had one row of stitching, whereas the new style had two rows (see Fig. 9.4).

Two factors led to the decision not to send through a pilot lot:

- The style, with the exception of neck stitching, was really a continuation of a style already being produced satisfactorily.
- The customer required the garments quickly, and management wanted to avoid the delay that would be introduced by having a pilot lot.

When it was eventually detected, the quality problem affected the neck facing. After in-line pressing, the appearance was poor. The facing was puckered and unsightly. As is often the case with problems

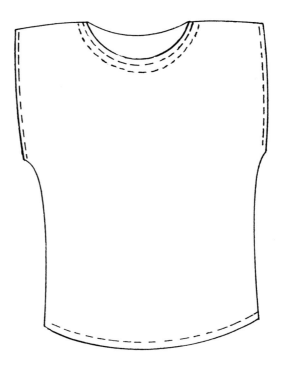

**Figure 9.4** Sketch of blouse with neck facing.

of this type, the puckering was variable. In the initial stages of production, there were few indications that a major problem would develop. This was probably because operators were taking extra care when sewing the facings when the style was introduced to the line. As the task became familiar, a rhythmical work cycle developed, and higher speeds of sewing were achieved. So in the initial stages of production, the garments did not look poor, but the signs indicating a problem became progressively more noticeable.

A further factor delayed the sounding of an alarm: the in-line presser was inexperienced and was not used to detecting faults. The presser merely completed the required work and passed the garments on for the next operation. The problem was actually detected by an intermediate examiner. Work coming through was noticed to be variable in its appearance and was sent back for repressing. When the problem did not go away, more concerted action to solve it was initiated.

Initially, effort concentrated on repressing faulty garments. Whilst this led to some improvements and was encouraging, the situation remained unsatisfactory. Additional work at final press was also investigated. However, all this time, more and more work was being fed to the in-line presser and a bottleneck developed. The customer requirement for rapid production was an additional factor that placed considerable stress on everyone concerned with this style.

It was eventually recognised that a revised pressing method would not solve the problem, and more drastic action was needed. The line was effectively stopped for a whole day, and effort was focused almost exclusively on the elimination of the puckered appearance.

A solution was found. The problematic neck seam was split into two separate operations: Topsew facing (1st row) and Topsew facing (2nd row). The second row was completed after the in-line press. In addition, more work was put into both intermediate press and final press. The relevant changes are listed in Fig. 9.5.

The 500 dozen contract was completed in 23 working days (plus two bank holidays). For each day, the standard minutes produced by the line has been determined, and knowing the daily direct labour costs for the line, the direct labour cost of producing one standard minute has been calculated. For details, see Tyler (1988).

Four distinct phases of the production period were identified:

1.  The start-up phase, days 1–6: although there was little new skill learning, all style changeovers can be disruptive with the need to clear out the old style and establish the new. By day 6, just before the line was stopped, a total of 120 dozen garments had been completed to operation 7 (Topsew facing) and about 50 dozen garments had reached intermediate examination.

2.  The quality problem, days 7–9: the excess costs were due almost entirely to waiting time, resulting from bottlenecks, stoppages pending solution of the problem, and the complete stoppage of the line on day 8. On day 9, work began again, but severe line imbalance and a general loss of

| Original method | | | Revised method | | |
|---|---|---|---|---|---|
| Operation no. | Description | SMV/unit | Operation no. | Description | SMV/unit |
| 7 | Topsew facing | 2.017 | 7 | Topsew facing (1st row) | 1.020 |
| 9 | Press neck facing and armhole | 0.600 | 9 | Press neck facing and armhole | 0.767 |
| 15 | Final press | 1.810 | 10 | Topsew facing (2nd row) | 1.104 |
| | | | 15 | Final press | 2.246 |
| **Total** | | **4.427** | **Total** | | **5.137** |

Figure 9.5 Work study details of changes in work content.

| | Excess costs in each phase of production | | | |
|---|---|---|---|---|
| | **1. Start-up** | **2. Quality problem** | **3. Re-work** | **4. Normal** |
| Excess direct cost (£) | 960.40 | 744.80 | 764.40 | −88.20 |
| % of total direct cost | 9.8 | 7.6 | 7.8 | −0.9 |

**Figure 9.6** Analysis of excess direct labour costs.

confidence meant that excess costs stayed high. In addition, work began on sorting through the garments already stitched.

3.  The re-work phase, days 10–14: waiting time in the line was low, and several operatives were engaged in paid re-work.
4.  Normal production phase, days 15–23: by this time, the re-work had been cleared and the line worked efficiently for the remainder of the time.

Using 10p/SM as the baseline, excess direct labour costs have been determined for each of the phases described above. The total direct wages bill during the period was approximately £9800.00, and the excesses are expressed in Fig. 9.6. in both absolute and percentage quantities.

From Fig. 9.6. it is apparent that the revised operation sequence, with the corresponding changes to the standard minute values, added 0.71 minutes per garment. For the contract of 500 dozen, this added £426.00 to direct costs, which represents 4.3% of the total wages paid.

A number of points emerge from this case study. We will limit comments to quality control procedures, product development and the role of technologists. The fact that a style has been manufactured successfully on a previous occasion may reduce the quality stress level, but it is no justification for reducing vigilance. Those who are not expecting quality problems are less well prepared to recognise them when they occur. Many quality problems do not allow simple decisions of *pass* or *fail*. Puckering is a case in point, as judgments about the quality of puckering have a strong ingredient of subjectivity. People get used to what they see in front of them, and recognition of a problem is delayed.

It generally takes a long while for operators to develop expertise to recognise and analyse faults. Experienced operators generally have a wealth of practical skill which one tends to take for granted. Consequently, it is easy to forget that inexperienced operators do not have these skills and that they need extra support. Time must be spent teaching them how to observe and analyse work passing through their hands.

When everyone is working to meet delivery deadlines, it is often easy to sacrifice pilot lots, routine checks and other functions that would normally be done as a matter of course. Production pressures will not go away – although management may well find it necessary to provide additional resources to ensure that normal quality procedures are not neglected.

As indicated earlier in this chapter, the design/production interface is often characterised by a lack of communication. It is not unusual in the clothing industry for production units to receive a cost sheet and a sample garment and to be informed that production starts in a few days. As a result, methods engineering (for efficiency and quality) tends to suffer as individuals respond to insistent pressures to meet deadlines. In this case study, excess costs of about 24 per cent occurred, nearly two-thirds of which was because of the quality problem. It is not possible in this case to say whether the puckering problem could have been foreseen and avoided, but a clothing technology input would have this as one of its objectives.

This case study is an example of a late-stage change associated with inadequate product development. Excess costs associated directly with quality failure and re-work amounted to nearly 15 per cent of the total direct labour cost. Additional costs associated with factory overheads and lost opportunities have not been taken into account. This example illustrates the graph shown in Fig. 9.2, and shows that there are cost drivers for changes to be made in product development practices.

## Concurrent product development

The product development process can be likened to a relay race, where a baton (the product) is carried by a succession of runners from the start (design concept) to the finish (in the hands of a satisfied customer) in the shortest possible time. Transfers of the baton from one runner to the next must be handled well so that there are no false moves and no delays. The analogy starts to look more complex when we think about who the runners are, and how the baton is passed from stage to stage.

Each leg of the relay race has a name: 'product concept', 'design sample', 'customer-approved sample', etc., as shown in Fig. 9.7. In each case, groups of people are responsible for completing each leg. Within traditional company structures, there are problems. Employees have only a limited understanding of their contribution to the product development process. In particular, there are weaknesses in relating their work to that of others, and of running to win the race rather than

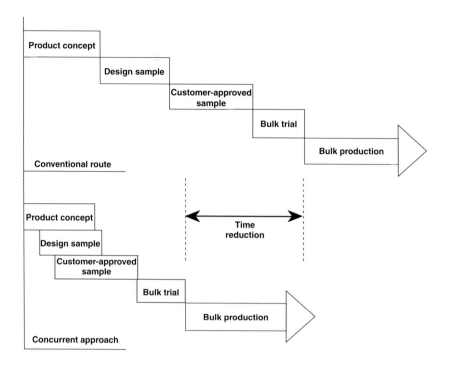

**Figure 9.7** Conventional and concurrent approaches to product development.

merely being a participant in their specific leg. As a result, the transfer of the baton is not performed well.

It is, of course, widely recognised that this complex process can be analysed and controlled. The danger is that the control system has an adverse effect on the timescales of the whole process, especially if the baton changes are specified to require the total completion of one task before starting the next, as illustrated in Fig. 9.7 as the 'Conventional route'.

The driving principle of concurrent product development is to deliver better, cheaper, faster products to eliminate waste and to improve communication throughout the product development process. This is achieved through planning and investment in early design activities and the use of multi-disciplinary teams from the beginning of a design project. This means that technologists do not have a late-stage role (which reduces to fire-fighting) but are working closely with other design development people soon after the design concept stage.

Figure 9.8 provides an overview of how product development might operate using the principle of concurrency. The starting point is a proposal for a new product (and associated manufacturing processes)

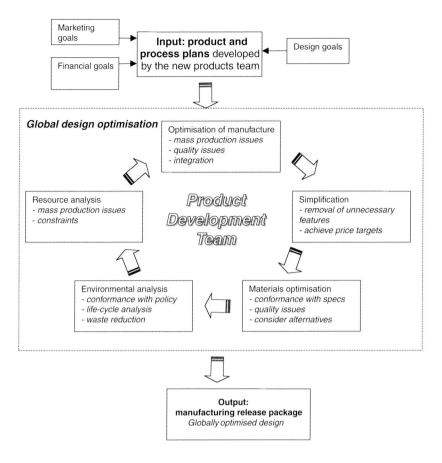

**Figure 9.8** Concurrent product development model.

from a new products team. This feeds into a global design optimisation procedure.

♦ *Stage 1* is *Optimisation for manufacture*. Product and process plans are scrutinised carefully to achieve integration, and the output is a product design plan.
♦ *Stage 2* is *Simplification*, where the product design plan is analysed in terms of its target customers and over-designed features are removed. At this stage, there may be simplification to achieve a retail customer's price point.
♦ *Stage 3* is *Materials optimisation*. This looks at the design plan in terms of materials selection, tolerances, performance in use, and so on. Alternative materials are considered and evaluated on performance and cost.
♦ *Stage 4* is the *Environmental analysis*. The product design plan is considered in the light of the environmental policies

of both company and customer. Abridged life-cycle analyses are carried out to address issues of waste in manufacture and in the supply chain. Alternative technologies are explored to improve the environmental profile of the product.

♦ *Stage 5* is the *Resource analysis*. This looks at resources required and available and produces a resource-dependent design plan.

The global design optimisation loop is entered again at Stage 1 and continues until a satisfactory outcome is agreed.

Technologists have a vital role to play in every stage of this product development model. Sometimes, the main channels of communication are with production people (as in the optimisation of manufacture and resource analysis); at other times the focus is on the design aspects of the product (as in simplification and materials optimisation). The environmental analysis promotes communication throughout the supply chain, and here the technologist has a major opportunity to contribute.

The major challenge with this approach is that companies are not used to a structured, managed process and there are often numerous pressures to make decisions pragmatically. Furthermore, people are not used to working in multi-disciplinary project teams, especially if they involve different companies in the supply chain.

Whatever the problems, all involved in the process of product development need to move away from fire-fighting modes of behaviour. They are time-consuming, expensive and they do not deliver a professional service to customers. The 'It'll press out' mentality is no longer valid. Seam pucker does not press out! Good quality must be designed into the products.

The globalised clothing industry is constantly changing and 'best practice' for new product development must be tailored to each specific case. Whilst teamworking is likely to be part of the picture, so much depends on product types, individuals, companies in the supply chain and leadership. Brand owners seeking to compress timescales for garment supply need to think very carefully about all these issues. Further discussion is in Tyler (2008).

# Chapter Ten
# Troubleshooting in the Sewing Room

Throughout Chapter 3, the emphasis was on correct selection of the various factors of stitch, seam, feed system, needle and thread, which together determine seam appearance and performance. At the same time, mention has been made of particular sewing problems that can arise and how one or other of these factors relates to each problem. It is the intention here to draw this information together by considering the range of problems that can arise, their causes and the various solutions available.

Sewing problems vary in their seriousness, with some causing only minor appearance problems, negligible in low price garments, but others causing damage to the material which it would not be economic to repair even if it were possible.

The problems are most conveniently divided into:

♦ problems of stitch formation that give rise to poor seam appearance and performance;
♦ problems of fabric distortion known as 'pucker', which also give rise to poor seam appearance;
♦ problems of damage to fabric along the stitch line.

## Problems of stitch formation

The main problems that arise from the actual stitch formation are:

♦ skip or slipped stitches
♦ staggered stitching
♦ unbalanced stitches
♦ variable stitch density
♦ needle, bobbin or looper thread breakage

Skip or slipped stitches arise from the hook or looper in the machine not picking up the loop in the needle thread. In a lockstitch, a slipped stitch will create a small gap in a seam or a poor appearance in top-stitching but it will not cause seam failure. In a 101 or 401 chainstitch, it produces a weak point in the stitching that will run undone during use of the garment. The causes of slip-stitching have been discussed in Chapter 3 under the heading of seam security.

| Causes of skip or slipped stitches | Possible solution |
| --- | --- |
| Bobbin hook fails to pick up loop | Check timing |
| Looper fails to pick up loop | Check timing |
| Thread does not form a good loop | Check thread tension & check spring |
| | Use better quality thread |
| Bent needles, damaged looper | Replace damaged needles |
| Deflection of needle | |
| Incorrect needle size | |
| Incorrect needle type | |
| Incorrect thread tension | Adjust tensioner |
| Poor material control | Throat plate hole too large |
| | Presser foot control is poor |
| | Needle is inappropriate for fabric |
| Clogged needle | Replace needle, avoid clogging |

Staggered stitching can be caused by yarns in the fabric deflecting the needle away from a straight line of stitching, giving a poor appearance. In some hard, woven fabrics, really straight stitching will only be achieved at a slight angle of bias.

| Causes of staggered stitches | Possible solution |
| --- | --- |
| Inappropriate size needle | Go up a needle size |
| Inappropriate needle point | Select sharper point |
| Inappropriate needle blade | Select tapered blade |
| Damaged needle | Replace needle |
| Poor material control | Check current settings |
| | Use alternative feed mechanism |
| Inappropriate seam for selected fabric | Redesign to sew at a slight angle of bias |

Unbalanced stitches in lockstitching can reduce the potential for stretch in a seam in a knitted fabric and, as explained earlier, lead to seam cracking. Unbalanced seams are often recognised by low extensibility leading to cracking. Bobbin tension should be adjusted until a full bobbin in its case will just slide down the thread when held by the end of the thread. Needle thread tension should be adjusted so that the threads interlock in the middle of the fabric, unless different colour threads are being used, for example in topstitching when a slight imbalance towards the underside may be needed to prevent the colour of the underneath thread showing on the top. Where maximum stretch is required in a lockstitch seam, careful adjustments of the type described earlier may be needed.

| Unbalanced lockstitch seams | Possible solution |
| --- | --- |
| Low extension, bobbin thread breakage | Reduce bobbin thread tension |
| | Check needle thread tension |
| Low extension, needle thread breakage | Reduce needle thread tension |
| | Check bobbin thread tension |

Variable stitch density may arise from insufficient foot pressure in a drop feed system, causing uneven feeding of the fabric through the machine. It can occur particularly with materials with sticky or slippery surfaces. Pressure must be adequate to enable even feeding but it will be realised from previous sections that with many fabrics and sewing situations, specialised feed systems are necessary to achieve even feeding of all the plies of the material. Operators may be able to contribute to consistency in stitch density by sewing at a constant speed, rather than in bursts.

Breakage of threads arises largely as a result of normally smooth metal surfaces in the machine becoming burred, chipped or otherwise damaged and then causing damage to the thread, whether needle, bobbin or looper. The guard over the hook in a lockstitch machine can become chipped, as can the needle hole in the throat plate, as a result of needle deflection. A variety of other causes have been identified, associated with incorrect settings, inadequate maintenance, or poor quality materials. Thread breakage during production is time-consuming for the operator, especially if a join in the stitching is not acceptable and he or she must unpick it and start again. Both the cause of the damaged machine parts and, if appropriate, the cause of the needle deflection, must be investigated.

| Variable stitch density | Possible solution |
| --- | --- |
| Poor material control using drop feed | Increase foot pressure |
| | Check feed dog setting |
| | Avoid sewing bursts |
| | Change to better feeding mechanism |
| Poor material control using specialised feed system | Increase foot pressure |
| | Check feed dog settings |
| | Avoid sewing bursts |
| | Change to walking foot mechanism |
| | Introduce puller |

| Thread breakage | Possible solution |
| --- | --- |
| Damage to thread guiding mechanisms | Polish or replace all damaged parts |
| Damage to throat plate | Polish or replace throat plate |
| Incorrect thread tension | Check and adjust thread tension |
| Incorrect settings for stitch forming | Check timing and adjust |
| Poor thread quality | Change thread |
| Poor cone of thread | Adjust guides, remove faulty cone |
| Wrong needle size for thread | Match thread with needle size |
| Needle overheating | Reduce speed of sewing |
| | Reduce needle size |
| | Improve sewability via fabric finish |

## Problems of pucker

The main problem that is solely appearance-related is that of pucker. To describe it like that is not to say that it is unimportant, for it can produce some very unsightly seams, but it does not actually cause any damage to the material being sewn.

Pucker is a wrinkled appearance along a seam in an otherwise smooth fabric. It generally appears as though there is too much fabric and not enough thread in the seam, as though the thread is drawing the seam in. For this reason the sewing thread is often blamed for causing the problem but there are several factors that contribute to pucker, including fabric structure, seam construction, needle size and feeding problems, as well as incorrect thread tensions and unsuitable thread. Pucker may show itself when the garment is first sewn or it may not appear until later when the garment is pressed, wetted or washed. It may show itself in all the plies of material that have been sewn together or only in some. It can also arise from more than one cause at the same time, which can make elimination extremely difficult. It could be said that there is pucker present in all sewn seams because it is impossible to introduce stitches into a fabric without it suffering some distortion, but in practice there are many fabrics of loose construction from soft yarns which show no visible pucker at all. By contrast, many of the modern smooth, fine, synthetic fabrics are almost impossible to sew without pucker. Indeed, so accustomed do people who work on these fabrics become to seeing some level of pucker at all times that they forget what a smooth seam looks like and may gradually accept a lower and lower standard.

The earliest detailed investigations into the causes of pucker are those by Dorkin and Chamberlain, who described five main causes which covered at least 90 per cent of pucker they found occurring in practice. Their descriptions are still relevant today.

### Seam pucker due to differential fabric stretch

In discussing sewing machine feed mechanisms, it was said that the prime requirement of a feeding system was that it should move the plies of fabric past the needle and that all the plies should move together. The feed mechanisms that were described have all been developed because the drop feed system does not consistently move the plies together. Thus one of the prime causes of seam pucker is differential fabric stretch caused by the feeding mechanism, often referred to as differential feeding pucker or just feeding pucker. If two fabric plies are being sewn together in a lockstitch sewing machine fitted with a drop feed mechanism, the feed dog rises up, presses the fabrics on to the underside of the presser foot against the spring pressure of that foot, and ideally carries both fabrics with it for the required distance, sliding them over the underside of the presser foot. The lower ply is engaged positively by the feed dog and moves with it by the same amount. For the upper fabric, the lower fabric effectively acts as a feed dog and exerts a frictional force tending to move it forward. The friction between fabric and fabric is never as great as between fabric and feed dog and in some cases is quite low. The upper fabric, being in contact on its upper side with the lower side of the presser foot, is subjected to a frictional force tending to impede its forward movement. Thus, as far as the feed mechanism itself is concerned, the amount that the upper fabric moves, relative to the lower, will be determined very largely by the balance between two frictional forces, one between upper and lower fabric tending to move the upper fabric forward, and the other between upper fabric and presser foot tending to hold it back. In general, therefore, the upper fabric would tend to be moved forward, but by an amount always less than the movement of the lower one.

The situation is further complicated by local distortions that take place during sewing between the actual stitch line and the areas either side of where the feed dog operates. These cause an extension of the upper fabric in the plane of that fabric immediately in front of the needle and a compression of the lower fabric in the same position. The relative amounts of extension and compression suffered by the upper and lower fabrics respectively are governed entirely by the relative extensibility and compressibility of the two materials. If, for example, the upper fabric is a readily extensible material like elastic net, and the lower is a relatively incompressible one like polyester satin, most of the distortion will appear as extension of the top fabric, and when the seam leaves the machine the lower fabric will be puckered by the contraction of the upper. In general, the compression and extension may be shared between the two in any proportions, subject to the fact that extension occurs more easily than compression because compression of the fabric in its own plane would require an increase in thickness which would be opposed by the presser foot pressure.

In order to ascertain whether the observed pucker in a seam is due to the presence of differential fabric stretch introduced by the feed mechanism in the manner described above, a simple test may be applied. Two strips of fabric should be cut from the warp direction and two from the weft direction of the fabric, about 10 cm wide and long enough to be marked with 25 marks at 1-cm intervals at right angles to the long edge. Each pair of fabrics is placed together with the marks face to face and in register and pinned at the starting end so that the register is not lost as sewing commences. The strips are seamed down the centre line, starting from the pinned end, removed from the machine and opened out. If differential stretch has occurred, the marks on the two pieces of fabric will gradually lose register along the line of the seam and the seam will be puckered to a greater or lesser extent. Half a mark gained in 25 indicates a differential extension of two per cent, which is sufficient to cause noticeable pucker in some fabrics.

The methods of overcoming pucker due to differential stretch are those of specialised feeding systems and operator handling described earlier.

### Seam pucker caused by differential fabric dimensional instability

The essential feature causing differential pucker is the relative change in dimensions of upper and lower fabric after the seam has been made. In the case discussed so far, this change is due to elastic forces brought into play by differential action of the sewing machine feed, but generally any relative alteration in the dimensions of the two fabrics after the seam is made will produce a comparable effect. Such changes can occur if one of the fabrics is dimensionally unstable whilst the other is not. In such cases, the seam may be perfectly flat and unpuckered as it leaves the machine but on subsequent washing one of the fabrics may shrink more than the other so that a differential pucker appears.

Differential pucker due to dimensional instability may be suspected when the two fabrics being joined are markedly different or when one shows noticeably more pucker than the other. The fabrics should be tested for dimensional stability by marking up sections of fabric and subjecting them to the washing process that the garment will undergo, or in the case of raincoat fabric to a simple wetting and drying process. Several washings may be needed as some fabrics shrink progressively. If the two fabrics show a difference in dimensional change of two per cent or more, pucker due to differential dimensional change may be expected to occur in finished garments after comparable treatment.

### Seam pucker due to extension in the sewing threads

In sewing a seam on a lockstitch sewing machine, two sewing threads are used and both are subjected to tension forces which tend to stretch them. The needle thread operates at a much higher tension than the bobbin thread because during the making of the stitch the upper thread has to snatch the lower thread up from below the fabric to form a loop midway between face and back of the seam and this requires considerable force. All sewing threads have some extensibility and they are thus extended by the action of the tension devices and pass into the seam in an extended state. When removed from the machine they will tend to contract. If the fabrics contract by the same amount this will have no visible effect, but if the sewing threads are particularly extensible and continue to contract after the fabric has reached its original unstretched length, pucker will result.

It is possible to test whether pucker is due to the extension of the sewing threads. A seam is sewn joining two test pieces of fabric, using the thread in question at the tension previously used. If this seam shows pucker, it is resewn with a sheet of paper on top of it, sewing through the paper as well as the fabric; after sewing the paper is torn away along the needle holes. The paper ensures that extra thread is fed into each stitch; when the paper is removed the extra length of thread is released into the seam. If the pucker previously was due to sewing thread extension, this seam should now be free of pucker. This only identifies the problem, of course, as it would not be practical to construct garments by sewing each seam through paper. Another test that can be used is to sew a seam in the normal manner, but with a larger stitch than usual, and then to cut every stitch on the face and back of the seam using very fine scissors, without disturbing the thread ends in the fabric. The tension in the sewing thread is now zero and if that was the cause of the pucker it will have disappeared.

Where thread extension is proved to be a cause of puckered seams, consideration must be given to the type of thread being used and to the tension settings on individual machines as these can cause the level of pucker to vary from machine to machine. Equipment is available to measure thread tensions in sewing machines and enable an attempt to be made to set all machines to the same satisfactory level.

### Seam pucker due to sewing thread shrinkage

This type of pucker was not included in the original work by Dorkin and Chamberlain but it should be mentioned here as the effect is exactly the same as the last situation described, although it does not appear until the garment has been pressed or washed. Cotton sewing threads increase in diameter and shrink in length when wet and these distortions may cause pucker in sensitive fabrics. Synthetic sewing threads have negligible wet shrinkage and should always be used for such fabrics. When selecting sewing threads for a fabric, it is important to match performance rather than fibre content. Thus, a non-shrink cotton fabric should be sewn with synthetic or corespun thread.

For dry conditions, synthetic threads are generally stabilised so as to have negligible shrinkage up to 150 °C but if garments are to be processed at higher temperatures, such as in a permanent press treatment, special threads may need to be requested.

*Seam pucker due to structural jamming*

Having considered the types of pucker attributable directly to distortion in one or other of the seam components (whether caused by the mechanical action of the feed dog and presser foot on the fabric, the action of the tension devices on the thread, or the shrinkage of the thread itself), there is a third possibility to be considered. The presence of the seam itself may introduce a distortion in no way dependent on the action of the sewing machine, but inevitably appearing as soon as the seam is formed. If a woven fabric has been constructed so as to be close to the practical weaving limit, i.e. with very little space left between the yarns either warp or weftways, it may be extremely difficult to force in any more threads in either direction.

For example, a fabric might be constructed with 45 warp yarns per centimetre and 24 weft yarns per centimetre, of a size such that there is no space within the construction of the fabric. If that fabric is then seamed on a lockstitch machine at five stitches per centimetre, five holes will be made in a line for each centimetre of fabric, and into each hole will be inserted side-by-side two threads whose diameter may be about the same as that of the yarns in the fabric. Along the line of the seam, instead of 24 picks per centimetre, an attempt is being made to insert 34. As the fabric has almost as many picks as it is possible to cram into it, there is not room in the structure for the insertion of sewing threads. Consequently the fabric along the line of the seam must be extended, although on either side of the seam and at a short distance from it no such extension occurs. The extension along the seam line must be accommodated by the fabric along the seam line assuming a buckled or puckered configuration. The term 'structural jamming' is given to this type of pucker because it results directly from the act of jamming extra threads into a structure which is already too closely set to accommodate them.

When sewing fabrics that suffer from structural jamming pucker, the problem is commonly more pronounced in one direction than the other. An important feature of the fabric that seems to relate to this is the crimp in the yarns. In a construction such as poplin, the warp yarns do all the bending while the weft yarns are nearly straight. As a result, the warp yarns can move sideways along the weft yarns with no crimp to prevent them, but the weft yarns cannot move in the seam way over the warp yarns because the sharp crimp of the warp yarns locks them and prevents such movement. In stitching a seam parallel to the weft, the space necessary for accommodating the sewing threads can be provided by such sliding of the warp yarns. When stitching parallel to the warp, such accommodation is not possible, and if sewing threads are inserted, the necessary space can be found only by extension of the warp, with consequent pucker.

An important point to note about structural jamming pucker is that it is entirely independent of the mechanics of the sewing machine and entirely inherent in the fabric structure. If the seam was made by hand, using the same sewing thread and the same stitch rate, the same pucker would appear. It is therefore essential that structural jamming pucker is identified correctly when it is present so that effort is not wasted in making adjustments to sewing machines in a vain endeavour to eliminate it.

Identification of structural jamming pucker, out of the other possible causes of puckered seams, requires following a sequence of steps that eliminate some of the other possibilities. Where two plies of the same fabric are being seamed, differential fabric stretch can normally be easily eliminated since it would show more on one ply of fabric than the other. Structural jamming pucker normally shows on both plies when they are the same fabric. If a seam is stitched through paper and the paper torn away, then if the pucker disappears it was caused by sewing thread tension. If the pucker remains, it is likely that the problem is one of structural jamming. Finally, a seam should be stitched at a lower stitch density than usual, about two to three per centimetre, and the stitches cut carefully on both the front and the back without disturbing the thread in the fabric. The pucker will remain, despite the removal of any possible thread tension, and will disappear only when the cut ends of thread are removed from the fabric with a pair of tweezers. This proves that the pucker was jammed into the seam by the inserted sewing threads, whose removal unjammed the structure and allowed the fabric to return to its original flat state.

It is clear that prevention of this type of pucker is a matter for the fabric designer rather than the garment manufacturer and where there is a choice of fabric it may be possible to prevent the problem. The worst types of fabrics are plain weaves constructed from hard yarns of a size similar to the size of the sewing thread. If the fabric is made from thicker yarns, then not only will there be relatively more room for the much finer sewing threads but the whole fabric will be stiffer and more rigid and pucker will be less likely on both accounts. The other problem is fabrics that are set close to the practical weaving limit; such fabrics show a high level of pucker whereas the more open types do not show so much. Constructing a slightly more open fabric however may not be acceptable as it will have a poorer appearance and less opacity. A different construction of fabric, away from a plain weave, will also improve matters providing the appearance is accept-able. Unfortunately, the opportunity to make radical changes of this sort to a fabric will be possible only in a situation of long-term fabric development or where it is possible to find alternative fabrics from stock that are also satisfactory in other respects.

When a garment maker has no choice in the matter of fabric, measures have to be taken in the design of the garment and the sewing of it to minimise the problem. The only step that will always produce a perfectly sewn seam is to sew the seam on the bias, i.e. at some definite angle to the warp or weft. A seam sewn on a 45 degree bias angle will encounter only 70 per cent of the yarns it would meet if it were sewn on the straight grain. It is unlikely to be necessary for the bias angle to be as high as 45 degrees, and in most cases 15–20 degrees is sufficient.

In garment design terms, of course, it may not be possible to angle the seams in this way without introducing problems of drape or uneven hems, or production problems of fitting pattern pieces into a marker. On the other hand, the amount of flare on some garment seams may be enough to help and some totally straight grain seams might be avoided if extra fabric could be used so that the seam can be eliminated altogether. When there is no choice but to make the garment up in a fabric and style that gives problems, it is unlikely that the problem can be eliminated completely, though it may be possible to reduce it. Synthetic threads have become stronger for their size in recent years and this enables finer sizes to be used while still producing satisfactorily strong seams. The fine fabrics that are often a problem used to be sewn with Tkt. 120 thread, but there are Tkt. 180 threads now with the same level of strength, which will cause less pucker. This will also enable a finer needle to be used so that there is less distortion of the fabric during sewing. The use of a lower stitch density may help but there will be a limit to how large a stitch gives an acceptable seam appearance.

So far it has been assumed that seaming is by means of a lockstitch machine. If a chainstitch could be used instead there would be no intersections of thread within the fabric in the way that there are with lockstitch and thus less bulk inserted into the fabric. Alterations in seam type might effect an improvement if fewer layers of fabric are sewn. An example would be the change in a shirt side seam from a lap felled seam to a superimposed seam sewn with safety stitch. This normally gives an improved appearance in terms of pucker, but moves away from the traditional construction of an expensive shirt.

Finally, the elimination of topstitching can reduce pucker and on garments such as workwear this is often done for reasons of appearance as well as cost, but it is unlikely to be possible on garments where topstitching is a design feature.

## Seam pucker due to mismatched patterns

Situations will occasionally be seen in a made up garment where there is pucker on some seams but not on others. If the patterns are checked carefully, it will be found that there is a discrepancy between the lengths of the stitching lines on the pattern pieces that go together in that seam and consequently a difference in the length of the cut parts which the machinist is sewing together. An experienced machinist will attempt to ease in the longer ply; if successful in doing so, the garment parts will appear to go together satisfactorily in the sense that the seam ends are level but the seams will have a puckered appearance on one ply. How much the problem shows depends to a great extent on the nature of the fabric, since, to quote an extreme contrast, a wool jersey would accommodate a considerable mismatch, whereas a pre-shrunk cotton poplin would not accommodate anything at all. If deliberate ease has been built into patterns designed for use with soft wool fabrics, these patterns must not be used for more rigid fabrics without adjustments being made to them to achieve the required shape of garment by means of pattern shape along a seam rather than pattern length.

The above discussion has made the assumption that having made the patterns, accurately or not, the materials are then cut out correctly to that shape and size. Instances of random pucker on seams may well occur as a result of inaccurate cutting of garment parts which are then eased together.

In discussing these causes of pucker, we have suggested ways to identify each of them out of the various possibilities. If this identification is carried out as an investigative process before production, it is possible to predict the extent to which pucker might be a problem in sewing a particular style and fabric, and to take steps to eliminate or at least minimise it before it happens. These simple test procedures can be carried out on new materials to indicate whether making-up problems are likely to be encountered and, if so, of what nature and severity. In addition to these simple procedures, very sophisticated instruments have been developed recently to assess the likelihood of such problems before production. These are described in the last section of this chapter.

It was suggested earlier that it is often difficult to assess the level of pucker that is present in garment production, particularly in a situation where it is almost impossible to eliminate it entirely, and consequently those working with it become accustomed to accepting a lesser or greater amount of it as normal all of the time. Whether a small amount of pucker is acceptable or not, it is essential to be able to grade puckered seams as objectively as possible.

For this purpose, a set of photographic standards has been produced by the American Association of Textile Chemists and Colorists, which shows five standards of pucker in a seam. Class 5 represents no pucker, while class 1 means very badly puckered. This 1 to 5 classification is similar to many others used in textile testing. In using the photographic standards, three test seams are compared with the standards by three observers under standardised lighting conditions. The use of three observers helps to level differences of opinion to which these types of assessment are liable. Attempts have been made over the years to develop instruments that could make a quantitative assessment of pucker in a seam but as yet none are available commercially. However, research is currently being undertaken into the problems of pucker, making use of computerised equipment that has not been available until recently. Such work may, in the future, provide instrumental methods of testing for pucker and for reducing or eliminating it.

| Puckering | Possible solution |
|---|---|
| Differential fabric stretch Slippage during feeding (Puckering appears after sewing) | Check presser foot setting Check feed dogs setting Explore use of PTFE-coated feet Use alternative feed mechanism |
| Differential fabric dimensional instability Differential shrinkage of fabrics (Puckering appears after washing) | Refinish fabrics to reduce shrinkage effects |
| Extension of sewing threads Thread is stretched during sewing but does not shrink until after the stitches are formed (Puckering appears after sewing) | Reduce thread tension Change to thread with reduced extensibility |
| Sewing thread shrinkage Thread is stretched during sewing but does not shrink until after washing (Puckering appears after washing) | Use a synthetic thread or core spun cotton |

| | |
|---|---|
| Structural jamming | |
| Thread is inserted to a tightly woven fabric which cannot accommodate it | Select finer thread |
| | Reduce stitch density |
| | Redesign (sew on bias, use different fabrics, modify construction) |
| (Puckering appears after sewing) | |
| | |
| Mismatched patterns | |
| Pattern dimensions not accurate | Ensure patterns are correct |
| (Puckering is not consistent) | Ensure cutting is accurate |
| | Ensure sewing ease is correct |

## Problems of damage to the fabric along the stitch line

The problem of damage occurring during sewing as a result of the use of unsuitable needles or of sewing unsuitable fabrics, or a combination of both, has already been outlined. It has also been mentioned many times in discussing needle points and thread types since the reasons for so many of these being available are, to a great extent, to overcome these kinds of problems. Sewing damage is a serious problem in garment production, leading to poor seam appearance and performance and, in a severe case, to complete breakdown of the seam. It remains now to summarise the basic needle damage problems which arise, to consider their causes, and to attempt to offer solutions.

It is worth stating again that the term 'needle damage' is used here because it is the terminology used in the clothing industry. However, it is not really the ideal term to describe what happens. The question of needles that become damaged has already been discussed as a straightforward problem with a simple solution. It is inevitable that damaged needles will damage the materials that they sew and the main problem is to establish the reason for the damage occurring and prevent its continued occurrence. The real problem is that a new and apparently perfect needle can cause damage because it is itself inappropriate in point type for the material being sewn, or because the combination of other factors (nature of the fabric, speed of the machine) is such that damage occurs. The problem is especially serious in knitted fabrics because they will ladder if damaged and because the damage is often not apparent when first sewn. It only becomes evident when flexing in wearing and washing causes the damaged or broken yarn to run back and become visible.

The problems that occur in sewing can be divided into those of mechanical damage and those of needle overheating damage.

*Mechanical damage*

The ways in which needles can strike and break fabric yarns and burst the loops in knitted fabrics have already been described and the appropriate set and ball point needles suggested as suitable for the sewing of woven and knitted fabrics respectively. It has also been suggested that needles should always be as small as possible.

The needle is not the only contributing factor to the problem of mechanical damage. A major problem is that the combination of the machine speed and the nature of the fabric prevents the yarns from moving out of the way of the needle sufficiently fast to avoid damage. The combination of reduced machine speed and a smaller needle diameter is often effective in reducing the incidence of mechanical damage but it is not a popular solution since it affects production levels if machines run more slowly. However, if a problem is not discovered until garments are actually in production, it may be the only possible action. Since sewing normally takes place for only 20 per cent of an operator's working time, a reduction in machine speed will not have as much effect as it would if sewing took place for the whole of the time.

Mechanical damage can usually be detected by manually stretching the fabric at the seam line. However, in some cases it is necessary to unpick the stitching and examine the yarns with a magnifying glass to detect the damage but it is precisely this level of damage that will begin to show after wearing and washing. While damaged garments are always a problem, those that are not detected until they have been worn and washed are a more serious problem because of the quantity that could have been made and sold up to the time of discovery. The problem could still be happening in production.

The most cost-effective (and long-term) solution is to enable the material to move out of the way of the needle more effectively. This is achieved by ensuring that the fabric is adequately lubricated at the finishing stage. Many fabrics have resin finishes applied to them and that, especially on a tightly woven fabric, additionally fixes the yarns tightly in the structure so that they cannot readjust to permit free passage of the needle. A level of lubricant of only 0.5–1 per cent is needed but it makes the fibres more mobile within the fabric structure and, in the case of knitted fabrics, enables the yarns from one loop in the fabric to move into the next loop during sewing so as to prevent bursting damage. If a problem such as this is not found until the garment is in production, and if measures such as the slowing down of the machine are unacceptable or ineffective, then it may be necessary to try a lubricant spray on the fabric ahead of the needle. This can give staining problems and, as with attempting additionally to lubricate sewing thread, it is potentially messy while not being nearly as effective as correct lubrication of the material beforehand. In an emergency, however, it may help.

The only real solution to the problems of mechanical damage is to test all sample lengths of fabric for sewability, to specify any necessary finishes to test before the bulk fabric is ordered, and to test bulk fabric before production to ensure that finishing treatments have been effective. Tests for sewability should be incorporated into the same testing programme that checks such properties as shrinkage and colour fastness. Unfortunately this assumes that materials are ordered other than from stock and that while the materials are being made these treatments can be included. In fashion manufacturing, where purchasing is usually from stock and lead time is short, many problems of sewability can arise. In high-volume bulk production, where the highest standards of seaming are required, there is usually time to get these matters right provided there is concern to do so.

| Mechanical damage | Possible solution |
|---|---|
| Needle size too large | Reduce needle size |
| Inadequate fabric finishing | Increase softener content on fabric |
| Inappropriate needle point | Select sharper set or finer ball point |
| Damaged needle point and/or throatplate | Replace damaged parts |
| Mismatch between needle size and throatplate hole | Reduce tightness of fit |

### Needle overheating damage

Needle overheating occurs as a result of friction between the needle and the fabric being sewn. In high speed sewing of sense materials, temperatures as high as 300–350 °C can be reached. At these temperatures, the needle may suffer damage and lose its hardness. Natural fibres in a fabric or thread can withstand these temperatures for a short time without serious effect, although some finishes or coatings may melt and spread to the needle surfaces, increasing friction and thereby producing higher temperatures. With synthetic fibres, the position is more critical since PVC fibres melt at around 100 °C, polyamide and polyester soften at about 230 °C; polyacrylics will withstand temperatures up to about 280 °C. Overheated needles can therefore soften the synthetic fibres in a fabric, weakening them and producing rough seams with harsh stitch holes. Melted fibres stick to the surface of the needle, increasing its friction and clogging the eye and grooves so that eventually no thread will sew because of breakage or skipped stitches. Before this state is reached, damage to the sewing thread by melting or abrasion may have produced weak seams.

Different approaches to the problem of needle overheating are possible, namely preventing the heating occurring, cooling down the needle as it heats, and preventing the heated needle from damaging the fabric or thread.

Since the heating is the result of friction, reducing the heating requires reducing the friction. The primary means of achieving this is by the incorporation of a suitable lubricant during fabric finishing. All other approaches provide only partial solutions. The sewing speed can be reduced but, as with mechanical damage, this is unpopular because of its effect on production. Reduction of friction can also be achieved by either changing the shape or surface of the needle or by changing the material it rubs against. Needles were described earlier which have a reinforced shoulder area and a bulged eye, both of which open up the needle hole in the fabric to allow freer passage of the main part of the needle blade. The extent to which the blade is reinforced is limited by the size of needle hole that is acceptable, since it can give a poor appearance in fine fabrics. The amount of reinforcement normally used enables an increase in stitches per minute sewing rate of 15 to 20 per cent above that which could be used with an ordinary needle without causing damage. The application of a roughened surface to the needle has also been found to reduce friction and heat development, and to resist the accumulation of any melted debris that does form. In fabric terms, there is the same need that there is with mechanical damage to enable the yarns to move away from the needle easily and the application of a lubricant to the fabric is again the answer. The length of seam sewn in a garment also has an effect on the temperatures built up in the needle. If long seams are sewn, high temperatures will be generated, and if there are only short time intervals between seams there will not be much opportunity for the needle to cool down. By contrast, short seams such as shoulder seams can be sewn at high speed without so much build-up of heat.

Air coolers have been used to reduce needle temperature, usually making use of existing compressed air lines within the factory. However, the effectiveness of air cooling is limited to marginal cases, and the air blast can lead to missed stitching and to operator discomfort. If needle overheating is accompanied by mechanical damage, as it often is, air cooling will not address the yarn breakage problem.

The sewing thread has a part to play in needle cooling with spun or corespun threads being the most effective. All threads cool the needle to some extent but if there are fibres on the surface they carry cooling air past the needle and also transfer more lubricant to the needle surface. If a thread break occurs for any reason, there is an immediate rise in needle temperature and if sewing conditions are near to, but not quite, critical, this hotter needle may produce damaged holes. Thus a section of fabric may become damaged in the distance it takes the operator to notice that the needle thread has broken and stop the machine. If the needle has picked up any molten fibres from the fabric at the same time, when the needle is rethreaded these deposits will produce higher needle temperatures and damage will continue until a new needle is fitted.

In terms of preventing the heated needle from damaging the fabric or thread, there is not a great deal that can be done to protect the fabric, the main action being needed in the areas already described. To protect the thread from damage, the use of corespun threads with a cotton covering ensures that the synthetic part of the thread is not exposed to the heat of the needle. As has already been explained, the development in thread lubricants is such that all threads, including those that are 100 per cent synthetic, have much greater resistance to high temperatures than they used to and the choice of threads that will not suffer from needle heating damage is now much wider. Needle overheating can occur with any fibre type but it is, of course, only a problem with synthetics. Thus many natural fibre fabrics are sewn without risk of damage to the fabric but they are in many cases sewn with synthetic or core-spun threads in order to achieve the necessary seam strength and minimising of pucker which these provide. Care must therefore be taken over thread selection and needle cooling so that no loss in strength occurs in the seams as a result of damaged thread. The production of jeans in cotton fabrics is typical of a situation where high speed machines are used on a natural fibre fabric and where considerable needle heat can be generated, particularly on the long seams. Corespun threads are normally used to achieve both strength and heat resistance.

The problems of fabrics becoming damaged during stitching have been described in detail here because the possibility of fabric damage is always present and it is important to know how to overcome it. It is essential to investigate fabrics before production to find out if damage is likely with that particular fabric. However, it should be said that the practical problems of damage experienced in sewing factories are not nearly as great as they used to be. Improvements in fabric finishes have made a great contribution to improved sewability, especially where needle heating is concerned. To a lesser extent, credit can be given to improved needles and threads.

| Needle overheating damage | Possible solution |
| --- | --- |
| Inadequate lubrication of fabric | Increase softener content on fabric |
| Excessive sewing speed | Reduce sewing speed |
| Needle size too large | Reduce needle size |

## Testing for sewability and tailorability

The question of testing materials before production for tailorability (largely pucker) and sewability (mechanical damage and needle heating damage) has been mentioned several times. Testing for such properties should be as routine as testing for other aspects of a material's performance that will affect a garment during making up, wearing and cleaning, but it is not often so. This is why time has to be devoted to palliative measures in the face of these problems when they are found to be occurring with garments that are already in production. In many cases, in-house, customised tests can be devised to determine performance and to assure quality. However, two instruments have been developed for investigating sewability, and two more have been developed to investigate tailorability.

### Sewability testing

The HatraSew was designed to be used in conjunction with a sewing machine. It measured the temperature reached by the sewing machine needle when sewing a particular fabric, making use of an infrared detection device. This machine is no longer offered for sale.

The L & M Sewability Tester operates independently of a sewing machine and measures the force required to push a needle through a fabric.

Both instruments enable the information obtained to be related to actual damage experienced during manufacture. Other test methods have been developed by companies for their own use. These involve sewing a piece of the test fabric with a specified machine, needle size and type, at a specified speed, through a specified number of thicknesses in a particular shape, which includes sewing in various directions on the sample. The sample is then inspected closely for damage.

### Tailorability testing

The Kawabata Evaluation System for fabrics (KES-f) was originally designed to measure a range of mechanical and physical properties of fabrics related to the handle of a fabric (in stretch and recovery). The system consists of four instruments, which between them measure the tensile, shear, compression, bending and surface properties of fabrics. Recent research has shown that these properties can also be used to predict how easily the fabric will make up into a garment, i.e. the 'tailorability' of the fabric. Based on prior experience on the factory floor, control charts are constructed which indicate the allowable limits for each of the mechanical properties before problems arise in cutting, sewing, pressing or in garment appearance. This equipment is a research tool and requires skilled technicians to use it. To make this equipment more accessible to industrial users, McLoughlin and Hayes (2007) have developed a computerised interface for the presentation and analysis of data. Examples of the screen displays are illustrated as Figs 10.1 and 10.2. These record the measured data and an interpretation of these data based on the chart.

The FAST equipment (Fabric Assurance by Simple Testing) was developed by CSIRO in Australia specifically to measure the mechanical properties of woollen and worsted fabrics which were relevant to tailorability. The system consists of three instruments to measure tensile, shear, bending and compressive properties of fabrics. A simple test for the dimensional stability of the fabric is also included. The results are plotted on a chart similar to that used for the KES-f

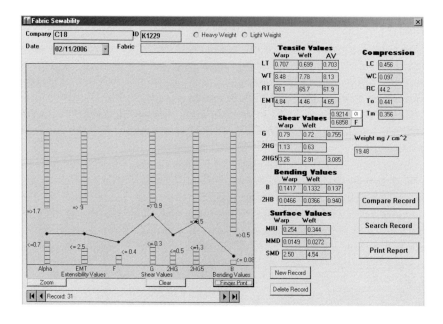

**Figure 10.1** Fingerprint for a fabric that sews well. All the data points occupy the comfort zone in the chart. (Image © McLoughlin and Hayes.)

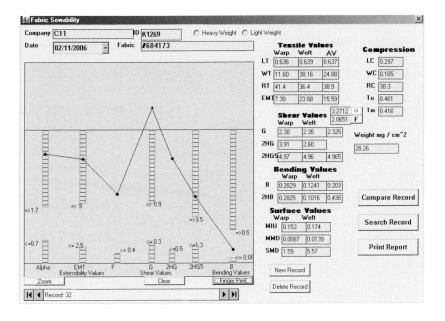

**Figure 10.2** Fingerprint for a fabric that can only be sewn with care. Many of the data points lie in the 'laddered' areas of the chart, indicating that the fabric properties are abnormally high. (Image © McLoughlin and Hayes.)

instruments, with upper and lower limits marked for each property. Fabrics whose properties lie within these limits should make up into garments without any problems. Where a fabric property falls outside a particular limit, the chart indicates the nature of the assembly problems that are likely to occur – for example, difficulty in setting sleeves or difficulty in obtaining satisfactory pleating. The FAST equipment is a cheaper alternative to KES-f, although it has no provision for detecting hysteresis effects. Nevertheless, it is gaining increasing acceptance as a tool for assessing fabrics before manufacture.

The terms sewability and tailorability have been used here in the sense given above but it should be noted that researchers in this field do use the terms somewhat interchangeably, and especially use the term tailorability to cover broader issues of general garment appearance.

# Bibliography

## References

### Chapter 3   Sewing

Grills, R. & Brown, S. (1975). *Productivity in Sewing Operations.* Shirley Institute.

### Chapter 4   Sewing machinery

Arthur D. Little Inc. (1965). *State of the Art Investigation of Automated Handling of Limp Fabrics.* Apparel Research Foundation, American Apparel Manufacturers Association.

Abernathy, F.H. & Pippins, D. (1986). (TC)$^2$: apparel, textile and education at its best. *Bobbin*, (September) **28**(1), 162–168.

*Automated Limp Fabric-Handling Devices: Report of the Limp Fabric-Handling Task Group,* 1987. Apparel Research Committee.

Bray, F. & Vento, V. (1986). Chapter two begins with Singer. *Bobbin*, (September) **28**(1), 170–174.

Brotherton, A.A. & Tyler, D.J. (1986). Clupicker performance and flexible apparel automation. *Hollings Apparel Industry Review*, **3**(2), 15–34.

Govindaraj, M., Chen, B. & Koechling, J. (1992). Fabric properties as control factors for flexible apparel production systems. *International Journal of Clothing Science and Technology*, **4**, 2/3, 34–38.

Grills, R. & Brown, S. (1975). *Productivity in Sewing Operations.* Shirley Institute.

Iype, C. & Porat, I. (1989). Fabric alignment using a robotic vision system. *International Journal of Clothing Science and Technology*, **1**(1), 39–43.

Leung, M., Black, D.H. & Lam, A. (1992). Evaluation of two pick and place devices used on clothing materials. *Hollings Apparel Industry Review*, **9**(1), 29–48.

Marlowe, P. (1992). Programmable sewing progresses: but where to? *Bobbin*, (January), **33**(5), 42–44.

Ono, E., Ichijo, H. & Aisaka, N. (1992). Flexible robotic hand for handling fabric pieces in garment manufacture. *International Journal of Clothing Science and Technology*, **4**(5), 16–23.

Taylor, P.M. & Koudis, S.G. (1987). Automated handling of fabrics. *Science Progress*, **71**, 351–363.

Taylor, P.M. & Taylor, G.E. (1992). Sensory robotic assembly of apparel at Hull University. *Journal of Intelligent and Robotic Systems*, **6**(1), 81–94.

Tyler, D.J. (1989). The development phase of the textile/clothing technology corporation automation project. *International Journal of Clothing Science and Technology*, **1**(2), 11–16.

Tyler, D.J. (1989). Managing for production flexibility in the clothing industry. *Textile Outlook International*, (September), 63–84.

## Chapter 5   Garment accessories and enhancements

BSEN 23758 (1994). *Textiles – Care Labelling Code Using Symbols.* British Standards Institution, London.

Miller, M. (1995). The embroidery industry, computerisation and education. *Text for the Study of Textile Art and History*, **23**, (Winter), 4–9.

Nergis, B.U. & Özipek, B. (1999). The behaviour of embroidery patterns on knitted fabrics after washing. *Knitting International*, **106**, (August), 41–43.

Consumer Safety Unit (1985). *A Guide to the Nightwear (Safety) Regulations 1985.* DTI, London.

## Chapter 6   Alternative methods of joining materials

Hayes, S.G. and McLoughlin, J. (2007). Welded and sewn seams: a comparative analysis of their mechanical behaviour. *85th Textile Institute World Conference, 1–3 March 2007, Colombo, Sri Lanka*, 131–142.

Shi, W., and Little, T. (2000). Mechanisms of ultrasonic joining of textile materials. *International Journal of Clothing Science & Technology*, **12**(5), 331–350.

Thorp, V. (2006). Seamless Knitting and stitch-free seaming technologies in performance apparel. *Performance Apparel Markets*, **16**(1), 17–37.

## Chapter 8   Technology and management of colour

ASBCI (2006). *Colour Clues, an Introduction to the Coloration of Textiles and Clothing.* ASBCI, Halifax.

ASBCI (2005). *Introduction to Colour in Clothing and Textiles.* ASBCI, Halifax.

Xin, J. (ed) (2006). *Total Colour Management in Textiles.* Woodhead Publishing Ltd.

## Chapter 9   Clothing technology and product development

Tyler, D.J. (1988). A quality problem during blouse production. *Hollings Apparel Industry Review*, **5**(1), 11–22. Reprinted in *Clothing*, 1988, **2**(6), 2–6.

Tyler, D.J. (2008). Advances in apparel product development. In Fairhurst, C. (ed) *Advances in Apparel Production*. Woodhead Publishing Ltd.

## Chapter 10    Troubleshooting in the sewing room

McLoughlin, J. and Hayes, S.G. (2007). Automating objective fabric reporting. *85th Textile Institute World Conference, 1–3 March 2007, Colombo, Sri Lanka*, 568–582.

## Further reading

The following books and articles will assist the reader in following the subject further. The bibliography of clothing manufacture has never been large but it has been expanded in recent years. Some earlier publications are still useful, even some from as long as thirty years ago, but unfortunately they are becoming increasingly difficult for the reader to locate.

Two general books that contain a wide range of detailed material, much of which is still useful despite their age, are *Apparel Manufacturing Handbook* by Jacob Solinger (Van Nostrand Reinhold, 1980) and *Sewn Products Engineering and Reference Manual*, edited by Manuel Gaetan (Bobbin Publications, 1977). A recently revised introductory book is Cooklin, G. (2006) *Introduction to Clothing Manufacture* (2nd ed), Blackwell Publishing, Oxford. Further books will be mentioned in relation to individual chapters.

A number of trade press journals made an important contribution to the subject during the 80s and 90s. *Bobbin*, published in the USA, covers a range of topics including technology. More recently, this journal has been renamed *Apparel*. The following four journals included useful articles from time to time and also reviews of machinery exhibitions around the world: *World Clothing Manufacturer*; *Clothing World*; *Textile Asia*; and *Apparel International*. Of these, only *Textile Asia* continues in print. A new journal for the European market is *Fashion Business International*. *StitchWorld* is concerned with technology and management in the sewn products industry; published in India. *Textiles* is the quarterly magazine of The Textile Institute, with most issues devoting some space to the topics discussed in this book.

*The Hollings Apparel Industry Review* (HAIR) was published by Hollings Faculty, Manchester Metropolitan University, and included industry statistical analyses as well as technical and research articles. It was the precursor to the commercial journal: *Journal of Fashion Marketing and Management*.

*Textile Outlook International* has mainly economics-related articles and company profiles that are useful as industry background, but occasionally carries useful technical articles. From the same publisher is the journal *Performance Apparel Markets*.

*International Journal of Clothing Science and Technology* publishes much of the scientific research currently being undertaken in the clothing field. Some useful technology papers appear in the *Clothing & Textiles Research Journal* and the *Journal of the Textile Institute*.

Specific articles are mentioned in the following sections but the reader is advised to monitor the journals on a regular basis in order to have the latest information and analysis.

An invaluable guide to terminology is *Textile Terms and Definitions*, edited by M.J. Denton and P.N. Daniels (11th ed, 2002, The Textile Institute, Manchester).

## Chapter 1    Background to the clothing industry

Up-to-date information on employment, output and other aspects of the clothing industry can be obtained from *Employment Gazette*, *Journal of Fashion Marketing and Management* and *Textile Outlook International.*

## Chapter 2    Cutting

A useful earlier work is:

Trautman, J.E. (1979). *Material Utilisation in the Apparel Industry.* Apparel Research Foundation Inc., Arlington.

The most comprehensive text, which contains substantial additional references, is:

Tyler, D.J. (1991). *Materials Management in Clothing Production.* Blackwell Scientific Publications, Oxford.

## Chapters 3 and 4    Sewing and sewing machinery

It is impossible to discuss sewing without the language and system of diagrams developed by the organisations who publish national and international standards. The British Standards Institution, 389 Chiswick High Road, London W4 4BR, UK, publishes:

BS 3870 (1991). *Stitches and Seams.* Part 1: *Classification and Terminology of Stitch Types.* Part 2: *Classification and Terminology of Seam Types.*
British Standard 3870 is identical with ISO 4915 (1991): *Textiles – Stitch Types: Classification and Terminology*, and ISO 4916 (1991): *Textiles – Seam Types: Classification and Terminology*, published by the International Organisation for Standardisation (ISO).

A comprehensive textbook with a full bibliography is *Stitches and Seams* by R.M. Laing and J. Webster (1998). The Textile Institute, Manchester. It is highly recommended.

Many of the Technological Reports published by the Clothing Institute contain useful research findings and are still relevant. A name that appears frequently among the authors of these reports is C.M.C. Dorkin who, in addition to carrying out a great deal of basic research herself, stimulated and managed a considerable body of work by others. Her influence on clothing research is immeasurable. Particularly useful technological reports are listed below:

Blackwood, W.J. & Chamberlain, N.H. (1970). The strength of seams in knitted fabrics. *Technological Report* No. 22, CI.

Burtonwood, B. & Chamberlain, N.H. (1966, 1967). The strength of seams in woven fabrics. Part 1, *Technological Report* No. 17, CI. Part 2, No. 18, CI.

Crow, R.M. & Chamberlain, N.H. (1969). The performance of sewing threads in industrial sewing machines. *Technological Report* No. 21, CI.

Deery, F.C. & Chamberlain, N.H. (1964). A study of thread tension variation during the working cycle in a lockstitch sewing machine. *Technological Report* No. 15, CI.

Dorkin, C.M.C. & Chamberlain, N.H. (1961). Seam pucker, its cause and prevention. *Technological Report* No. 10, CI.

Dorkin, C.M.C. & Chamberlain, N.H. (1962). Lockstitch seams in knitted fabrics. *Technological Report* No. 11, CI.

Dorkin, C.M.C. & Chamberlain, N.H. (1963). The facts about needle heating. *Technological Report* No. 13, CI.

Townsend, T. & Chamberlain, N.H. (1974). More light on structural seam pucker in lightweight fabrics. *Technological Report* No. 16, CI.

In addition:

ASBCI (no date). *Make or Break*. ASBCI, Halifax.

Dobilaite, V., Juciene, M. (2006). The influence of mechanical properties of sewing threads on seam pucker. *International Journal of Clothing Science and Technology*, **18**(5), 335–345.

Escott, D. (1978). The mechanics' guide – stitches, seams and stitchings. *Bobbin*, (October), **20**(2), 84–108.

Hurt, F.N. & Tyler, D.J. (1973). The influence of fabric finishing conditions on sewing needle temperatures. *Clothing Research Journal*, **1**(1), 47–52.

J&P Coats Ltd. (1978). Seam pucker – why always blame the thread? *Bobbin*, (November), **20**(3), 188–192.

Pavlinic, D.Z., Gersak, J., Demsar, J. and Bratko, I. (2006). Predicting seam appearance quality, *Textile Research Journal*, **76**(3), 235–242.

Recent research into seam pucker, using modern techniques such as KES-f and laser measurement of seam appearance are reported in various articles in the *International Journal of Clothing Science and Technology*.

## Chapter 5   Garment accessories and enhancements

ASBCI (no date). *Caring for your Clothes*. ASBCI, Halifax.

ASBCI (no date). *Joining Forces*. ASBCI, Halifax.

BS 3084 (1992). *Specification for Slide Fasteners*. BSI.

Kyllo, K. (2003). Care labeling: where in the world are we? AATCC Review, **3**(10), 9–15.

Labels and labelling (1992). *Manufacturing Clothier*, (May), **73**(5), 23–27.

Russell, E. (1999). Labelling: seeking a secure solution. *World Clothing Manufacturer*, **80**(2), 12–15.

Schneider, C. (1978). *Embroidery: Schiffli and Multi-Head*. Coleman Schneider, New Jersey.

Schneider, C. (1990). *The Art of Embroidery in the '90s*. Coleman Schneider, New Jersey.

Coats North America website has information regarding embroidery threads: http://www.coatsna.com

Useful guidance on care labelling is at: http://www.ftc.gov/bcp/conline/pubs/buspubs/comeclean.htm#For%20More%20Information

Some useful trade press journals for embroidery and garment decoration are *Printwear & Promotion* (in the UK), and *Stitches Magazine* (in the US).

## Chapter 6   Alternative methods of joining materials

The main part of this chapter is about fusing, for which there is some useful literature. There are a number of the Clothing Institute's *Technological Reports* which are relevant:

Dorkin, C.M.C. *et al.* (1968). The practical performance of fusing presses. *Technological Report* No. 19, CI.

Dorkin, C.M.C. *et al.* (1968). The testing and utilisation of fusible interlinings. *Technological Report* No. 20, CI.

Morris, P.A. (1971). The physical properties of textile laminates made from fusible interlinings. *Technological Report* No. 23, CI.

A relevant textbook is:

Cooklin, G. (1990). *Fusing Technology*. The Textile Institute, Manchester.

The British Interlining Manufacturers' Association (BIMA) has produced a useful series of Bulletins which collectively cover most of the issues in fusing technology, including base cloths, the chemistry and application of fusible resins, methods of fusing, fusing equipment, testing procedures, trouble-shooting and some typical garment construction applications.

The Association of Suppliers to the British Clothing Industry (ASBCI) has five spiral-bound books dealing with different aspects of interlinings, and another with the title *Joining Forces*, which considers the varied types of fastenings that are currently on the market.

## Chapter 7   Pressing and related garment finishing techniques

*CTC Technology Review* No. 5. (1990). Evaluating steam pressing. Clothing Technology Centre, Kettering, (July).

Friese, R. (1992). State-of-the-art pressing and finishing. *Manufacturing Clothier*, (March), **73**(3), 24–27.

Wilford, A. (1999). *Non-Iron Garments Best Practice Guide*. Satra Technology Centre, Kettering.

## Chapter 9   Clothing technology and product development

Bhamra, T., Heeley, J. & Tyler, D. (1998). A cross-sectoral approach to new product development. *The Design Journal*, **1**(3), 2–15.

# Index